P9-CME-447

OLD TESTAMENT MESSAGE

A Biblical-Theological Commentary

Carroll Stuhlmueller, C.P. and Martin McNamara, M.S.C.
EDITORS

Old Testament Message, Volume 20

THE BOOK OF WISDOM, SONG OF SONGS

James M. Reese, O.S.F.S.

Michael Glazier, Inc.
Wilmington, Delaware

First published in 1983 by: MICHAEL GLAZIER, INC., 1723 Delaware Avenue, Wilmington, Delaware 19806
Distributed outside U.S., Canada & Philippines by: GILL & MACMILLAN, LTD., Goldenbridge, Inchicore, Dublin 8 Ireland

Library of Congress Catalog Card Number: 82-83726
International Standard Book Number
Old Testament Message series: 0-89453-235-9
WISDOM — SONG OF SONGS
0-89453-254-5 (Michael Glazier, Inc.)
7171-1184-9 (Gill & MacMillan, Ltd.)

Cover design by Lillian Brulc
Typography by Peg McCormick
Printed in the United States of America

Contents

The Song of Songs

INTRODUCTION

COMMENTARY

Editors' Preface

Old Testament Message brings into our life and religion today the ancient word of God to Israel. This word, according to the book of the prophet Isaiah, had soaked the earth like "rain and snow coming gently down from heaven" and had returned to God fruitfully in all forms of human life (Isa 55:10). The authors of this series remain true to this ancient Israelite heritage and draw us into the home, the temple and the marketplace of God's chosen people. Although they rely upon the tools of modern scholarship to uncover the distant places and culture of the biblical world, yet they also refocus these insights in a language clear and understandable for any interested reader today. They enable us, even if this be our first acquaintance with the Old Testament, to become sister and brother, or at least good neighbor, to our religious ancestors. In this way we begin to hear God's word ever more forcefully in our own times and across our world, within our prayer and worship, in our secular needs and perplexing problems.

Because life is complex and our world includes, at times in a single large city, vastly different styles of living, we have much to learn from the Israelite Scriptures. The Old Testament spans forty-six biblical books and almost nineteen hundred years of life. It extends through desert, agricultural and urban ways of human existence. The literary style embraces a world of literature and human emotions. Its history began with Moses and the birth-pangs of a new people, it came of age politically and economically under David and Solomon, it reeled under the fiery threats of prophets like Amos and Jeremiah. The people despaired and yet were re-created with new hope during the Babylonian exile. Later reconstruction in the homeland and then the trauma of apocalyptic movements prepared for the revelation of "the mystery hidden for ages in God who created all things" (Eph 3:9).

While the Old Testament telescopes twelve to nineteen hundred years of human existence within the small country of Israel, any single moment of time today witnesses to the reenactment of this entire history across the wide expanse of planet earth. Each verse of the Old Testament is being relived somewhere in our world today. We need, therefore, the *entire* Old Testament and all twenty-three volumes of this new set, in order to be totally a "Bible person" within today's widely diverse society.

The subtitle of this series—"A Biblical-Theological Commentary"—clarifies what these twenty-three volumes intend to do.

Their *purpose* is theological: to feel the pulse of God's word for its *religious* impact and direction.

Their *method* is biblical: to establish the scriptural word firmly within the life and culture of ancient Israel.

Their *style* is commentary: not to explain verse by verse but to follow a presentation of the message that is easily understandable to any serious reader, even if this person is untrained in ancient history and biblical languages.

Old Testament Message—like its predecessor, *New Testament Message*—is aimed at the entire English-speaking world and so is a collaborative effort of an international team. The twenty-one contributors are women and men drawn from North America, Ireland, Britain and Australia. They are scholars who have published in scientific journals, but they have been chosen equally as well for their proven ability to communicate on a popular level. This twenty-three book set comes from Roman Catholic writers, yet, like the Bible itself, it reaches beyond interpretations restricted to an individual church and so enables men and women rooted in biblical faith to unite and so to appreciate their own traditions more fully and more adequately.

Most of all, through the word of God, we seek the blessedness and joy of those

who walk in the law of the Lord!...
who seek God with their whole heart (Ps. 119:1-2).

Carroll Stuhlmueller, C.P. *Martin McNamara, M.S.C.*

THE BOOK OF WISDOM

INTRODUCTION

1. Origin and Genre of the Work

The Book of Wisdom (Wis) is one of the most learned books of the Bible. It was accepted into the canon of the Catholic Church and included into the Vulgate, its official text. The work appears as part of the writings that are found in the earliest Greek biblical manuscripts, and this is no doubt its original language. In other words, Wis is not a translation from Hebrew or Aramaic, and so is not technically part of the Septuagint Greek (LXX) translation.

Its wide-ranging vocabulary of 1734 different words, including technical terms characteristic of philosophical and scientific tracts of the hellenistic period, point to its origin in the Jewish community living in cosmopolitan Alexandria, Egypt. Its apologetic approach and learned vocabulary point to a period of crisis for Jewish intellectuals torn between the values of their ancestral religion and culture on one hand and the attraction of popular hellenistic societies on the other. The anonymous author (whom I designate for convenience as the Sage) wrote to motivate young Jewish intellectuals to remain in their ancestral faith rather than opt for hellenistic cultural ideals.

The Sage's choice to write in Greek prevented his book from being incorporated into the Jewish canon of Scripture.

That Hebrew canon was drawn up by rabbis only after the fall of Jerusalem. But Wis was accepted as part of Scripture by the early Christian church along with the prevailing Greek translation of the Hebrew Bible—the so-called Septuagint—as its "Old Testament."

While remaining within the subject matter of biblical tradition, the Sage organized his material in literary forms—both larger and smaller—from hellenistic literature. He employed a vocabulary highly influenced by contemporary philosophy and prevailing Greek science. About one of every five terms in Wis appears nowhere within the Greek translation of the Hebrew Bible. Such a high percentage shows literary independence from the LXX as well as a creative effort to communicate in the language of contemporary culture.

USE OF DIATRIBE TECHNIQUE

For modern readers to understand the Sage's approach, they must acquaint themselves with the literary technique of diatribe. Diatribe is a method of arguing that creates imaginary opponents to argue with, uses irony freely, and wanders over a wide range of topics with great liberty of style. The diatribe was a literary method developed by Stoic philosophers so that they could deal with a wide range of topics in a flexible framework.

The Sage found this method useful in handling traditional biblical topics, especially apocalyptic judgment themes that had become popular after the Babylonian Exile. During long centuries of political subjection, Israelite writers started to hope for and portray striking end-time interventions of God to save his people and punish their enemies.

The overall literary genre chosen by the Sage for this scholarly essay comes from Greek philosophy; it is called a *protreptic* or rhetorical exhortation. Most examples of this genre have been lost, including the one composed by Aristotle and paraphrased in dialogue form in Cicero's *Hortensius*. From Christian Egypt the *Protreptic* or *Exhortation to the Greeks* of Clement of Alexandria has survived. The protreptic genre suited the purpose of the Sage because he wanted to display his encyclopedic learning as he dealt with a wide variety of topics in an apologetic manner.

Despite its far-ranging reflections, Wis exhibits a strong unity of composition. The Sage passes logically from one topic to another and links all his parts by the technique of "flashbacks." He begins from an eschatological perspective with a picture of the final destiny of humans in the divine plan of salvation. He then moves into a celebration of Lady Wisdom, that female figure found in earlier biblical writings. The striking feature of Lady Wisdom in this work is that she takes on features of the pagan goddess Isis, popular patron of human wisdom during that period. After a diatribe against the folly of idolatry, the Sage contrasts in great detail the activity of God's saving power and wisdom for the benefit of his people against their enemies.

The text to be explained is the Revised Standard Translation (RSV). This translation has been checked on the basis of the excellent critical Greek text prepared by Joseph Ziegler for the Göttingen *Septuaginta* edition of 1962. Key places where manuscript readings are disputed will be noted in the commentary. Since Wis is a carefully developed writing, most of its text will be commented on and special effort be made to show the flow of thought.

2. *Purpose of the Book*

The Book of Wisdom is essentially an appeal to believe in the God of revelation. This complicated and sophisticated rhetorical exhortation was composed to justify the activities of the God of Israel in the eyes of intelligent, cosmopolitan Jewish students—some of whom were being tempted to abandon their revealed religion in favor of prevailing secular culture. This purpose accounts for the Sage's prominent display of hellenistic culture—philosophy, psychology, anthropology, religion. He knows the many attractions they face but assures them that their traditional faith with its solid hope, '*full of immortality*' (3:4) is better.

The Sage bolsters his apologetic by arguments from history, philosophy and theology. Above all, he appeals to the unique nature of the God whom Jews worship as all-powerful, all-knowing, and consequently all-merciful. Only this God knows and answers human needs and brings his creatures to their real destiny. Both the tragic history of pagan idolatry and the repeated loving interventions of God in favor of his chosen people teach believers to remain loyal to the God of revelation. '*For in everything, O Lord, thou has exalted and glorified thy people*' (19:21).

3. Author and Date

A variety of data—subject matter, method of developing topics, literary and historical allusions—point to its author as a teacher in the synagogue schools of Alexandria in Egypt. He is familiar not only with the whole range of Israelite history but also with Egyptian religious practices and with topics of speculation popular in hellenistic philosophy and science in the period before the birth of Jesus. With great skill he is able to integrate qualities of the goddess Isis, popular guardian of civilization, into his praises of Lady Wisdom, savior of God's chosen people (Wis 7-10). This commentary will show the importance of links made by the Sage between Lady Wisdom of the biblical tradition and the popular prose poems called aretalogies that celebrated Isis for her gifts to humanity.

Even as he reaches out to acknowledge the values of other cultures, the Sage continues the ancient Jewish tradition of appropriating all wisdom to the '*God of the Fathers*' (9:1). He climaxes this approach by the final series of narratives about seven decisive interventions of this saving God on behalf of his chosen people. These interventions are formulated in the form of a *syncrisis* or rhetorical comparison. While the subject matter of this syncrisis comes from the biblical book of Exodus, the Sage modified details and order radically. He updated them with psychological motifs and terminology from contemporary hellenistic culture and turned them into powerful religious appeals for fidelity.

Can we pinpoint the chronological moment at which such a daring project would have been undertaken? My study of the technical vocabulary of Wis points to a date soon after 28 B.C., the beginning of the Imperial Roman period. The Sage is obviously concerned about the survival of his people. He feels a personal responsibility to keep them faithful to their destiny. One aspect of his apologetic is to make himself appear familiar with every area of human knowledge. One way to do that was to employ contemporary scientific vocabulary. In a book that has slightly less than 7,000 Greek words, the Sage uses 1,003 only once. Such an approach was sure to make an impression on students who admired the syncristic philosophical style of that age.

One significant example will illustrate this characteristic of the Sage. It is his use of the term *threskeia* for '*cult*' (14:18, 27). This was a term coined long before from the proper name Thrace. It was found in Herodotus to portray people who live like Thracians, that is, who are models of piety. But it dropped completely out of usage until it was revived at the beginning of the Roman period in both literary texts and inscriptions. Only an author who was in touch with the religious revival of that period and who wanted to exploit popular religious feelings would have appreciated the force of this term.

The Book of Wis shows other marks of an academic origin, especially heaviness of style. Its first part was evidently revised and polished, but the last part points to a failure to eliminate ambiguity and excessive wordiness. Nevertheless, it remains as perhaps the best example of the learned piety of a hellenistic Jewish sage on the eve of the Christian era. As part of the convention of biblical wisdom writing, the Sage assumes the identity of Solomon: see 9:1-18, imitating the famous prayer of 1 Kgs 3:6-9. He also imitates Solomon's encyclopedic knowledge. The fixing of the origin as Egypt is reflected in the polemics against animal worship and idols shaped as animals—cults linked especially to Egypt.

4. Structure and Division of the Book

Scores of divisions have been proposed for Wis. Lack of familiarity with the literary genre of protreptic or rhetorical exhortation was responsible for much of the disagreement among earlier commentators. But failure to master unusual characteristics of the Sage's style continues to lead to disagreement about the structure of Wis, especially as to how to fit its major parts together.

The book is difficult to divide because of its dynamic flow and its emotive nature. It is not a static meditation of a disinterested expositor of a philosophical theory, but an expressive plea aimed at convincing sophisticated and cultured readers. The Sage casts his net wide to provide his readers with as many motives as possible for choosing to remain loyal to traditional Israelite faith. As a result, the book may appear as a collection of four disparate essays tied together by literary devices such as interlocking paragraphs, literary inclusions and "flashbacks" to earlier scenes. Underlying all these techniques, however, is a profound unity of purpose.

Only the major sections of Wis are listed here. A more detailed introduction will be provided at the beginning of each of these parts.

Part I (1:1—6:11 + 6:17-21). The Book of Eschatology—a diatribe to portray the final goal of the upright and their enemies.

Part II (6:12-16 + 6:22—10:21). The Book of Wisdom Proper—an aporia or philosophical inquiry to investigate the nature and role of Lady Wisdom in God's plan.

Part III (11:15—15:19). The Book of Divine Justice and Human Folly—a diatribe exposing the folly of idolatry, and tracing the moral decadence it brought upon the world.

Part IV (11:1-14 + 16:1—19:22). The Book of History—a syncrisis or series of seven contrasts showing how God used nature to benefit his people and punish their enemies.

5. *Message of the Book of Wisdom*

The author of Wis was not a professional theologian. Nor was he a professional philosopher whose vocabulary shows technical precision. Rather, the Sage was a religious thinker, a pious teacher in the tradition of writers like Qoheleth and the Son of Sirach—but more influenced by cosmopolitan culture. As a teacher he is so into his message that commentators cannot extract the conceptual element without weakening the dynamic power of his appeal for action. Writing in a climate of political uncertainty and intellectual skepticism, the Sage packaged traditional faith in an expression of personal mysticism that still evokes admiration and confidence.

His extremely personal method of reflecting on material from biblical revelation led him to believe that no opposition existed between fidelity to '*the incorruptible light of the law*' (18:4) and openness to the religious quest of his contemporaries. He undertakes to build a bridge between his vision of revelation and an audience wavering in their faith. He establishes connections by concentrating on three areas:

a) eternal union with God as the destiny of human existence;
b) God's incorruptible image in mortals as inviting them to embrace this union;
c) organizing events from both biblical tradition and human culture in a way that illustrates God's call to this union.

a) The Sage's message is ultimately rooted in the prophetic appeal to '*seek the Lord*' and to '*be concerned*' about God's will in all aspects of life (1:1). This command binds not only the chosen people but all '*the judges of the earth,*' that is, sincere seekers of truth among every nation. This quest for God is built into the very '*nature*' that God has given to every human being. Consequently, all who remain in '*ignorance*' of God are '*empty*' or false to this nature (13:1). The Sage is the first biblical writer to employ this sense of the term '*nature,*' popular in Greek philosophy. He does so to bring the natural condition and destiny of all humanity under the direction of God's wisdom and power (7:20; 19:20).

By endowing every created species with stability, God in some way communicated to them a saving role in his creation. But humans are unique. They receive a nature that will abide not only for a short period on earth. No; God created humans '*in incorruption,*' as the '*image of his own eternity*' (2:23). Again the Sage appropriates a technical term from hellenistic philosophy to formulate his message in a way that would appeal to an educated audience. Epicureans attributed the superiority of the gods to the quality of '*incorruption*' which their nature possessed. The Sage affirms that God has bestowed that gift on humans so they may share his life and happiness forever.

In making use of these terms from popular contemporary philosophy, the Sage transformed their significance by inserting them into the horizon of revealed religion. His young students needed to know that they are not bound by material limits in their goals. Their lives and destinies are gifts of a loving creator, who loves all that he has made and maintains it in existence by his own '*incorruptible spirit*' (12:1).

b)The Sage does not transfer the fulfilment of human destiny from this world into afterlife only, however. Life upon this earth is not our total destiny, but it plays an essential part in the happiness God plans for his children. Drawing upon his own religious experience to portray the nature of union with God, the Sage describes it as a marriage with Lady Wisdom. Greek philosophy at that time celebrated the search for wisdom and described it by contrast with the tempestuous sexual unions that produced worry, pain and frustration.

The Sage's elaborate description of his blessed union with Lady Wisdom draws upon descriptions of Isis, a favorite Egyptian goddess whose cult was revitalized by Egyptian priests in the second century B.C. at shrines throughout the Aegean area. Isis was praised as guardian of culture and source of all forms of benefits for humanity. What pagan devotees were seeking from Isis, the Sage found as gift of Lady Wisdom, God's '*throne partner*' (6:14; 9:4, a technical term found nowhere else in the Bible). His quest for Lady Wisdom brought him all virtue, the '*justice*' celebrated by the prophets. In this union the Sage fixes the bond between the first two parts of his exhortation.

PROGRESSIVE THEOLOGY

In both of these developments the theological direction is clear. He pursues what Alexander DiLella calls "progressive theology," in contrast with the conservatism of Qoheleth; see *Catholic Biblical Quarterly* 28 (1966) 139-154. In other words, the Sage deliberately sets out to update the expression of traditional theology and to demonstrate its relevance to the situation in contemporary Alexandria. This approach was apologetic. It did not mean to compromise or express lack of trust in biblical faith. The Sage was familiar enough with prevailing attempts at religious syncretism to know that they offered no hope in an unstable world. But he was also realistic enough to see that he could not ignore the achievements of hellenistic culture. He draws upon them, especially the richness of the Greek language, to exalt the truths of revelation. In the final analysis, all enduring knowledge is God's gift (7:15-22). The ultimate purpose of this knowledge is to bring humans to the '*kingdom*' of God (6:20).

c) The explicit goal of the Sage's long exhortation is the practical or pastoral guidance he gives for the pursuit of human destiny. He appealed to a sense of traditional responsibility in his readers. They needed motivation to work toward receiving eternal life '*from the hand of the Lord*' (5:16). This kind of immortality is not a natural quality of the human soul but God's reward for an upright life (5:15).

The sorites or extended syllogism that forms the appendix to the first book of Wis traces growth in practical wisdom, a necessary condition for complete union with God (6:17-20). This stress on God's creative presence and initiative through the process of achieving union with himself lays the foundation for the later theological teaching on *graita praeveniens*—spontaneous divine favor preceding all human activity. This same truth underlies the image of union with Lady Wisdom. She anticipates her devotee's search for her and enters into a spousal communion with him (8:3, 9, 16).

Imitating this inventiveness of Lady Wisdom, the Sage undertakes to make traditional revealed truths available by using all resources at his disposal. He embraces traditional values of biblical tradition but recasts them in the literary style of popular religious hymns of Isis and the vocabulary of hellenistic science and philosophy. He assumes the person of King Solomon, founder of the wisdom movement in Israel, to illustrate the transforming power of union with Lady Wisdom (9:1-18). The scientific knowledge she gave him is subject to ethical gifts, including the four cardinal virtues of popular philosophy (8:6-7).

Another source of material for the Sage's praises of Lady Wisdom were hellenistic "Kingship Tracts." These were manuals for the ethical guidance of future rulers, written to enflesh Plato's dictum that a people will be happy only when its philosophers are kings and its kings philosophers.

All in all, then, the Sage spared no effort in formulating a message appealing to well-educated contemporary Jews. He received freely from Lady Wisdom and now shares without jealousy all she taught him (6:22-25). Grateful recognition that all true wisdom is gift of God separates the Sage from the self-confidence of hellenistic philosophers. Thus he is not ashamed to end his long description of all that he has to offer by reciting a long prayer begging to receive Lady Wisdom. This prayer links Book II of his exhortation to the great truths celebrated in biblical revelation that God is unique savior of all. Humans do not create their own destiny but are '*saved by wisdom*' (9:18).

The Sage expands upon this insight by the empassioned ode to Lady Wisdom as God's agent throughout salvation history (10:1-21). This poetic summary of biblical scenes unfolds with great skill and serves to orient readers toward the specific scenes based on the Exodus from Egypt that brings his long exhortation to a close in the form of an address to God. Before offering God's own conduct as model in the concluding syncrisis or comparison (Wis 16—19), however, the Sage inserts a long diatribe against all forms of pagan religion, which he portrays as senseless idolatry. With great skill he organizes material from hellenistic philosophy and popular religious practice to expose them as expressions of folly incapable of satisfying the true religious spirit of believers. The completed exhortation forms a masterpiece of theological insight and rhetorical persuasion.

6. *Features of Style*

Stylistically the Book of Wisdom illustrates the pedantic school style of late hellenistic philosophical tracts. The Sage deliberately strives for this effect by multiplying artificial rhetorical figures. This feature is one of the strongest proofs that he wrote in Greek. In addition, the first part of his work utilizes the characteristic feature of Hebrew poetry, known in modern times as parallelism. Parallelism is the method of repeating each statement so that every verse has two (rarely three) *stichs* or sense lines, each with the same concept. The latter part of Wis, in which the Sage addresses God directly to praise him for accomplishing the wonders of the Exodus, abandons parallelism. The sentences become more complicated and are overloaded with images and allusions.

The most frequently used stylistic figure is *hyperbaton,* the artistic ordering of words. The words are arranged—often with an artistic use of the article—to achieve some literary effect like emphasis or surprise or special sound effect. Frequently hyperbaton involves manipulating the definite article to introduce whole phrases into the attributive position, that is, to make an entire phrase into an adjective. Since this figure is foreign to English style, the pedantic mood created by hyperbaton disappears in translation, and the sense may come across as quite flat or strained.

A figure of speech frequent in Wis is *litotes* or understatement, often for emphasis. The very first sentence in the work uses this figure to describe God. Translated literally, the lines involved read: '*he is found by those not tempting him and manifests himself to those not mistrusting him*' (1:2). What the Sage means is that believers must make a conscious effort to seek God by their pursuit of justice and uncompromising confidence in him. This same figure of litotes closes the entire book. Its final couplet, which is also in the form of an apostrophe or direct address, reminds God, '*You do not neglect to make your presence felt in any time or place*' (19:22, my translation). Again, this is a respectful understatement to praise the powerful protection that God always exercises toward his chosen people.

Another favorite rhetorical device of the Sage is *paranomasia* or punning assonance, a figure that occurs more than a hundred times. Paranomasia creates a melodious quality in the text but its effect is lost in translation. Chapter 10 is characterized by the striking *anaphora* in the repetition of the emphatic '*she,*' referring to Lady Wisdom at the beginning of each new statement. A related figure is *antonomasia* or deliberate avoiding of proper names; it is frequent in chapters 10—19. Because many of its rhetorical figures can scarcely be translated, and because modern readers are not familiar with its literary allusions, the style of Wis comes across as heavy and obscure. Part of its lack of popularity comes from the failure of translations to communicate the enthusiasm that the Sage's artistry must have aroused in his original readers.

He was skillful in coining words, especially compounds, a feature that recalls the poetry of Aeschylus. He often structured literary units by means of an *inclusion,* putting the same key word or expression at the beginning and end. But the most striking stylistic device—the one that assures the unity of this well-planned work—is the presence of *flashbacks.* These are literary allusions in the later part to tie events of salvation history to earlier reflections on God's mastery over all creation. This is a common technique in movies and TV. It helped the Sage make his exhortation a justification of the ways of God with men.

PART I:
THE BOOK OF ESCHATOLOGY
(1:1—6:11 + 6:17-21)

Introduction

The opening major section of Wis is a carefully constructed diatribe composed of five concentric reflections plus an appendix. It is entitled the Book of Eschatology because it paints the destiny of those who obey God's will as enjoying life forever '*in the hand of God*' (3:1). The Sage has arranged its five parts in chiasmic or inverted order around a long description of how God vindicates the '*just*' (3:1—5:1). To make his appeal for loyalty to God more striking, the Sage describes the happiness of fidelity in three paradoxical models: the barren but unsoiled wife; the childless but virtuous parent; the youth who dies despite his refusal to sin.

As an inclusion binding these examples together, the Sage affirms that God will not allow those who trust in him to be harmed by foes. At the final judgment, '*the souls of the righteous are in the hand of God*' (3:1), and so, '*the righteous man will stand with great confidence in the presence of those who inflicted him*' (5:1).

Within this set of examples the Sage uses the technique of digression to link this diatribe with the second half of Wis. First, he interjects briefly the principle of divine retribution—'*the ungodly will be punished as their reason-*

ing deserves' (3:10)—to anticipate Part Three of his book, "The Book of Divine Justice and Human Folly" (11:15—15:19). Later he interjects the example of Enoch, the ancient patriarch who '*was caught up lest evil change his understanding or guile deceive his soul*' (4:11). This notice anticipates the Sage's long prayer reciting a series of seven examples of God's saving intervention in Part IV.

The opening and closing sections that frame this centerpiece of apologetics are both exhortations. The opening exhortation is to '*righteousness,*' which alone assures mortals of their God-given destiny (1:1-15; a piece set off with an inclusion by the repetition of '*righteousness*' in verses 1 and 15). The closing piece is an exhortation to pursue practical wisdom (6:1-11). It is also addressed to the upright but under the titles of '*rulers,*' '*judges*' and '*monarchs*' (6:1, 9).

Between these two exhortations is another balanced set of descriptions. Wis 2:1-20 is a long mocking diatribe voicing the unsound logic of '*ungodly men,*' surrounded by the Sage's short comments that they are '*blinded*' by wickedness (1:16; 2:21-24). After God's intervention in favor of the righteous, the Sage skillfully pictures the wicked as being forced to admit their blind folly. He then describes in apocalyptic terms the saving intervention of the Lord to wipe out evil (5:2-23).

This whole opening polemic—directed against unbelieving Hellenists whom the Sage equates with the ungodly—serves as an apologia for the Jewish faith, which reveals God's saving justice to the world.

1. AN EXHORTATION TO RIGHTEOUSNESS
Wis 1:1-15

1 Love righteousness, you rulers of the earth,
think of the Lord with uprighteousness,
and seek him with sincerity of heart;
[2]because he is found by those who do not
put him to the test,
and manifests himself to those who do not distrust him.
[3]For perverse thoughts separate men from God,

and when his power is tested, it convicts the foolish;
[4]because wisdom will not enter a deceitful soul,
nor dwell in a body enslaved to sin.
[5]For a holy and disciplined spirit will flee from deceit,
and will rise and depart from foolish thoughts,
and will be ashamed at the approach of unrighteousness.

[6]For wisdom is a kindly spirit and will not free a blasphemer from the guilt of his words;
because God is witness of his inmost feelings,
and a true observer of his heart,
and hearer of his tongue.
[7]Because the Spirit of the Lord has filled the world,
and that which holds all things together knows what is said;
[8]therefore no one who utters unrighteous things will escape notice,
and justice, when it punishes, will not pass him by.
[9]For inquiry will be made into the counsels of an ungodly man,
and a report of his words will come to the Lord,
to convict him of his lawless deeds;
[10]because a jealous ear hears all things,
and the sound of murmurings does not go unheard.
[11]Beware then of useless murmuring,
and keep your tongue from slander;
because no secret word is without result,
and a lying mouth destroys the soul.
[12]Do not invite death by the error of your life,
nor bring on destruction by the works of your hands;
[13]because God did not make death,
and he does not delight in the death of the living.
[14]For he created all things that they might exist,
and the generative forces of the world are wholesome,
and there is no destructive poison in them;
and the dominion of Hades is not on earth.
[15]For righteousness is immortal.

This exhortation to '*righteousness,*' which acts as the prologue to the entire Book of Wisdom, is a carefully constructed appeal in a poetic style that imitates Hebrew poetry. The lines are composed in the characteristic feature of Hebrew verse, namely, parallelism: each image is stated in two successive sense lines, called *stichs*. Ordinarily two stichs make up one verse, but sometimes there are three as in verses 1, 5, 6cde, 9. This manner of expression slows the pace to give the poetry a reflective mood.

In the original Greek text this exhortation consists of only two sentences (1:1-11 and 1:12-15). The first sentence—a string of motives for seeking '*righteousness*'—is tied together by repetition of the conjunction '*for*' (*gar*) six times. Each of these motives illustrates an aspect of the image of God that the Sage elaborates in this work. The second and shorter sentence develops the ultimate practical motive for seeking '*righteousness*,' namely, that it is '*immortal*' (v. 15). As such, it is the condition for humans to achieve their final destiny, a state of eternal companionship with God. The subject of the first major part of Wis will be to examine the nature of '*righteousness*' as gift of the all-powerful God of Israel to his people. As is the practice of most translations, the Revised Standard Version (RSV) breaks this prologue into shorter sentences—in keeping with good English style.

The opening address to '*you rulers of the earth*' is a literary feature—a borrowing from Ps 2:10 (LXX)—equating the audience of Jewish students with philosophers, the true rulers of the world. Israel's prophets often addressed their oracles to pagan nations as a way of affirming the superiority of the God of Israel. The Sage imitates that way of thinking. By addressing earthly '*rulers*,' he reminds his Jewish readers of the unique destiny they have received with their religious heritage. He thus sets an apologetic tone that prevails throughout his book.

The exhortation to '*love righteousness*' is rooted deep in biblical tradition. For example, the psalmist speaks to the ideal king as : you who '*love justice and hate wickedness*' (Ps 45:7). The verb '*love*,' one of the author's favorites, occurs in his book nine times to describe both human and divine striving. But this exhortation would also remind readers of the Platonic 'imitation of God' theme; it proposed as the highest human ideal the effort to become as much like the divine as possible. This double allusion at the outset of Wis illustrates an important characteristic of the Sage: he makes a conscious effort to write in images with links to both the biblical and the Greek religious traditions.

'*Righteousness*' in the biblical tradition describes a life lived in conformity with God's will as expressed in the Mosaic commandments and in imitation of God's method of ruling the world '*in holiness and righteousness*' (9:3). In keeping with the poetic style, this opening appeal is repeated by parallelism in two synonymous commands:

(1) '*think of the Lord with uprightness.*' The Greek words have a more affectionate tone, namely, to '*cherish*' the Lord by '*goodness,*' a quality attributed to God in 7:26 and 12:22. '*Cherish*' is related to the cardinal virtue recommended in 8:7.

(2) '*seek him with sincerity of heart.*' The admonition to '*seek the Lord*' also appears in connection with a plea for righteousness in Isa 55:6. Below, the Sage will describe the true religious attitude to which all are called as '*sincerity of heart*' (13:6)—an example of his "progressive theology" that seeks to link human values with God's saving plan. David described himself as sincere of heart in his final prayer recorded in 1 Chronicles 29:17 (LXX). Since other allusions to this Greek version occur in Wis, the Sage no doubt read his Scripture in that translation. It is identified in the commentary by the designation of LXX.

His conscious effort to follow LXX terminology makes it significant when he substitutes terms from hellenistic ethical and anthropological vocabulary. He always operates on the supposition that human science must submit to the norm of faith in order for humans to know themselves and their condition truly and thus advance toward that '*wisdom*' which '*will not enter a deceitful soul nor dwell in a body enslaved to sin*' (v. 4). In this first appearance '*wisdom*' has the practical sense of a quality of human conduct. But in 1:6 '*wisdom*' is already a synonym for God (and hence better capitalized), the ruler and creator of human destiny as a '*kindly spirit.*' The '*kindly*' of the RSV fails to capture the distinctively Greek dimension of this picture of God. He is identified by an adjective characteristic of hellenistic moral philosophy, *philanthropos* (lover of humans), in the sense of one kindly disposed toward them—a term that celebrates the ideal of a God who lavishly bestows benefits upon those deserving (see 7:23; 12:19). In Part II the Sage will treat personified Lady Wisdom, sent by God into human history to guide humanity in its search for himself (Wis 6—10).

Because this first part of Wis is written in the style of parallelism, the question arises whether the terms '*soul*' and '*body*' (v. 4) are synonyms, both signifying the human person. Since the Sage clearly distinguishes between '*soul*,' which he mentions 25 times, and '*body*,' which appears only five times, the answer seems to be that the Sage distinguishes them here. He always gives priority to the '*soul*' in determining human conduct because it supports human personality (8:19-20) and is the origin of decisions that shape human righteousness (1:11). Although he is influenced by Greek dualism, the Sage does not see the '*soul*' as operating virtuously by its own power but only by the '*power*' of God, which '*convicts the foolish*' (v. 3). A better way of understanding the phrase is to read it not as '*his power*,' but "the Power," a proper name for God. The Sage likes to multiply synonyms that refer to both persons and things. He designates God by this synonym again in 5:23 and 11:20, although the RSV translates the term differently in those texts.

A Religious View of Humanity

The Sage looks on every human being as a religious creature responsible to the one God—the '*Power*,' the '*Wisdom*,' the '*kindly Spirit*,' he who '*is Witness of his inmost feeling*,' and who punishes '*a blasphemer*' (v. 6). He will expand and clarify this relationship to God in 11:21-26. The biblical belief in final judgment plays a decisive role especially in these opening scenes of Wis, because that is the occasion when God will separate forever the wise from the foolish, saints from sinners (3:1, 19; 4:7, 16; 5:2-16). God can pass judgment because he is '*witness*' of the sinner's '*inmost feelings*' as well as '*hearer of his tongue*' (v. 6). The Sage attributes this divine knowledge to the presence of '*the Spirit of the Lord,*' which '*has filled the whole world*' (v. 7). In contrast to verse 5, the RSV capitalizes '*Spirit,*' a feature that recalls to Christian readers the truth of the Holy Spirit. But original readers of Wis would have no such concept. '*The Spirit of the Lord*' here is the all-pervading creative and saving presence of God (see Gen 1:2). In fact, throughout this prologue the Sage plays with various conceptualizations of how God relates to mortals: Lord, power, wisdom, spirit, witness, observer, hearer, justice, jealousy. He is already anticipating Part III, his criticism of idolatry, which deifies God's creatures and thus cuts humans off from communion with their one source of life and salvation.

This term '*spirit*' also had links with various philosophical and religious ideas current when the Sage was writing. Pythagoreans had a theory that a spirit existed in the realms of space to sustain the breathing of the cosmos, which they viewed as a living animal, because it had '*spirit*' (*pneuma*; the Greek word means both breath and wind). Spirit played an important role also in Stoic philosophy as vivifying both human bodies and the whole cosmos, and as distinguishing between each level of existence. The Sage was aware of such speculation. In treating Lady Wisdom he will go into detail in attributing to her qualities of the Stoic world spirit. In this opening exhortation he seems to be giving play to a kind of stream of consciousness. By tracing briefly the glories of the God of revelation, he reminds Jewish students that their God is source of all life and wisdom.

The Sage's purpose in beginning this way is not primarily didactic, that is, to give a lesson in theodicy. Rather, his goal is pastoral: to encourage the practical faith and ethical response that God demands of those who acknowledge him as creator and final judge. This prologue elaborates what is implied in carrying out the initial command to '*love righteousness,*' and that is the reason for the long opening sentence. Only in obedience will his readers experience the import of the command—that it cannot be accomplished except in total surrender to the will of God and to the dynamism of his transcendent presence in their lives.

In diatribe style this opening sentence ends with a series of warnings beginning with '*therefore*' (v. 8). The RSV refers to this '*justice*' with the neuter pronoun, '*when it punishes.*' But the Sage puts forth '*justice*' (*Dikē;* see 11:20) as a title for God in his role as the punisher of those who refuse to live according to the intelligence he gives them. The Sage is developing a picture of the unique personal God who condemns all forms of idolatry. The disobedient thus become the '*ungodly*' (v. 9, that is, the impious, a term that identifies them 14 times). Humans are by their very nature religious beings with responsibilities to the God who created them.

Modern readers may feel that the Sage needlessly belabors his point in heaping up terms that are practical synonyms. But this device of style has two aims: (1) to multiply vocabulary and thus introduce contemporary words foreign to the biblical tradition, and (2) to repeat distinctive terms in different parts of the book as a means of reinforcing its unity by his "flashbacks." Given this technique, the RSV's translation '*a jealous ear*' obscures the Sage's title for God (v. 10). The Greek text reads "ear of jealousy," a phrase that should not be handled as a Semitic idiom like 'king of kings' to mean the greatest king. On the contrary, God is '*jealousy*' in the sense that he allows no rivals to his claims.

The Sage concludes his warnings by stating the fundamental reason for an upright life, namely, because sin '*destroys the soul*' (v. 11). He lists only sins of the tongue, but includes all impious conduct, as is implied in the repetition of '*murmuring.*' That is the biblical term for the sin of Israel in the desert and so epitomizes all rebellion against God (Exod 16:8; Num 17:5-10). This list of sins includes three terms never found in the LXX translation. These are: '*slander,*' the first recorded use, but frequent in early Christian writings; '*secret,*' in the sense of spoken against God; '*lying,*' as a false accusation against God. The warning is against trying to fool God.

This closing sentence of the prologue explains the ultimate destiny of humans and how they can lose it by sin, which drives '*uprightness*' from '*your life*' (v. 12). A double imperative balances the opening exhortation of the book but now it is given in negative terms: do not '*seek death*' or '*bring on destruction*' by turning from God to '*the works of your hands*'—the biblical term for idols (see 13:10). The Sage is not speaking in terms of a Platonic natural immortality. Rather, he is urging his readers to seek blessed immortality, a gift of God's grace—as he will explain (see 2:23; 5:1). Since their lives are not limited to this world, they must be guided by the truth and values that are from God who '*created all things*' (v. 14). He will expand this veiled warning against idolatry of all kinds in Part III.

In stating that '*God did not make death*' (v. 13), the Sage alludes to the biblical story of the fall, which is the result of the disobedience of Adam and Eve. He warns against the '*error of your life*' that invites death—error not in an intellectual sense but in the Greek sense of going astray in one's '*life*' (v. 12; see 12:24). Real '*life*' is not the external activity in which they are involved but the fulness of personal communion with God. What this communion involves will be described in the examples of uprightness that the Sage will soon picture and in his praise of Lady Wisdom, who communicates endless '*life*' to believers.

Enemy of immortal '*life*' is '*death,*' conceived not primarily in terms of the end of physical existence on earth but as eternal separation from God (vv. 12, 13). In this sense, '*God did not make death*' (v. 13; see 12:20). Here the parallelism equates '*death*' and '*destruction.*' The statement, '*God did not make death*' is litotes or understatement to affirm that God provides humans with all they need to remain in his love. The vagueness of the statement stirs up curiosity and prepares for the later theological reflections on how God empowers the just to remain with him forever. The Sage is still laying the groundwork by brief comments, as when he states God's creative purpose: '*he created all things that they might exist*' (v. 14).

This last statement refers to the physical universe. The Sage means that individual species, translated as '*generative forces,*' are '*wholesome,*' that is, survive. His terminology is similar to hellenistic philosophical theories for the existence of a providence within the cosmos. Once again he appeals to aspects of secular thought and popular religious attitudes that were able to be reconciled with his biblical faith. The '*destructive poison*' apparently alludes to harmful effects of popular healing rites (v. 14; see the elaboration in 11:23-25).

Specific interest in final destiny appears in the statement that God has given '*Hades*' no '*domination*' on earth. '*Hades,*' representing Death as in Job 38:17 LXX, is the final personification in the prologue. It designates not simple physical decay but Death as cosmic enemy, dreaded obstacle to the eternal life God gives to those who trust in him.

With a short clause that has no parallel sense line, the Sage quickly brings his prologue to a close: '*For righteousness is immortal*' (v. 15). This phrase looks both backward and forward: backward to the book's opening line, with which it forms an inclusion; forward to the following explanation of human immortality as God's great grace to human beings. In contrast to Death that sinners foolishly seek (v. 12) the Sage will now show readers how to find the '*immortal*' bliss of '*righteousness.*'

2. THE WAY OF THE WICKED
Wis 1:16—2:24

> [16]But ungodly men by their words and deeds
> summoned death;
> considering him a friend, they pined away,
> and they made a covenant with him,
> because they are fit to belong to his party.
> **2** For they reasoned unsoundly, saying to themselves,
> "Short and sorrowful is our life,
> and there is no remedy when a man comes to his end,
> and no one has been known to return from Hades.
> [2]Because we were born by mere chance,
> and hereafter we shall be as though we had never been;
> because the breath in our nostrils is smoke,
> and reason is a spark kindled by the beating of our hearts.
> [3]When it is extinguished, the body will turn to ashes,

and the spirit will dissolve like empty air.
[4]Our name will be forgotten in time,
and no one will remember our works;
our life will pass away like the traces of a cloud,
and be scattered like mist
that is chased by the rays of the sun
and overcome by its heat.
[5]For our allotted time is the passing of a shadow,
and there is no return from our death,
because it is sealed up and no one turns back.

[6]"Come, therefore, let us enjoy the good things that exist,
and make use of the creation to the full as in youth.
[7]Let us take our fill of costly wine and perfumes,
and let no flower of spring pass by us.
[8]Let us crown ourselves with rosebuds before they wither.
[9]Let none of us fail to share in our revelry,
everywhere let us leave signs of enjoyment,
because this is our portion, and this our lot.
[10]Let us oppress the righteous poor man;
let us not spare the widow
nor regard the grey hairs of the aged.
[11]But let our might be our law of right,
for what is weak proves itself to be useless.

[12]"Let us lie in wait for the righteous man,
because he is inconvenient to us and opposes our actions;
he reproaches us for sins against the law,
and accuses us of sins against our training.
[13]He professes to have knowledge of God,
and calls himself a child of the Lord.
[14]He became to us a reproof of our thoughts;
[15]the very sight of him is a burden to us,
because his manner of life is unlike that of others,
and his ways are strange.
[16]We are considered by him as something base,
and he avoids our ways as unclean;
he calls the last end of the righteous happy,
and boasts that God is his father.
[17]Let us see if his words are true,

and let us test what will happen at the end of his life;
[18]for if the righteous man is God's son, he will help him,
and will deliver him from the hand of his adversaries.
[19]Let us test him with insult and torture,
that we may find out how gentle he is,
and make trial of his forbearance.
[20]Let us condemn him to a shameful death,
for, according to what he says, he will be protected."

[21]Thus they reasoned, but they were led astray,
for their wickedness blinded them,
[22]and they did not know the secret purposes of God,
nor hope for the wages of holiness,
nor discern the prize for blameless souls;
[23]for God created man for incorruption,
and made him in the image of his own eternity,
[24]but through the devil's envy death entered the world,
and those who belong to his party experience it.

A new section of the opening diatribe begins at 1:16—a reminder that the chapter and verse numbers are not part of the original. The chapter divisions were created by a medieval scholastic commentator, and the verse numbers were inserted by an early French printer to identify passages conveniently. In a number of instances in Wis these divisions do not mark the natural movement of the text and have contributed to disagreement about interpreting verses. Usually the Sage moves so skillfully from one development to the next that it is difficult to make a clean break. His artistic transitions contribute greatly to the power of his message.

As noted in the introduction to Part I, this description will be balanced by the picture of the final judgment (5:2-23), in which the wicked will see their lives exposed as foolish by those who chose wisdom in this life. The Sage begins with a vivid image—carried to the point of a caricature—of the lifestyle of '*ungodly men*' (1:16), enemies of '*the righteous man*' (2:12), whose '*wickedness*' has blinded them (2:21). In diatribe style the Sage presents these ungodly men as voicing their own motives (2:1-20). This technique sustains reader interest. It also dramatizes the moral chasm existing between a life faithful to God's covenant and one motivated by sinful ambition.

The whole picture is developed artistically in the form of an introduction (1:16—2:2) plus seven paragraphs consisting of eight to ten stichs or sense lines each. The first three paragraphs detail the errors of these '*ungodly men*' (2:3-9); the next three describe their malice (2:10-20). A final paragraph presents the Sage's short refutation (2:21-24; expanded in the corresponding description of the last judgment in 5:2-23). The entire development is set off by a literary inclusion that features the key words '*death*' and '*party*' (1:16; 2:24).

The accusations in this section could apply equally well to apostate Jews or to worldly pagans. Only the larger context makes clear that the Sage is making an appeal to educated Jews who are tempted by the allurements of pagan culture. Much of the power of this self-portrait of the pagan depends upon its figures of speech—most of which are lost in translation. If some of the arguments appear weak and the Sage seems to be building a straw man, modern readers should recall that he is an artist employing literary skills not evident in the English.

The designation of the opponents as '*ungodly men*' (1:16; see 1:9) is to link moral malice to the failure to develop a vision of reality based on faith, for the Sage believed that an intimate connection existed between not believing in the God of Israel and leading an evil life. Their godlessness was not confined to an attitude of mind but manifested itself in '*words and deeds*' that summoned '*death*' (1:16). The RSV text is based on the Latin, which inserts the noun '*death.*' The RSV note gives the Greek text, '*summoned him,*' namely, the personified Death of 1:13. This personification implies their opposition to the God of Israel who made a covenant of life with Abraham and Moses. The Sage is elaborating a contrast between the deceitful promises of Death and the power of God, who alone can reward those who trust in him. In Part II the Sage will specify Lady

Wisdom as the one who empowers '*God's friends*' to share life-giving gifts (7:27).

The malice of the ungodly results in their reasoning '*unsoundly*' (2:1). This soliloquy against them embodies philosophy popular at that time. It should not be studied as though it were a scientific exposition on one particular school of thought. Its eclectic nature can be recognized in these examples: the practice of oppressing the '*poor*' is seen in Ps-Heraclitus (v. 10); Plato speaks about the doctrine that '*might*' makes '*right*' (v. 11); that our breath is '*smoke*' and that a person should be tested to find how '*gentle*' he is both appear in Epicurus (v. 19). Yet many of the views are simply commonplaces of hellenistic ethics and appear here in keeping with the apologetic aim of the Sage—to prove the superiority of Israel's revealed truth and morality over paganism in any form—even its great philosophers.

The ungodly starts out by voicing paganism's most foolish mistake: assuming that human life ends with death and so thinking that '*there is no remedy when a man comes to his end,*' for the world is governed '*by mere chance*' (2:1-2), a teaching attributed to the Epicureans. The root of this mistake is implied in his colorful description of '*reason*' as a '*spark*' whose failure reduces the whole human body to '*ashes*' and '*empty air*' (vv. 2-3). The Epicurean error is to deny the reality of the spiritual and to reject any principle that is not material. In personal conduct they translate this shallowness into the maxim, "Eat, drink and be merry for tomorrow we die." The Sage elaborates their *carpe diem* philosophy in the form of seven wishes (vv. 6-9).

His vocabulary in them employs five hellenistic terms never found elsewhere in the Bible, including the terms translated: '*crown ourselves,*' '*rosebuds,*' '*to the full*' and '*meadow*' (v. 9, if the reconstruction based on the Latin is correct: '*let no meadow be barred from our revelry*'). The description ends on a tone of biting irony when the ungodly proclaim, '*this is our portion and this our lot.*' Both '*portion*' (1:16; 2:9, 24) and '*lot*' are traditional designations of Israel's covenant with God and so convey a contrast between the abiding gifts true believers receive and the emptiness of pagan existence.

Underlying this strong criticism of pagan lifestyle is the Sage's presupposition that ignorance and malice go hand in hand. Which comes first? Malice breeds ignorance and yet ignorance is responsible for their shameful existence. Only a break with ignorance can improve the moral quality of their life. The dark side of paganism appears in its violence against the weak: '*the righteous poor...the widow...the aged*' (v. 10).

Thc portrait of the ungodly emerging from this harangue is composite. Their '*sins against the law*' point to them as Jews, but '*sins against our training*' (*paideia*, v. 12) point to formation in Greek culture. This combination reflects the syncretism of the age. Jewish and Greek ideas interacted so closely that it is often impossible to isolate their influence. For example, the phrase '*inconvenient to us*' alludes to Isaiah 3:10, but in the LXX translation. Allusions to the Suffering Servant of Isaiah 53 are possible only if the Greek word *pais* is understood as '*servant*' with the RSV note (v. 13).

Teaching On The Afterlife

The crucial difference in attitude between the '*righteous*' and the '*ungodly*' is their understanding of what happens at death. The ungodly resent the hope found in the '*last end of the righteous*' (v. 16), a hope that sustains believing Jews. The Sage will show the validity of this hope in his vivid picture of the righteous enjoying God's favor forever (see 5:2-23).

The ungodly end their diatribe against the believer by mockingly planning to do away with him (vv. 17-20). The ironic tone and bitter words of this plot make clear that the Sage's intended readers are not pagans. Such style would only alienate them further against pious Jews. Hence, this is an academic, inhouse Jewish composition addressed to students familiar with their long religious tradition and still open to its validity and healing power, even if they waver somewhat.

Belief in the afterlife is decisive in placing formal judgment on the quality of earthly existence. The ungodly group presumes that the upright must fear death just as they do. So they think their violence will shake '*the righteous*' man's belief in being '*God's son*' (v. 18). Since no one on earth can see believers enjoying heavenly happiness, the ungodly mock God's ability to '*deliver*' those who trust in him '*from insult and torture*' with bold and blasphemous language (vv. 18-19). Some commentators see these verses as literary models for the description of the mocking of Jesus on the cross, but the language is too different to prove direct influence.

The qualities of the righteous that these persecutors seek to test are virtues extolled by Greek ethical writers: '*how gentle he is*' and '*his forbearance*' (v. 19). The term translated '*gentle*' is the ordinary technical term for "equity," a virtue celebrated by Greek ethical philosophers. Epictetus made a comment similar to this when he wrote that a bad neighbor exercises a person in equity. The term never appears in biblical books translated from Hebrew. Nor does '*forbearance*' appear again in the Bible except in 2 Tim 2:24. This terminology shows the Sage's familiarity with hellenistic ethics.

This long outburst of the ungodly ends, however, on a biblical tone, although it is obscured in the RSV. The victim is reported as saying that '*he will be protected*' (v. 20). What he claims is that he will have a "visitation" from God. This is a common biblical term to designate God's saving intervention for those who trust him. It can be either to rescue him or to punish his enemies. Wis uses this biblical term '*visitation*' seven times, either for final salvation (3:7, 9, 13; 4:15) or for final punishment of God's enemies (14:11; 19:15).

The Sage gives a brief commentary on this violent diatribe to refute how the ungodly '*reasoned*' (vv. 21-24). He says they '*were led astray, for their wickedness blinded them*' (v. 21; see 11:15). He sees their malice as coming first;

it '*blinded*' their judgment. As a result, they could not '*know,*' that is, believe in '*the secret purposes of God,*' which alone nourish '*hope*' and lead to '*the prize for blameless souls,*' namely, blessed immortality (v. 22).

The Greek word expressing God's '*secret purposes*' is *mysterion,* a technical term from the mystery cults. By picking this word the Sage presents Israelite religion as response on the part of believers to God's wisdom that rules this world. In contrast to pagan worshipers, who act in ignorance, the chosen people enjoy the light of God's revealed truth. Yet, the Sage draws upon hellenistic religious thought when he describes the fruits of these '*secret purposes*' as being the gift of '*incorruption*' to '*blameless souls*' (v. 22) because:

(1) he chooses the term '*souls*' as recipient of God's reward (v. 22, picked up in 3:1). The '*soul*' is the philosophical term for the moral, intellectual and spiritual principle that differentiates humans from brute animals. By this term the Sage in no way denies the unity of human beings but proclaims the priority of the spiritual element in their nature (see 1:11).

(2) he appropriates the technical Epicurean term '*incorruption*' that designated the transcendental quality that characterized the gods. '*Incorruption*' was their name for the power gods had to overcome forces that dissipate atoms; and so they could survive forever in contrast to mortals. For the Sage '*incorruption*' was the power that God originally gave humans to enjoy his friendship forever. Human immortality is not part of human nature but a special gift by which God transforms humans into '*the image of his own eternity*' (v. 23; or, according to some Greek manuscripts, into his own "nature" or "identity").

In saying that God '*created man for incorruption,*' the Sage is not speaking of a future goal. He affirms rather that God gave mortals the state of '*incorruption*' as a condition that empowered them to enjoy eternal life. This nuance, which is clear in the Greek text, affirms that immortality is not an innate or natural quality of human '*souls,*' but rather a free divine gift. Alluding again to the biblical story of the fall of Adam and Eve, the Sage is the first writer to identify the snake with '*the devil,*' who was envious of this gift of '*incorruption*' and actively encouraged the sin by which '*death entered the world*' (v. 24). This '*death*' extends beyond the purely physical; it brought about the corruption of the spiritual realm, the world of the soul. In the original '*secret purposes of God,*' humans would not have been subject to the power of personified Death. Now, all who sin '*experience*' this Death with its power to blind and corrupt (v. 24; see 1:13).

3. THE TRIUMPH OF THE RIGHTEOUS
Wis 3:1—5:1

3 But the souls of the righteous are in the hand of God,
and no torment will ever touch them.
[2]In the eyes of the foolish they seemed to have died,
and their departure was thought to be an affliction,
[3]and their going from us to be their destruction;
but they are at peace.
[4]For though in the sight of men they were punished,
their hope is full of immortality.
[5]Having been disciplined a little, they will receive
great good
because God tested them and found them
worthy of himself;
[6]like gold in the furnace he tried them,
and like a sacrificial burnt offering he accepted them.
[7]In the time of their visitation they will shine forth,
and will run like sparks through the stubble.
[8]They will govern nations and rule over peoples,
and the Lord will reign over them for ever.
[9]Those who trust in him will understand truth,
and the faithful will abide with him in love,
because grace and mercy are upon his elect,
and he watches over his holy ones.[a]
[10]But the ungodly will be punished as their
reasoning deserves,
who disregarded the righteous man[b]
and rebelled against the Lord;

[11]for whoever despises wisdom and
instruction is miserable.
Their hope is vain, their labours are unprofitable,
and their works are useless.
[12]Their wives are foolish, and their children evil;
[13]their offspring are accursed.
For blessed is the barren woman who is undefiled,
who has not entered into a sinful union;
she will have fruit when God examines souls.
[14]Blessed also is the eunuch whose hands
have done no lawless deed,
and who has not devised wicked things against the Lord;
for special favour will be shown him for his faithfulness
and a place of great delight in the temple of the Lord.
[15]For the fruit of good labours is renowned,
and the root of understanding does not fail.
[16]But children of adulterers will not come to maturity,
and the offspring of an unlawful union will perish.
[17]Even if they live long they will be held of no account,
and finally their old age will be without honour.
[18]If they die young, they will have no hope
and no consolation in the day of decision.
[19]For the end of an unrighteous generation is grievous.

4 Better than this is childlessness with virtue,
for in the memory of virtue is immortality,
because it is known both by God and by men.
[2]When it is present, men imitate it,
and they long for it when it has gone;
and throughout all time it marches crowned in triumph,
victor in the contest for prizes that are undefiled.
[3]But the prolific brood of the ungodly will be of no use,
and none of their illegitimate seedlings will strike a deep
root or take a firm hold.
[4]For even if they put forth boughs for a while,
standing insecurely they will be shaken by the wind,
and by the violence of the winds they will be uprooted.
[5]The branches will be broken off before they come to
maturity, and their fruit will be useless,

not ripe enough to eat, and good for nothing.
[6]For children born of unlawful unions are witnesses of
evil against their parents when God examines them.
[7]But the righteous man, though he die early, will be at rest.
[8]For old age is not honoured for length of time,
nor measured by number of years;
[9]but understanding is grey hair for men,
and a blameless life is ripe old age.

[10]There was one who pleased God and was loved by him,
and while living among sinners he was taken up.
[11]He was caught up lest evil change his understanding
or guile deceive his soul.
[12]For the fascination of wickedness obscures
what is good,
and roving desire perverts the innocent mind.
[13]Being perfected in a short time, he fulfilled long years;
[14]for his soul was pleasing to the Lord,
therefore he took him quickly from the midst
of wickedness.
[15]Yet the peoples saw and did not understand,
nor take such a thing to heart,
that God's grace and mercy are with his elect,
and he watches over his holy ones.

[16]The righteous man who has died will condemn
the ungodly who are living,
and youth that is quickly perfected will condemn the
prolonged old age of the unrighteous man.
[17]For they will see the end of the wise man,
and will not understand what the Lord purposed for him,
and for what he kept him safe.
[18]They will see, and will have contempt for him,
but the Lord will laugh them to scorn.
After this they will become dishonoured corpses,
and an outrage among the dead for ever;
[19]because he will dash them speechless to the ground,
and shake them from the foundations;
they will be left utterly dry and barren,

and they will suffer anguish,
and the memory of them will perish.

[20]They will come with dread when their sins are reckoned up, and their lawless deeds will convict them to their face.

5 Then the righteous man will stand with great confidence
in the presence of those who have afflicted him,
and those who make light of his labours.

[a] The text of this line is uncertain, and it is omitted here by some ancient authorities. Compare 4.15

[b] Or *what is right*

Continuing the technique of developing his argument by means of short paragraphs, the Sage describes the ongoing struggle between good and evil. After presenting the problem of suffering in the example of the suffering just man—a traditional biblical theme (3:1-9)—the Sage resolves the tension in a striking but unbiblical way. He creates an intricate series of three contrasting illustrations that offer a paradoxical view of the triumph of righteousness. The contrasts are: apparent sterility with real barrenness (3:13 + 3:16—4:6); apparent and real fruitfulness (3:14-15); apparent and real stability (4:7-9 + 15-16).

Inspiring these contrasts is the Sage's absolute certainty about eternal life with God as the destiny of those who obey his will. The contrasts are interrupted at two points by digressions. The first, on the folly of rejecting wisdom (3:10-12), prepares for Part III, the Book of Divine Wisdom and Human Folly. The second digression, on Enoch, without using his name (4:10-14), links this opening part of Wis with the seven historical contrasts in Part IV.

In these illustrations the Sage continues to draw upon popular hellenistic philosophy—which by his time had become theosophy, a mystical syncretism of philosophy and theology—and uses it to show the superiority of traditional revealed religion of the covenant. He addresses the concerns of the young Jewish intellectuals and shows how the principles of their traditional beliefs can answer them by incorporating terminology from prevailing currents of hellenistic religion. By such illustrations he shows how the '*secret purposes*' (2:22) of God's plan are still operative.

His opening illustration operates like the chorus of a Greek tragedy. It vindicates the righteousness of God by explaining how divine wisdom surpasses and confounds the cleverness of the ungodly (3:1-9). God does not fail to reward those who entrust themselves to him, but only after death will it be clear to them that '*the souls of the righteous are in the hand of God*' (3:1). The term '*soul*' here is practically equivalent to the later philosophical concept of a person in the sense that the '*soul*' is the sustaining principle that enables humans to commune with God.

The Sage goes on to remind readers that the '*foolish*' are mistaken when they look upon the passing of the righteous as '*affliction*' and '*destruction.*' On the contrary, those who trust in God are '*at peace*' in the biblical sense of enjoying the experience of God's favor (3:2-3). More important, they will dwell in this favor forever. In the light of his belief in blessed immortality the Sage reinterprets prophetic passages like Isaiah 57:1-2. The Greek of Wis 3:4 can be rendered as in the RSV, '*their hope is full of immortality,*' but the translation, "their hope of immortality is satisfied," is more in line with the Sage's previous statement that '*righteousness is immortal*' (1:15). This translation contrasts the hope of the upright with that of the ungodly, which is '*vain*' (3:11).

In this wider eschatological horizon of looking at reality in terms of its final goal, the Sage explains the sufferings of this life as one's being '*disciplined a little*' by God in order that one's personal fidelity might be '*tested*' and be found '*worthy of himself*' (3:5). This testing is described in two images: the smelting '*furnace*' (see Mal 3:2) and the '*sacrificial burnt offering*' (3:6, a phrase never found in the LXX). Earthly sufferings are a discipline by which God prepares his saints for final judgment—here accurately translated as a divine '*visitation*' (3:7; contrast 2:20). The just will then radiate like '*sparks*'—the unusual image of 2:2 repeated here with positive connotations. The image enhances the contrast between the joy of the upright and the despair of the wicked. The Sage ends this introductory illustration with a variety of images to make blessed immortality desirable to his readers (3:8-9). The righteous will experience God's divine existence '*in love*'; they will participate in God's power to '*rule over peoples*'; they will enjoy God's '*grace and mercy*'; they will have an experiential knowledge of '*truth.*' The wicked will allude to this final aspect of immortality when they contrast their life of error, which was to stray from '*the way of truth*' (5:6).

Because the final sense line of 3:9 comes as an anticlimax, the RSV notes that it is uncertain. It is lacking in some manuscripts, and many modern editors omit it. The paragraph as a whole conveys in florid language the Sage's affirmation that eternal happiness is an exercise of the human faculties of intellect and will, namely, of knowing and loving.

Before going on to his three specific examples, the Sage inserts a short digression, a kind of footnote (3:10-12). He introduces the principle that evil carries its own punishment, an insight that he will develop in Part III (11:16-12:27). Such digressions act as bonds to unify the entire exhortation. This one is based upon an insight from Proverbs 1:7 LXX that '*whoever despises wisdom and instruction is miserable,*' the same adjective that describes idolaters in 13:10.

The following three vivid examples of how God disciplines his loyal followers are complicated by the insertion of the foolish conduct of sinners. The Sage adds the contrasts to prove that a life of righteousness is superior to following the path of paganism. First, in contrast to the '*grievous*' end of an '*unrighteous generation*' (3:19), the fruitfulness of a '*eunuch*' is '*blessed*' (3:14-15). Why? Because he will enjoy God's enduring '*fruit,*' but adulterers will have neither '*honour*' nor reputation. The prophet had promised the eunuch a share in Israel's worship (Isa 56:3-5), but the Sage enlarges the reward of '*understanding*'—that is an upright life—to embrace intimacy with God in the heavenly '*temple of the Lord.*'

The second example (introduced first but then deferred) is the blessedness of the '*barren*' but '*undefiled*' wife, for she will enjoy immortality as a person of '*virtue*' (3:13 + 3:16—4:6). She will never have the disappointment of '*fruit*' that is '*useless...and good for nothing.*' The two contrasting examples are intermingled and hard to disentangle because the style is so emotive. The RSV translation adds to the confusion by adding to the '*better*' of 4:1 '*than this.*' Actually, the untainted wife is contrasted not only to the preceding '*children of adulterers*' (3:16) but also to the '*prolific brood of the ungodly*' who '*are witnesses of evil against their parents*' (4:3-6).

The basis of the contrast is sharing eternal life, '*for in the memory of virtue is immortality*' (4:1). '*Memory*' is not used in the weak sense of what humans recall (as in 8:13) but in the saving sense of being known by God, who alone has power to communicate his own eternity to mortals (see 2:23). But the Sage also extols the worth of '*virtue*' (a term from philosophical ethics) in human relationships: it wins admiration, arouses imitation and stirs those who have witnessed it to action (4:1-2). The image of '*virtue*' being '*crowned in triumph*' recalls the fleeting joys of the ungodly who crowned themselves with fading rosebuds (see 2:8). The two kinds of joys differ in their origin and goal. The Sage does not oppose human discipline as long as it rests upon complete trust in God. On the other hand, ungraced human effort, like mere physical fertility, cannot produce either contentment or enduring renown before God. The image of '*seedlings*' that do not '*strike a deep root*' is a commonplace. The Sage is simply multiplying motives for fidelity to God in order to influence his audience of students to remain loyal to their Israelite heritage.

Problem Of Early Death

The third example defends the type of divine testing most difficult to explain: the problem of the early death of good-living persons, although '*the unrighteous man*' lives to a '*ripe old age*' (4:7-9 + 15-16). Rejecting the traditional view that a long life in itself is necessarily a blessing, the Sage insists on examining the quality of life. The true goal of life, which is to be '*at rest,*' is achieved not '*by number of years*' but only by '*understanding*' and '*a blameless life*' (4:7-9). Again he rejects external criteria as a basis for forming judgments; human happiness depends on qualities of spirit. The term translated '*understanding*' denotes not intellectual acumen but practical prudence, the ability to choose wisely. It is one of the hellenistic cardinal virtues that the Sage will attribute to Lady Wisdom as gift (8:6-7).

Whether moral life is summed up in the single biblical term of '*uprightness*' or in the four virtues which hellenistic philosophers saw as perfecting the four key human potencies was not an important consideration for the Sage. His stress was to attribute goodness to God as its unique source. At the same time, by employing this technical term of Greek ethics ten times, '*understanding/prudence,*' he shows his admiration for the analytic skills of philosophy.

In the midst of this third example appears another short digression. It concerns a great biblical model of '*understanding,*' Enoch, again without the proper name (4:10-14; see Gen 5:24). The digression provides a proof for the assertion that those pleasing to God may die young. God himself showed this by snatching Enoch from this world not as punishment but because he was '*one who pleased God and was loved by him.*' Enoch is an especially appropriate example because Wis teaches that physical death is not the end of human existence. And so God '*took him quickly from the midst of wickedness*' in this world '*lest evil change his understanding.*' God thus deepened his friendship with Enoch by confirming him in this '*understanding*' (*synesis,* a different term from verse 9). *Synesis* was a common term in both biblical wisdom literature and Greek ethical tracts for the insight needed to live an upright life (see 9:5).

The example of antonomasia, that is, omission of proper name, in the digression on Enoch points to a readership familiar with the Bible. The insert serves as a forerunner to the seven comparisons on salvation history that form the topic of Part IV, where the Sage celebrates God's care for his people. It is also a subtle confirmation of the unity of the entire book because Enoch will be omitted from the roster of those heroes aided by Lady Wisdom in history (Wis 10).

This footnote digression also raises the question of how modern editors preparing editions of Wis for readers unfamiliar with the Bible should present the text. Should the proper names be inserted into the text or should footnotes be used? In any case, the Sage's encyclopedic learning is reflected in his constant use of allusion, which makes Wis a difficult book and helps account for its lack of popularity. A similar problem arises in the book's vocabulary. The Sage deliberately picks words that had an appeal to readers familiar with contemporary hellenistic learning. For example, his observation about why God snatched Enoch contains three words never found elsewhere in the Bible (marked with *): '*The fascination* of wickedness* obscures what is good, and roving desire* perverts the innocent mind.*' Such words were chosen for their evocative power, that is, their ability to elicit reader reaction. But such nuances are lost upon modern readers. How can a modern editor recapture the original impression?

With 4:15 the Sage returns to his third example—the '*righteous man*' who dies '*early*' in life. The second half of this verse repeats 3:9cd, except that '*elect*' is substituted for '*holy,*' although RSV translates both terms as '*holy ones.*' The digression is ignored because what '*the peoples saw and did not understand*' was not the case of Enoch but the early death of the righteous—whenever such a case occurs. Again, the Sage solves the problem by appealing to blessed immortality, which will include for the '*righteous man*' a role in passing judgment upon the '*ungodly who are living*' (4:16). From what follows, this act of judging is not to deliver a guilty verdict but to appear publicly as enjoying God's favor.

The Sage finally concludes this long, complex section with a summary judgment to show that the ungodly will never be able to appreciate God's protection of his own (4:17—5:1). This scene is painted in apocalyptic style, that is, with terrifying cosmic images. The ungodly see only the surface action and so '*will have contempt*' for the '*wise man.*' This is the first time the righteous is called '*wise.*' The pagan Alexandrians did not value the wisdom of faith. Lest his readers imitate them, the Sage reminds them, '*the Lord will laugh them to scorn*' (4:18).

The descriptions in Isaiah 53-57 seem to have served as basis for this development, but the Sage extends the struggle into the arena of eternal destiny. Even cultured pagans do not have stability, for God will '*shake them from the foundations.*' They may appear flourishing to young Jewish intellectuals, but they do not have lasting values and so '*the memory of them will perish*' (v. 19). What is even more fearful is that their death will become a moment of judgment. Their own '*lawless deeds*' will stand as accusers and '*convict them to their face*' (5:1).

This section concludes with '*the righteous man*' standing calmly before those who misjudged him and who '*made light of his labours.*' Although the medieval editor who devised chapter divisions put this verse at the beginning of chapter 5 and thus sees it as opening a new scene, it really forms the climax of the section beginning with the affirmation that '*the souls of the righteous are in the hand of God*' (3:1—5:1). The Sage marks the limits of this section by means of a literary inclusion, that is, by repeating the key term '*righteous man.*' Now he will contrast God's care for his worshipers with a verdict to prove that the ungodly are foolish.

Modern readers may find this series of contrasts to be overdone, polemical, even bordering on caricature. That is because of a lack of feeling for the charged atmosphere of Alexandria at the beginning of the Roman era when the Jewish community was in danger of losing its identity. The Sage knew that his readers needed to be shocked into an awareness of their unique religious heritage.

4. JUDGMENT ON THE WICKED
Wis 5:2-23

[2]When they see him, they will be
shaken with dreadful fear,
and they will be amazed at his unexpected salvation.
[3]They will speak to one another in repentance,
and in anguish of spirit they will groan, and say,
[4]"This is the man whom we once held in derision
and made a byword of reproach—we fools!
We thought that his life was madness
and that his end was without honour.
[5]Why has he been numbered among the sons of God?
And why is his lot among the saints?
[6]So it was we who strayed from the way of truth,
and the light of righteousness did not shine on us,
and the sun did not rise upon us.
[7]We took our fill of the paths of lawlessness and destruction,
and we journeyed through trackless deserts,
but the way of the Lord we have not known.
[8]What has our arrogance profited us?
And what good has our boasted wealth brought us?

[9]"All those things have vanished like a shadow,
and like a rumour that passes by;
[10]like a ship that sails through the billowy water,
and when it has passed no trace can be found,
nor track of its keel in the waves;
[11]or as, when a bird flies through the air,
no evidence of its passage is found;
the light air, lashed by the beat of its rushing flight,
is traversed by the movement of its wings,
and afterward no sign of its coming is found there;
[12]or as, when an arrow is shot at a target,
the air, thus divided, comes together at once,
so that no one knows its pathway.
[13]So we also, as soon as we were born, ceased to be,
and we had no sign of virtue to show,

but were consumed in our wickedness."

[14]Because the hope of the ungodly man
is like chaff[a] carried by the wind,
and like a light hoarfrost[b] driven away by a storm;
it is dispersed like smoke before the wind,
and it passes like the remembrance of
a guest who stays but a day.

[15]But the righteous live for ever,
and their reward is with the Lord;
the Most High takes care of them.
[16]Therefore they will receive a glorious crown
and a beautiful diadem from the hand of the Lord,
because with his right hand he will cover them,
and with his arm he will shield them.
[17]The Lord[c] will take his zeal as his whole armour,
and will arm all creation to repel[d] his enemies;
[18]he will put on righteousness as a breastplate,
and wear impartial justice as a helmet;
[19]he will take holiness as an invincible shield,
[20]and sharpen stern wrath for a sword,
and creation will join with him to fight
against the madmen.
[21]Shafts of lightning will fly with true aim,
and will leap to the target as from a well-drawn
bow of clouds,
[22]and hailstones full of wrath will be hurled
as from a catapult;
the water of the sea will rage against them,
and rivers will relentlessly overwhelm them;
[23]a mighty wind will rise against them,
and like a tempest it will winnow them away.
Lawlessness will lay waste the whole earth,
and evil-doing will overturn the thrones of rulers.

[a] Or *dust*
[b] Other authorities read *spider's web*
[c] Gk *He*
[d] Or *punish*

In the second scene above the wicked had mocked the suffering just man in a long speech that revealed their malice and ignorance (2:1-20). Now, to balance that pompous display of '*arrogance*' (v. 8) and pseudo-learning, the Sage brings these wicked men back on stage at the moment of final judgment. By the technique of palinode they modify their earlier speech. These '*fools*' now ironically confess '*in anguish of spirit*' the '*unexpected salvation*' of the just man, who is now enjoying the fruits of his upright life (vv. 2-3). In lyrical language they picture the life that had '*no sign of virtue to show*' but consumed them in their '*wickedness*' (vv. 4-13).

Above, the Sage had briefly passed judgment on the wicked for their erroneous reasoning—'*for their wickedness blinded them*' (2:21)—and assigned them to the '*party*' of the devil (2:24). At the end of this speech he summarizes in a series of images their emptiness (v. 14). Then he goes on to elaborate upon the transformation of the upright, using apocalyptic imagery to show how God employs nature both to bless his worshipers and to punish their enemies (vv. 15-23). This theme of how God makes nature a source of both blessing and punishment is the basis of the seven comparisons in Book IV (see 11:5; 16:17, 24; 17:15; 18:8; 19:6, 10-12, 18-21). This is one of the techniques that makes the book such a powerful and unified protreptic to encourage fidelity to ancestral Jewish religion.

The wicked are described by the use of psychological language with emphasis on the '*fear*' that the Sage will define in the long comparison about how God uses light and darkness for friend and against foe (v. 2; see 17:12). This fear is '*dreadful*' in the sense that it causes horror, as will be seen in the dreams of the wicked (see 18:17). Why should the '*unexpected salvation*' of the '*righteous man*' cause such amazement? Because it reversed the foolish view of those who thought that everything was subject to fate or '*mere chance*' (2:2). Their response is now '*repentance*,' a term borrowed from the religious vocabulary of hellenistic mystery cults (v. 3). It is not the inner conversion demanded of sinners by Jesus but only an intellectual regret of having made the wrong decision in conducting their lives—as their explanation shows.

Does their designation of the upright man as being numbered both '*among the sons of God*' and '*among the saints*' make these two terms synonyms for the elect in God's presence? No, because the Sage never calls mortals in glory '*saints*.' Hence '*saints*' here refers to members of God's heavenly court. A better English translation would be "angels," creatures popular in Jewish piety of that period, as the Qumran documents attest (see 10:10).

The ungodly speak with poetic eloquence as they use the journey image to describe their wandering from the '*way of truth*' (v. 6), which is '*the way of the Lord*' (v. 7). But it is not clear how the Sage understands their status. Since they do not possess '*the light of justice,*' they cannot enjoy immortality, which is linked to '*uprightness*' (1:15), a gift limited to God's friends. He voices an opinion about their situation when he describes their feelings of frustration (4:9-14). This is a long periodic sentence—one of the most complicated in Wis. The three illustrations that describe their emptiness serve as conditional clauses in the sentence, which lead up to one final statement of condemnation. The first two examples—the ship and the bird—are found in Prov 30:19, suggesting that the Sage may have been thinking of that passage. But he elaborates upon the biblical imagery. Not until the final condemnation does it become clear that the whole sentence forms an answer to their rhetorical question about what good was their '*arrogance*' and '*wealth*' (v. 8).

By placing on their lips the Greek ethical term '*virtue*' (v. 13; see on 4:1), the Sage pictures these mockers as pagans, not apostate Jews. When they speak of a '*sign*' of '*virtue,*' they are using the term '*sign*' not in the biblical sense of a deed of divine power but in the philosophical meaning of a perceptible token from which logical conclusions can be drawn. As he does frequently, the Sage uses irony. They state the prophetic principle that sin embodies its own destruction when they recognize: we '*were consumed in our own wickedness*' (v. 13). This principle is introduced because it forms the basis of the polemic against idolatry in Part III.

The punishment of the '*ungodly man*' is spelled out in four images that illustrate their empty hope (v. 14). The image of '*hoarfrost*' is repeated in the '*wintry frost*' of 16:29. The final striking image of the '*guest who stays but a day*' and is quickly forgotten recalls Jeremiah's complaint addressed to God as '*hope of Israel,*' and yet treats his people '*like a wayfarer who turns aside to tarry for a night*' (Jer 14:8). Again, this is a learned image that assumes readers are familiar with biblical imagery.

Apocalyptic Triumph

At this point the ungodly fade from the scene and the rest of this section is an apocalyptic celebration of the final victory of the '*righteous.*' It begins by recalling that '*the Most High takes care of*' his own in a way only he can do: '*the righteous live for ever*' (v. 15; see 3:1). Their life with God is a dramatic reversal of the mocking picture painted in the section that balances this one (1:16—2:24) in Part I. The RSV translates, '*their reward is with the Lord,*' but the Greek text says it is '*in the Lord,*' a life of personal union that surpasses the promises of God to Israel in Isaiah 40:10 LXX. God will not only exercise his power toward believers but let them enjoy his personal companionship without end.

Again the Sage balances a biblical image with one from the hellenistic kingship tracts when he speaks of God's '*care*'—their term to describe a good king's concern for his people. The '*glorious crown*' God gives recalls the "crown of Hades" that sinners subject themselves to (1:14, there translated '*dominion of Hades*'). The '*diadem*' they wear recalls the diadem of Israel's high priest that protected him from foes—mentioned below in the comparison that spells out God's care for his people (18:24). Verse 16 provides an excellent example of how the use of parallelism slows up the movement of a verse and allows readers to savor the triumph of the upright. It is the pause before the powerful apocalyptic intervention of God next described.

In his opening exhortation the Sage had warned rulers not to '*invite*' death by foolish living (1:2). Now he pictures God as arming himself with '*zeal*' to visit '*destruction*' on sinners. In creating, God had not put any '*destructive poison*' into the world (1:14), but at the last judgment he '*will arm all creation to repel his enemies*' (v. 17). The imagery seems to be borrowed from the description of God's punishment of sinners in Isaiah 59:16-18 (see Eph 6:10-17), although the vocabulary introduces hellenistic terms not found elsewhere in the Bible. Thus, God's justice is '*impartial,*' and his "holiness" (rather than his '*shield,*' as in the RSV) is '*invincible,*' and his wrath is '*stern.*' God shared his power to rule with the just (3:8); now he shares his power to judge with all of his creation, which he joins with himself '*to fight against the madmen*' (v. 20).

This vivid picture of the certainty of God's victory and of the impossibility of escaping his power is a warning to Jewish readers to keep focusing on their final destiny and not to let temporary advantages of hellenistic culture corrupt their judgment. The extravagant apocalyptic imagery makes this sober scene more urgent. From the angle of the natural advantages the Jews may seem to be helpless. But their opponents prove themselves '*madmen*' by fighting against the Lord of the universe. A better translation for this term would be "deranged" (v. 20), because in Greek the term is a poetic word that recalls the tragic heroes who were driven mad by the gods.

Apocalyptic writers generally borrow their imagery from earlier biblical passages. In this case '*shafts of lightning*' (v. 21) could be an allusion to Hab 3:11 or Zech 9:14. But the thrust of the image depends upon common hellenistic cosmology that conceived of the universe as one living animal. Again the Sage links this contemporary scientific image to belief in God as creator who alone can control the cosmos and make it respond to his care for those who worship him. By showing how popular cosmology can be integrated into belief in creation, he affirms that only faith gives integral vision to reality.

This passage has other touches of poetic diction, such as the Homeric attribute '*well-drawn bow of the clouds*' (v. 21) and the Aeschylean-like compound '*well-aimed*' shafts (v. 21, but which does not appear in the RSV). Readers familiar with Greek literature would appreciate this artistry, but it escapes modern readers. The phrase that appears as '*mighty wind*' could also be rendered as "wind of the Almighty" by taking the Greek term for "might" as a personification for God as in 1:3 (see 11:20).

The final couplet, repeating the idea of sin as an empty '*shadow*' (v. 9), is a moralizing comment that blames the '*waste of the whole earth*' on '*lawlessness*' and '*evildoing,*' rather than upon the lightning intervention of God (v. 23). It voices the apologetic concern underlying the entire book of Wis. Evil is not God's creation but fruit of '*lawlessness.*' Against it righteous persons must direct all their energy—all the while motivating themselves to persevere in loyalty to God and to the believing community. This couplet acts as a bridge: it both repeats warnings found in 1:12 and 6:21, and introduces a new term for '*rulers,*' who will be amazed at "Solomon's" wisdom in Part II (8:11).

5. EXHORTATION TO WISDOM
Wis 6:1-11

6 Listen therefore, O kings, and understand;
learn, O judges of the ends of the earth.
[2]Give ear, you that rule over multitudes,
and boast of many nations.
[3]For your dominion was given you from the Lord,
and your sovereignty from the Most High,
who will search out your works and inquire
into your plans.
[4]Because as servants of his kingdom you did not rule
rightly, nor keep the law,
nor walk according to the purpose of God,
[5]he will come upon you terribly and swiftly,
because severe judgment falls on those in high places.
[6]For the lowliest man may be pardoned in mercy,

but mighty men will be mightily tested.
[7]For the Lord of all will not stand in awe of any one,
nor show deference to greatness;
because he himself made both small and great,
and he takes thought for all alike.
[8]But a strict inquiry is in store for the mighty.
[9]To you then, O monarchs, my words are directed,
that you may learn wisdom and not transgress.
[10]For they will be made holy who observe holy
things in holiness,
and those who have been taught them will find a defence.
[11]Therefore set your desire on my words;
long for them, and you will be instructed.

Commentators are divided about the role this section holds in the over-all structure of Wis. But the particle '*therefore*' and the vocabulary are decisive in recognizing that this paragraph serves as the opening half of the conclusion to Part I. The concluding exhortation serves to balance the prologue rather than to open Part II. The Sage concludes his long introductory diatribe, which was addressed to '*rulers of the earth*' (1:1) by again addressing the same group as '*kings.*' As mentioned above, this is a sophisticated way of speaking to learned students, a *noblesse oblige* approach encouraging them with constant reminders that God has given them unique gifts to reach their exalted destiny. The phrasing is modeled on Psalm 2:8-10 LXX, a royal psalm that contains the terms '*kings,*' '*judging*' and '*ends of the earth.*' This psalm also uses in parallel the phrases '*now, kings, understand*' and '*rulers of the earth*' which are distributed between Wis 1:1 and 6:1.

The Sage continues to mingle these familiar biblical phrases with terms from hellenistic philosophical writings, like: '*boast*' (v. 2, although better translated "exalt"); '*dominion*' and '*search out*' (v. 3); '*severe*' (v. 5). The concepts are easily understandable. What the modern reader misses is *why* these particular images were chosen. The answer is that their inclusion communicated a conscious effort to reach out to Greek culture without abandoning ancestral faith.

The prevailing style of this exhortation has been that of biblical poetry, which is based on parallelism, as the double divine names in verse 3: '*Lord*' and '*most High.*' Its thrust displays apocalyptic urgency: walk '*according to the purpose of God*' and '*keep his law*' because he is final judge (v. 4). The tone is one of warning, for it puts readers in the same category as enemies of God's people. This emphasis shows how seriously the Sage considered the danger of these intelligent Jewish students compromising their responsibilities as God's chosen people. The pull of hellenistic secular humanism was strong. Yet a decision to identify with it would be foolish because the Lord '*will search out*' their plans and demand reckoning (v. 3). The second '*therefore*' rounds out the plea with a literary inclusion and hints that the remainder of the book is going to provide motivation for the choices offered now to them (v. 11).

Both verses 3 and 4 begin with the same causal particle, translated by different words in the RSV: '*for*' and '*because.*' They are best understood as coordinate, offering parallel motives for heeding this advice. The first looks to the power of God who will demand an account for the '*dominion*' he has given to them. The second is built on their failure to utilize these gifts by the witness of their lives. In this development verses 5-8 form a single sentence to reinforce this warning. Thus, the whole paragraph is carefully constructed to justify the '*severe judgment*' of God upon '*those in high places*' (v. 5). The RSV keeps the play on words in the Greek by translating '*mighty . . . mightily*' (v. 6). Another bridge to secular culture is the word '*pardon,*' a term never found elsewhere in the Bible; it is a legal term from contemporary Greek.

The affirmation that God '*will not stand in awe of any one*' (v. 7) gives the same criterion that God told Moses to use in choosing judges: they must not show partiality (Deut 1:17; see Exod 23:21, of the angel guiding the Israelites). By employing the Greek term for '*master*' in the title '*Lord of all*' (v. 7; also in 8:3; 11:26; 13:3, 9), God is compared to hellenistic rulers who were pictured as protectors of justice. To prepare their sons to carry on that role, these rulers engaged philosophers as their tutors. The Sage thus reminds his readers that they have a royal mission in remaining loyal to the God who '*takes thought for all alike*' (v. 7).

The exhortation comes to a close with a direct address that gives the readers a new title, '*monarchs*' (v. 9, "tyrants" in the technical sense; also found in 8:15; 12:14; 14:16). "Tyrant" denotes an absolute ruler who had no hereditary rights to his throne. Generals of Alexander the Great who set themselves up as kings would belong to this category. This multiplication of titles provides further evidence that they are to be understood in the figurative sense. The Sage loves to multiply synonyms as a way to display his learning and give his exhortation the flavor of a philosophical tract addressed to the elite.

All these devices have as their goal to illustrate that the appeal to '*learn wisdom*' looks not to abstract principles but to a practical religious stance toward life (v. 9). Without '*wisdom*' they '*transgress,*' a term which in Greek implies committing apostasy, the worst sin for a Jew. The best '*defence*' against apostasy is '*holiness*' (v. 10, with another play on words). The final plea is to '*set your desire*' and to '*long for*' holy things. Ordinarily these two verbs have persons as their object. Their choice is not accidental because the Sage is already preparing for Part II, devoted to desiring and searching for Lady Wisdom, whom his '*words*' are now going to describe.

6. LADY WISDOM—WHY SEEK HER
Wis 6:12-16

[12]Wisdom is radiant and unfading,
and she is easily discerned by those who love her,
and is found by those who seek her.
[13]She hastens to make herself known to
those who desire her.
[14]He who rises early to seek her will have no difficulty,
for he will find her sitting at his gates.
[15]To fix one's thought on her is perfect understanding,

> and he who is vigilant on her account will soon be free
> from care,
> [16]because she goes about seeking those worthy of her,
> and she graciously appears to them in their paths,
> and meets them in every thought.

Logically, this short paragraph belongs to Part II of Wis. But, to connect the variety of forms that make up his exhortation, the Sage has interlocked his four books. So this commentary follows his literary order of justifying the ways of God.

The second major part of Wis begins abruptly with the presentation of Lady Wisdom, who is implicitly equated with the quality of '*righteousness*' and even with God himself, whom readers have been urged to '*seek*' from the first sentence. In fact, three verbs of that opening sentence are repeated in this opening of Part II: '*seek*...*love*...*find*.' This dramatic opening description of Lady Wisdom encourages readers to attach themselves to her. She is a mysterious companion of God who offers them personal communion with him now and for ever. The characteristic feature of Part II of Wis is her personification as God's unique, pre-existing companion. In the other three parts wisdom is simply a quality of God or of the upright, except in 1:6, where it is one of the titles of God. In this part Lady Wisdom is mentioned explicitly 24 times.

The Greek text begins emphatically with the adjective '*radiant*,' never found elsewhere in the Bible—although it is common in pagan literature since Homer and appears in one of the Isis hymns. Religious writers called stars that provoked illustrious births '*radiant*.' The following description of Lady Wisdom will draw heavily upon hellenistic philosophical and religious texts. M.E. Boismard holds that this passage influenced the Gospel of John 1:35-42 and 14:18-21. However, John's style and vocabulary in those passages have little in common with this description of Lady Wisdom or her role on behalf of the Sage.

'*Unfading*,' the other adjective describing Lady Wisdom, is also a biblical *hapax legomenon*, that is, it appears only here in the Bible. It contrasts her beauty to the transient pleasures of sinners, which quickly '*wither*' (2:9, a verb from the same root). The saying that Lady Wisdom is '*discerned by those who lover her*' means that her lovers willingly contemplate her in much the same way as philosophers contemplate truth with their intelligence (see 13:5). But the contemplation or discernment of those who pursue Lady Wisdom is with '*love,*' that is, with an affectionate concern that includes dedication of will and self-mastery (v. 12).

The rest of this short opening paragraph explains the power of Lady Wisdom to initiate and seal an intimate spiritual bond with those who are '*worthy of her,*' that is, righteous. This initiative of Lady Wisdom, a constant theme of Part II of Wis, lays the foundation for the technical theological concept of *gratia praeveniens*—the doctrine of the absolute priority of divine action in human salvation. Lady Wisdom has both the power and the desire '*to make herself known,*' that is, '*beforehand,*' as the compound verb in Greek clearly states (v. 13; also in 8:8; 18:6). She offers a religious experience that calls for total response as will be illustrated in Abraham (10:5).

'*Rising early*' is virtually an idiom in the religious vocabulary of the Greek LXX to describe devotion in prayer, as in Ps 77:34 LXX (see Luke 21:38). When Lady Wisdom brings it about that her lovers '*have no difficulty,*' she does so by communicating to them a quality she has even when she '*toils*' with them (9:10; the RSV translates the same term in different ways). The image is that her worshipers do not grow weary because of the comfort she offers them (compare Matt 11:28). She displays this power of comfort when she appears '*sitting*' at the gates of God's worshipers (v. 14). This simplified translation obscures the presence of a technical term found in the Greek, '*throne partner*' (again of Lady Wisdom in 9:4), a divine consort that guarantees religious and moral values by her influence. Part II of Wis will spell out in detail the values she brings into the lives of believers.

The two final verses offer additional motives to whet the appetites of readers for undertaking a whole-hearted pursuit of Lady Wisdom.The text implies that this will be a more rewarding challenge than the pursuit of philosophy—to which pagan counterparts were devoting their talents. Using allusions to Lady Wisdom's hymn to herself in Proverbs 8:4-36 (especially v. 34), the Sage urges them to be '*vigilant*' and to devote their '*thought*' to this quest (vv. 15-16).

An implicit contrast lies under the surface, namely, to those who are tied down to the cares of raising a family and providing for physical needs (see Sir 42:9). Those material tasks create a burden, but Lady Wisdom's comfort makes her pursuers '*free from care*' as she '*graciously*' supplies their needs. '*Graciously*' is found in both kingship tracts and hellenistic inscriptions praising public benefactors for being well-disposed toward serving others. Those who seek Lady Wisdom are called to imitate her generosity '*in every thought*' and to persevere in serving God's people (v. 16).

7. APPENDIX TO PART I
Wis 6:17-21

> [17]The beginning of wisdom is the most
> sincere desire for instruction,
> and concern for instruction is love of her,
> [18]and love of her is the keeping of her laws,
> and giving heed to her laws is assurance of immortality,
> [19]and immortality brings one near to God;
> [20]so the desire for wisdom leads to a kingdom.
>
> [21]Therefore if you delight in thrones and sceptres, O
> monarchs over the peoples,
> honour wisdom, that you may reign for ever.

After a short, striking introduction to Lady Wisdom, the text suddenly shifts back again to one final reflection on wisdom as a human quality. Hence, this paragraph serves as a conclusion, a kind of footnote to Part I of Wis. By such interlacing, the Sage joins the first two major parts of his rhetorical exhortation and gives his readers one more literary signal that this entire work is a carefully constructed whole, despite its diversity in style and content.

A theological message was also at work in the insertion of this final recommendation to the '*judges of the ends of the earth*' to seek wisdom (6:1). The introduction of Lady Wisdom pointed out that only her initiative, and not unaided human achievement, makes the quest for eternal life possible. Divine grace brings humans to their destiny with God for ever. Greek philosophy considered human virtue to be the triumph of self-actualization. Even the Platonic ideal to "become as much like God as possible" was achieved by unaided human effort. The Sage never denies the need for human effort as this paragraph shows—but places its roots in God's graciousness, which arouses even the desire for wisdom and creates inner capacity for personal union with God himself.

To show that faith in God does not hinder integral human development and virtue, the Sage has constructed this footnote in the form of a sorites or abridged series of syllogisms. In other words, the predicate of the first syllogism becomes the subject of the second and so forth to form a chain argument. Actually, the series does not form a rigid sorites, but synonyms are freely substituted in keeping with the Sage's flexibility and love for a large and varied vocabulary.

The opening subject, '*beginning of wisdom,*' is common in the Bible as object of the biblical ideal of piety, '*fear of the Lord*' (see Prov 1:7; 9:10: Ps 110:11 LXX; Sir 1:14). The Sage omits the term '*fear*' because he prefers to understand it in the Greek psychological sense (see on 17:12). Since wisdom depends upon '*the most sincere desire for instruction,*' it is attained only by those who '*long for*' it, as the Sage urged (v. 11; '*desire*' and '*long for*' are from the same root). This sorites, then, simply spells out the exhortation that the readers '*be instructed*' because '*desire*' or '*concern for instruction*' leads to '*love*' (v. 18). The Greek text does not say '*love of her*' but simply '*love,*' that is, affectionate concern for others and not the quest for Lady Wisdom. This '*love*' is other-directed, '*the keeping of her laws*' (v. 18; compare the test for love as keeping of Christ's commands in John 14:15, 23; 15:10).

The terminology in the last part of verse 18 comes from Greek law, and may be translated: "devoting one's attention to her laws is warranty of incorruption." '*Incorruption*' (rather than RSV's '*immortality*') was the technical Epicurean term explained above (see on 2:23). This '*incorruption*' is the climax of the transformation effected by wisdom that '*brings near to God*' for ever (v. 19). The concluding verse summarizes the argument of this sorites: '*so the desire for wisdom leads to a kingdom*' (v. 20). The pursuit of wisdom is the way to receive the reward of God's promise that the upright will '*rule over peoples*' (3:8). The pursuit of blessed immortality is a dynamic experience.

The Sage finally draws the long opening diatribe that makes up Part I of Wis to a close by one final appeal to undercut the prevailing theme of Epicurean philosophy—that pleasure is the highest good. On the contrary, only God and his gift of eternal '*wisdom*' can satisfy the deepest need of humans, the longing for happiness. This polemic purpose explains the choice of the verb '*delight in,*' common among Greek philosophers. They speculated that the gods experienced only pleasure. For example, Philodemus in this tract *On Piety* says that the life of the deity is the height of pleasure. The invitation of the idea that there is something better to '*delight in*' prepares for the long development on Lady Wisdom, who brings pleasure to those who woo her. The direct address to readers as '*monarchs*' is a compliment to their intelligence: choosing '*wisdom*' makes them supreme celebrants of life (v. 21; repeating the title from v. 9).

PART II:
THE BOOK OF LADY WISDOM (6:12-16; 6:22—10:21)

Introduction

This part of Wis stands out because it alone features Lady Wisdom, a personification found elsewhere in biblical wisdom literature: Job 28; Prov 8:1-36; Sir 1:1-18; 24:1-17; Bar 3:9—4:4. The Sage, however, has endowed this mythic figure with features not typical of her biblical role and accented her association with God in his work as creator and savior. He shows that union with Lady Wisdom is the only way to insure perfect communion with God. He maintains his style of writing in short paragraphs, linked together in a chain-of-consciousness style. The interaction of themes and images often suggests a variety of insights in the give and take style of a diatribe.

The literary genre of this part is *aporia* or "problem literature." The Sage treats union with Lady Wisdom as creating a series of problems that must be solved before he can lead readers to their destiny of unending happiness with the Lord. Although it is difficult to fix the exact limits of the units that make up this Book of Lady Wisdom, the movement of the whole is clear. It consists of four major sections:

(A) A prologue introducing Lady Wisdom and appealing to readers to follow her (6:12-16, 22-25).

(B) A celebration of the praises of Lady Wisdom in the encyclopedic, academic style of hellenistic religious writing, especially as found in hymns to the goddess Isis. Lady Wisdom is described: in herself (7:22—8:1); in her effects on behalf of human beings (8:2-18).

(C) A prayer for Lady Wisdom, spoken by "King Solomon," with whom the Sage identifies in an "autobiographical" description of how he came to see his need for her (8:19—9:18).

(D) An ode to praise the activity of Lady Wisdom throughout salvation history, showing how she blessed and saved believers who trusted in her (10:1-21).

Why and how did the Sage put these sections together as he did? The *why* is in keeping with his overarching goal: to encourage young Jewish students to remain faithful to their ancestral revelation, but in a way compatible with living in a metropolitan milieu. In other words, he wanted to show them how to integrate the achievements of the sophisticated culture of Alexandria into a living faith in the God of revelation.

The *how* of Part II of Wis is to portray the quest for Lady Wisdom in terms of Solomon's experience of her, especially as expressed in his prayer for her. Yet, the Sage updates this quest by means of resources with which his readers were familiar from contemporary hellenistic religion. Instead of a prayer for wisdom as a quality of soul or spirit, Solomon reaches out to Lady Wisdom and describes her in ways never found elsewhere in biblical writing. He thus creates a new picture of Lady Wisdom by integrating into the traditional personification features of style and vocabulary from the flourishing cult of Isis, the Egyptian goddess of wisdom.

This part of Wis illustrates how familiar the Sage was with the so-called aretalogies or praises of Isis circulating at that time throughout the Aegean area among religious pagans. Drawing on their vocabulary, structure and style, he pictures Lady Wisdom as benefactor of humanity. In this way he spells out the role she plays in both the individual life of the believer and in the salvation of God's people. Without reducing the picture of Lady Wisdom to that of Isis, he skillfully incorporates elements of hellenistic religion. Thus he challenged his sophisticated audience to reflect upon the choices faith demands.

The Sage's goal can thus be compared to the one Milton set out for himself in composing *Paradise Lost:* to justify the ways of God with men. This goal influenced his whole book but plays a decisive role in the presentation of Part II, because here the Sage deals most directly with the temptation to apostasy that these young Jews faced. He seems to have pinpointed the appeal of hellenistic religion to those on the threshold of manhood. Then he organized this long *aporia* to lay out their problems and to counter the hellenistic intellectual and emotional attraction. The exciting feature of his solution was to incorporate qualities of pagan culture in a positive way. Rightly employed, Greek culture promised to reinforce the faith of Jewish believers.

The Kingship Tracts

Religious choices are not made in a vacuum. They involve relationships to all levels of creation, including intellectual talents that mold civilization. The intellect, in turn, depends upon moral guidance and social concern. Since the time when the generals of Alexander began to set up kingdoms in the Middle East, they hired philosophers as tutors to prepare their sons to become benevolent kings. These philosophers composed the so-called kingship tracts, manuals of advice about how to rule wisely and justly as representatives of the gods and guardians of the cosmic order.

One great danger to this respect for cosmic order was the growing skepticism within Greek society. As philosophy became less abstract and tended to turn into theosophy, that blend of theology and mysticism, these philosopher-tutors became more and more propagandizers. A number of rival schools sprang up, each with its own theory about the way to achieve happiness. Such plurality furthered the prevailing skepticism and helped to fragment hellenistic society. Traditional religious values had less and less influence on human conduct, and human power became all important. The Sage states the prevailing attitude in blunt terms in the soliloquy of the ungodly, '*Let our might be our law of right*' (2:1). Now he wishes to offer a refutation of this view on the basis of his faith in God as unique source of all wisdom, whether religious or profane.

By this approach the Sage, as Thomas Finan demonstrated, fits into the apologetic tradition of Eupolemus and Ps-Aristobulus (2nd century B.C.) and of Artapanus (1st century B.C.). The establishment of the great library at Alexandria exposed Jewish students to the fruits of Greek humanism. As they matured and prepared to enter society, they had to make a choice between contemporary man-centered culture and the traditional revealed religion of Israel. Without composing a philosophical tract on the situation, the Sage composed a rhetorical exhortation that welcomed Greek humanism as long as it remained subject to the scrutiny of Lady Wisdom. That ecumenical tone of Wis is most evident in this Book of Wisdom proper.

Having argued against the might-makes-right attitude of pagans by means of the diatribe that forms Part I, the Sage now moves to construct the theoretical basis for his faith approach. Part II constitutes his affirmation that God's gift of Lady Wisdom provides the ordering principle on every level of creation, physical, ethical and spiritual. Using terminology from hellenistic religion, he portrays her as God's '*throne partner*' (9:4). Yet he does not consider her to be a transcendent being distinct from God, but only a literary figure to dramatize the effective and saving presence of God, which is at once transcendent to and immanent in creation. She attaches herself to those who believe in her as principle of their spiritual activity.

Precisely because God's wisdom is his personal gift to transform human destiny can the Sage personify it as Lady Wisdom, who offers herself to believers as their bride. He recognizes all true religious experience as a gift of God and capable of being brought under her influence because she '*reaches mightily from one end of the earth to the other*' (8:1). Her transforming presence adds saving dimensions to all human activity. The believer encounters her in every element of creation—seasons of the year, solstices, cycles of years, animal activities, powers of plants (7:17-20). Whoever is wise knows that all workings of the cosmos come under the guidance and concern of God.

What the Sage celebrates in the lyrical Part II, he will spell out by practical illustrations in the remainder of Wis. Part IV will offer seven comparisons showing how God makes nature work both for the good of his chosen ones and against their enemies. In those comparisons, however, the Sage will present not Lady Wisdom but God himself as molding events. The fact that he can attribute the same saving wisdom either to God or to Lady Wisdom shows that for him they represent the same reality. She is no second deity.

The *how*, then, or method of the Sage is, as Finan explains, basically that of "humanism." Displaying a profound knowledge and appreciation of the complex culture surrounding him, the Sage skillfully integrates historical, philosophical, scientific and cultic elements of Hellenism into "a speculative monism, in that they make Wisdom the source of all knowledge, profane as well as sacred."

The question that may intrigue a modern reader is why the Sage should choose to present this "monism" in the form of praises of Lady Wisdom rather than in an abstract philosophical *aporia*. The answer is that he was a religious thinker and a teacher rather than a professional philosopher. By attaching his theological insights to the figure of Lady Wisdom—familiar to his students who knew their Bible well— the Sage opted to identify with the long tradition of biblical wisdom. It was a literature composed to prepare each new generation of the chosen people to take its place as recipients of God's favor in the world. When the Sage reminds his student readers that even the '*perfect*' mortal '*will be regarded as nothing*' without Lady Wisdom (9:6), he provides a basis for later theological speculation on divine grace. Those who deny her access into their lives cut themselves off from friendship with God and from his saving presence that was operative throughout creation and history (7:14). Lady Wisdom shines forth as bearer of freedom to humanity.

In Part II the Sage is struggling to provide satisfactory answers to the profound religious questions that each age of believers proposes in its own way. He is not waging polemics against political authorities about restrictions on his people but rather illustrating "liminality as a social setting for wisdom literature," as Leo G. Perdue suggests. In other words, his problem approach recognized that his young readers were at the point of embarking upon the transition into becoming mature believers. He offers them Lady Wisdom as the only one able to provide all that is necessary to become mature believers.

The Sage's literary identification with King Solomon in these "autobiographical" passages clarifies the metaphorical nature of his address to '*kings.*' He identifies himself with the patron saint of wisdom so that his readers will take steps to become the true '*rulers of the earth*' (1:1), who manage well all the gifts God places at their disposal. He puts his whole literary exhortation into perspective by finishing this part with an ode to the work of Lady Wisdom, who was active throughout salvation history. She brought salvation to all biblical heroes, beginning with Adam. Each Israelite willing to submit to her guidance experienced her power to save. Now too, any Jewish student willing to take Lady Wisdom as his bride will enter into this parade of heroes and enjoy their reward—eternal life.

In introducing this ode of Lady Wisdom that occupies chapter 10, the Sage introduces into the text for the first time the characteristic biblical term '*save.*' The remainder of his book will center around the seven reflections to compare God's use of creation to help his people and punish their foes.

1. PROLOGUE TO THE QUEST FOR LADY WISDOM
Wis 6:22-25

> [22]I will tell you what wisdom is and how she came to be,
> and I will hide no secrets from you,
> but I will trace her course from the beginning of creation,
> and make the knowledge of her clear,
> and I will not pass by the truth;

[23]neither will I travel in the company of sickly envy,
for envy does not associate with wisdom.
[24]A multitude of wise men is the salvation of the world,
and a sensible king is the stability of his people.
[25]Therefore be instructed by my words,
and you will profit.

This short paragraph serves as an introduction to the contents of Part II, the so-called "Book of Wisdom Proper." It celebrates Lady Wisdom as God's intermediary in establishing friendship between himself and the righteous. The Sage has already introduced her (6:12-16; commented on above). Now he proceeds to impress upon his readers their responsibility to commit themselves to her and to accept her claims upon their lives. Here he spells out the radical incompatibility between a life spent in the service of Lady Wisdom and a life bent upon personal pleasure or glory. Her gifts are a powerful motive to reject the appeal of hellenistic philosophies and to choose a life of faith and self-discipline.

The promise to tell readers: (1) '*what wisdom is*' and (2) '*how she came to be,*' and (3) to '*trace her course from the beginning of creation*' is an artistic way of announcing the three sections of this *aporia* or problem section of the book (v. 22). The Sage carries out this promise only after his "autobiographical" revelation of his own marriage to Lady Wisdom (7:1-22). Then he (1) gives the portrayal of '*what wisdom is*' (7:22—8:1); (2) explains '*how she came to be*' in his own life as model of an upright worshiper (8:2-18 plus 9:1-18), and (3) hails her activity on behalf of the patron saints of God's people from Adam until the liberation of the Exodus under Moses (10:1-21).

In 6:22 '*wisdom*' should be capitalized to show that the topic of this paragraph is Lady Wisdom. The Greek verb that opens the verse has the technical meaning in the Isis hymns of proclaiming her wise and beneficent wonders—a dimension lost in the banal English verb '*tell.*' The Sage reinforces his promise by restating it in the negative—again alluding to the style of the praises of Isis, who does not '*hide*' her wonders on behalf of humanity (v. 22). The '*secrets*' of

Isis are her '*mysteries,*' another term borrowed from hellenistic religion. Only Lady Wisdom was capable of giving the protection that pre-scientific people felt they needed against hostile forces. She had been giving divine blessings '*from the beginning of creation*' (v. 22)—thus implying her pre-existent cosmic power. This combination of '*hidden*' and '*clear*' occurs again at the end of the Sage's long "autobiography" explaining his experience of Lady Wisdom (7:21).

In this introductory passage the Sage establishes a high level of solemnity by repetition in the form of antithetical parallelism. Parallelism, the characteristic feature of Hebrew poetry, is the practice of stating the same thought or image in two or even three expressions in the successive "stichs" or verse lines that form a single Hebrew verse. The verb translated '*pass by*' here and in verse 10:8 is to be understood in the metaphorical sense, much like the English idiom "by-pass." This figurative usage is prolonged by the verb '*travel*' in the next line (v. 23). This common English word gives no indication that the Greek term was extremely rare—in fact, this is its first recorded use. It resonates religious overtones because the related noun means familiarity with God in the Jewish writer Philo. The Sage rejected the advances of '*sickly envy,*' a term better capitalized because it is the personified rival of Lady Wisdom. '*Envy*' was the "evil eye" of hellenistic inscriptions, a quality of the devil who brought sin into the world (see 2:22). Envy is pictured as '*sickly*' in the sense of pining after those who fall under her spell, and so '*consuming*' their lives by her overpowering spell because she prevents them from becoming companions of Lady Wisdom.

Such sophistication indicates that the Sage's audience was made up of intelligent Jewish scholars. He takes every opportunity to remind them of their responsibility to witness to God's saving power as a '*multitude of wise men*' living in a pagan society (v. 24). He builds on an idea he expressed in his opening exhortation about the '*generative forces*' of creation being '*wholesome*' (1:14; the Greek term is "saving") by extending the realm of salvation to future life. Thus he hurls a challenge to each reader as a '*king*' in the universal plan of God for the '*salvation*' of his creatures. What he is about to tell them demands a hearing, for it '*will profit*' them if they allow themselves to '*be instructed*' by the words he has learned from Lady Wisdom (v. 25). This introductory paragraph ends with one of the Sage's favorite figures of speech, litotes or understatement. The '*profit*' he refers to is not the practical advantage of everyday wisdom but the endless joy of eternal life.

2. PERSONAL EXPERIENCE OF LADY WISDOM Wis 7:1-14

7 I also am mortal, like all men,
a descendant of the first-formed child of earth;
and in the womb of a mother I was moulded into flesh,
[2]within the period of ten months, compacted with blood,
from the seed of a man and the pleasure of marriage.
[3]And when I was born,
I began to breathe the common air,
and fell upon the kindred earth,
and my first sound was a cry, like that of all.
[4]I was nursed with care in swaddling cloths.
[5]For no king has had a different beginning of existence;
[6]there is for all mankind one entrance into life,
and a common departure.

[7]Therefore I prayed, and understanding was given me;
I called upon God, and the spirit of wisdom came to me.
[8]I preferred her to sceptres and thrones,
and I accounted wealth as nothing
in comparison with her.
[9]Neither did I liken to her any priceless gem,
because all gold is but a little sand in her sight,
and silver will be accounted as clay before her.
[10]I loved her more than health and beauty,
and I chose to have her rather than light,
because her radiance never ceases.
[11]All good things came to me along with her,

> and in her hands uncounted wealth.
> [12]I rejoiced in them all, because wisdom leads them;
> but I did not know that she was their mother.
> [13]I learned without guile and I impart without grudging;
> I do not hide her wealth,
> [14]for it is an unfailing treasure for men;
> those who get it obtain friendship with God,
> commended for the gifts that come from instruction.

Up to this point the Sage has addressed his readers as '*kings*' or '*monarchs*' (tyrants) or '*rulers of the earth.*' Now he reveals that he himself is also a king—in fact, he is Solomon, the model of Israelite wisdom. This identification of himself with the traditional creator of wisdom literature is further confirmation of the literary fiction being used in this intensely hellenistic exhortation. Throughout this whole "Solomon" section (7:1—9:18), the Sage plays on this identification by organizing his insights into short paragraphs, each reinforcing the thrust. The force of his argument depends upon his readers being familiar with hellenistic ideas circulating in the cultured milieu of Alexandria. The following comments point out elements in this situation that will assist present-day readers in getting a feel for the Sage's urgency.

He offers a wordy introduction in the form of "autobiographical" details. This literary device gives his readers a better feel for their historical tradition and for the values he wants them to celebrate in their lives and perpetuate in the world. In this passage he explains how he came to appreciate the need all humans have for an experience of Lady Wisdom to transform their lives. The physiology expressed departs from that presupposed in the Hebrew Bible. The Sage's presenting himself as skilled in hellenistic science is part of his agenda to convince the Jewish intelligentsia that fidelity to the faith of their fathers in no way cuts them off from participating in the best cosmopolitan knowledge of Alexandria.

He states his link to humanity by calling himself '*mortal*' (v. 1), a term found only five times in the Bible available to the Sage, including a passage in his favorite prophet (Is 51:12). The '*first-formed child of the earth*' is a non-traditional way of referring to Adam. '*First-formed*' is a new compound, which the Sage applies to Adam again in his poem describing Lady Wisdom's activity in history (10:1). In this "autobiography" the Sage strives for variety by introducing eleven words into biblical literature. His description of gestation and conception in that order mirrors contemporary scientific speculation on conception as a process of being '*moulded into flesh within the period of ten months*' (v. 2). Neither the image nor the time duration are biblical. The same unusual adjective to indicate a pregnancy of '*ten months*' is found in one of the aretalogies in praise of Isis. Thus the Sage adopts the conclusion of hellenistic science about the length of pregnancy and about the male as sole active agent.

The description of the birth of a king as being no different from that of any other '*mortal*' was a philosophical commonplace in hellenistic philosophy to proclaim both human equality and the contingency of all life. Even the king had to '*breathe the common air*' and to be received by '*thy kindred earth*' at birth and begin life with '*a cry*' like other mortals (v. 3). This description of his birth reads like a parody of statements found in a variety of the Sage's contemporaries. It provides convincing evidence that he is deliberately recalling popular kingship tracts rather than writing for existing rulers. His technical terminology establishes a tone that is almost impossible for modern translators to capture.

The allusion to crying at birth (v. 3) had become a mark of every authentic human being—in contrast to Zoroaster, who was recorded as laughing at birth. By detailing this account of his birth, the Sage is preparing for the passage attributing his exaltation to Lady Wisdom. Every believer's real dignity comes not from earthly prestige or advantage or even from any natural talent, but solely from her power and goodness. The Sage's protestations about the ordinary quality of his condition end with a proverbial remark on death as the great equalizer. His play on words might be captured by saying that all humans have the same "ingress into and egress from life."

Having experienced his own weak humanity, the Sage recalls that he wisely '*prayed.*' This is the only time he uses the common biblical term for a prayer of request (v. 7; also found on an Isis inscription). As a reward he received the gift of '*understanding,*' which was both a title for Isis and a technical philosophical term for prudence (see 8:7). The parallelism of verse 7 suggests that he personifies this term and intends it to refer to Lady Wisdom. His mention of the '*spirit*' of Lady Wisdom coming to him recalls his identification of wisdom as a '*kindly spirit*' (1:6). But he may also allude to the praise of scribes who study the Law (see Sir 39:1-11). In either case he anticipates his prayer for Lady Wisdom in chapter 9.

He begins to elaborate upon the impact that her transcendence made upon him. As yet he has not described her but is using expressive language to vocalize his personal feelings toward what she communicated to him. The imagery is in keeping with his literary device of assuming the role of King Solomon. He '*preferred*' Lady Wisdom to '*sceptres*'—a term to be understood in the figurative hellenistic sense of "power" (v. 8). In the parallel line, the term '*comparison*' is also a technical term for a genre of Greek oratory (*syncrisis*) that the Sage will employ in the final part of Wis—the seven comparisons of the activity of God toward his people and their enemies.

In verse 9, with a striking progression of tenses—past, present, future—the Sage prolongs his detailed reaction to Lady Wisdom's entrance into his life. This particular image is found already in classical Greek: '*all gold is but a little sand,*' rather than coming from biblical examples. When he compares Lady Wisdom to '*health and beauty*' (v. 10), his allusion is to the Greek ideal of a sound mind in a sound body. Yet he rejects that maxim as the ultimate criterion of conduct because she is better than '*light, because her radiance never ceases*' (an idea repeated in 7:29-30). The RSV fails to capture the epic diction of the phrase in Greek,

"The radiance which comes from her never sleeps." '*Radiance*' is a quality attributed to Isis. The phrase '*never sleeps*' translates a common Greek alpha-privitive, that is, an adjective formed by prefixing the equivalent of "non"—here, "non-sleeping." This kind of formation was a favorite of the poet Aeschylus and praised as a mark of lofty style by Aristotle. The Sage has over 70 examples of this kind of adjective or noun, including six in this paragraph. It is one of the poetic features lost in translation.

The Sage continues to rejoice in describing his encounter with Lady Wisdom by announcing all the benefits she brought into his life before he knew about her (vv. 11-12). The wealth she gave him was '*too great to be counted,*' as the adjective is translated in 18:2, rather than '*uncounted,*' as it is rendered here. As the context makes clear, '*wealth*' is not limited to material possessions but extends to all values, for Lady Wisdom '*leads them*' and '*was their mother.*' Mother is one of five feminine titles that the Sage gives to her. The others are '*craftswoman*' (7:22; 8:6; 14:2; never elsewhere in the Bible), '*initiate*' and '*chooser*' (8:4; only here in the Bible), and '*throne-partner*' (6:14; 9:4, the only times this daring title appears in the Bible). The term translated '*mother*' is a late form; in fact, this is the first recorded use in Greek. It may have been coined by the Sage by analogy with other feminine agent nouns. Hence, a better translation would be a more unusual word, like "begetter."

The Sage concludes this account of his personal experiences with Lady Wisdom with a promise to be as generous in communicating her as he was in receiving her into his life (vv. 13-14). He repeats the same expression that appears near the opening of Part II (6:22), not to '*hide.*' And he reminds his readers of the personal moral and intellectual honesty needed to accept Lady Wisdom into one's life. She can be received only '*without guile.*' Because her gifts are never exhausted, the Sage does not have to hold back in fear of impoverishing himself by teaching others to welcome Lady Wisdom as '*an unfailing treasure*' for all who receive her. What she offers is inexhaustible, namely, '*friendship with God*' himself. In the Greek this '*friendship*' is not stated as a general situation in the present, as the English indicates, but as a once-for-all acquisition in the past, implied in the aorist tense. The point is that the Sage is appealing to the example of all holy believers who obtained friendship with God down through history (see 7:27).

What Lady Wisdom brings are not human accomplishments but '*gifts that come from instruction,*' that is, from the discipline of responding to the covenant by carrying out the law of Moses. The term '*instruction*' also appeared in the chain syllogism or sorites of 6:17-20, as one step in obtaining the '*kingdom.*' It is also the common Greek word for "culture." Its implication would be that true culture must embrace the religious dimension of human existence because only through it will humans '*obtain*' the wealth that leads to '*friendship with God*' (v. 14). Instead of '*obtain,*' most manuscripts read "use," a more dynamic word. The adjective that describes this friendship as an '*unfailing*' treasure is one of those negative (alpha-privitive) terms that the Sage loves. This one appears nowhere else in Greek literature; evidently he coined it, probably without realizing that it was a new formation (7:14; again in 8:18).

3. DESCRIPTION OF LADY WISDOM
Wis 7:15—8:1

> [15]May God grant that I speak with judgment
> and have thoughts worthy of what I have received,
> for he is the guide even of wisdom
> and the corrector of the wise.
> [16]For both we and our words are in his hand,
> as are all understanding and skill in crafts.
> [17]For it is he who gave me unerring knowledge
> of what exists,
> to know the structure of the world and
> the activity of the elements;
> [18]the beginning and end and middle of times,

the alternations of the solstices and the changes of the seasons,
[19]the cycles of the year and the constellations of the stars,
[20]the natures of animals and the tempers of wild beasts,
the powers of spirits[a] and the reasonings of men,
the varieties of plants and the virtues of roots;
[21]I learned both what is secret and what is manifest,
[22]for wisdom, the fashioner of all things, taught me.

For in her there is a spirit that is intelligent, holy,
unique, manifold, subtle,
mobile, clear, unpolluted,
distinct, invulnerable, loving the good, keen,
irresistible, [23]beneficent, humane,
steadfast, sure, free from anxiety,
all-powerful, overseeing all,
and penetrating through all spirits
that are intelligent and pure and most subtle.
[24]For wisdom is more mobile than any motion;
because of her pureness she pervades
and penetrates all things.
[25]For she is a breath of the power of God,
and a pure emanation of the glory of the Almighty;
therefore nothing defiled gains entrance into her.
[26]For she is a reflection of eternal light,
a spotless mirror of the working of God,
and an image of his goodness.
[27]Though she is but one, she can do all things,
and while remaining in herself, she renews all things;
in every generation she passes into holy souls
and makes them friends of God, and prophets;
[28]for God loves nothing so much as the man who lives with wisdom.
[29]For she is more beautiful than the sun,
and excels every constellation of the stars.
Compared with the light she is found to be superior,
[30]for it is succeeded by the night,
but against wisdom evil does not prevail.

8 She reaches mightily from one end of the earth
to the other,
and she orders all things well.

[a] Or *winds*

As he does frequently, the Sage edges into his principal subject, so that the description of Lady Wisdom does not begin until verse 22. Up to that point he continues his autobiographical approach, but now shifting into her gifts to him personally. All of this is leading up to that special moment when he recognized her in his life.

Overwhelmed by her majesty, her beauty, her unique ability to empower him to be king of God's chosen people, the Sage prays that he may be able to portray her worthily. He adopts a formal mode of presentation, asking God to allow him to '*speak with judgment,*' that is, to render correct legal opinion on this situation. He repeats the verb from the sorites, '*to have many thoughts worthy*' of the gifts he received through her (7:15; see 6:15). These enable him to explain the moral demands that she makes.

At this point the Sage takes care that his readers do not isolate Lady Wisdom from the God of their fathers, '*for he is the guide even of wisdom,*' just as he was the '*guide*' who led his people out of Egypt (v. 15; see 18:3). Never does the Hebrew Bible apply the word '*guide*' to God, but pagans called Hermes the guide of souls, and it was one of the titles of Isis. The Sage will apply the corresponding verb to Lady Wisdom (9:11; 10:10, 17). As he gets deeper into his description of her, he borrows extensively from the vocabulary of hellenistic religion. His portrait of her abounds in expressions found in the popular aretalogies or praises of Isis.

Earlier he had said that '*a multitude of wise men is the salvation of the world*' (6:24). Now, again multiplying titles for God, the Sage presents him as '*corrector of the wise,*' another late hellenistic compound. It appears first in Diodorus Siculus but never again in the Bible. Repeating the image found in 3:1, that '*the souls of the righteous are in the hand of God,*' the Sage affirms continuity in God's friendship extending from life on earth under the guidance of Lady

Wisdom to everlasting happiness with God. His is a holistic understanding of the saving presence of God, which embraces nature, world history and the destiny of believers. The Sage creates no dichotomy between what later theologians call the order of nature and the order of grace, but sees Lady Wisdom active in both.

Imperceptively he glides from the power of God that sustains the cosmos and grounds all scientific knowledge into his celebration of Lady Wisdom's role in saving humanity. What he attributes to God in verse 17, he attributes to '*wisdom,*' that is, to Lady Wisdom, in verse 22. It is important that this young Jewish intelligentsia see the God of the fathers as giver of all human learning. The wonders of nature that hellenistic science seeks to explain derive their order and harmony from the God of nature and of creation. In these introductory verses to the description of Lady Wisdom (vv. 16-21), the Sage covers all major areas of hellenistic scholarship, but refers them to God's guidance. They all exist for human betterment and fall within the wider horizon of the divine plan.

The Sage had already urged his readers, '*set your desire on my words*' (6:11). Now he says that '*our words*' are in God's '*hands*' (v. 16). In contrast to the all-powerful word of God by which he '*made all things*' (9:1), human '*words*' have only the power he grants them through Lady Wisdom. The same is true for human '*understanding and skill in crafts.*' '*Understanding*' is the prudence or moral quality needed to lead an upright life; '*skill*' is the practical know-how to master the secrets of creation (v. 16). This is the first recorded use of the word translated '*crafts,*' but it came into popular usage as the name of a feast celebrating the "labors" of Hercules.

The Sage now holds himself up as a model in every science, saying he possesses '*unerring knowledge of what exists.*' He summarizes briefly what Ps-Aristotle will discuss at length in the tract *De mundo.* He does this in a set of seven parallel or related phrases describing the key features of this learning:

1) '*the structure of the world and the activity of the elements*' (v. 17). '*Structure*' is a modern term that updates the Platonic concept of order. The phrase '*structure of the world*' expresses the content of Isis' teaching in the hermetic hymn *Kore kosmou* (Daughter of the Universe). Isis is a teacher of the "constitution of the universe," that is, the physical make-up of the world. The parallel phrase, '*activity of the elements,*' expands and specifies that the Sage learned all about the fundamental '*elements*' that constitute the universe (see 19:18 for a more popular use of '*elements,*' never found in the LXX).

2) '*the beginning and end and middle of times*' (v. 18), that is, all the signs of the zodiac and astronomical dating. Again the Sage employs contemporary scientific terminology.

3) '*the alternations of solstices and the changes of seasons*' (v. 18). Knowledge of such technical matters would flatter his students, since Jewish legends portrayed Abraham as father of astronomy.

4) '*the cycles of the year and the constellations of the stars*' (v. 19). One motive for praising Isis was for her regulation of the year. Below, the Sage will picture Lady Wisdom as more beautiful than '*every constellation of stars*' (7:29).

5) '*the natures of animals and the tempers of wild beasts*' (v. 20). The philosophical term '*nature,*' a favorite with the Stoics, and which the Sage uses again (7:20; 13:1 19:20), never appears in the Greek LXX translation of the Hebrew Bible. Interest in properties of the living soul of both humans and brutes was strong among hellenistic philosophers.

6) '*the powers of spirits and the reasoning of men*' (v. 20). Whether the Greek term *pneuma* should be translated '*spirits*' or '*winds*' (as in the RSV margin) is disputed, depending upon how this verse is interpreted. There is not enough context to decide whether the Sage is speaking about '*spirits*' inhabiting the universe and influencing events, or about characteristics of '*winds*' that could play an important part in human lives. The expression occurs in the tract *De mundo* mentioned above; there it refers to winds.

7) '*the varieties of plants and the virtues of roots*' (v. 20). This combination favors the translation '*winds*' in the previous line. Then the whole list deals with natural science.

The next verse serves both as a summary of the Sage's encyclopedic knowledge and as a transition into his description of Lady Wisdom, whom he praises as his teacher—in contrast to attributing this knowledge to God in verse 15. The ambiguity proclaims that in some fashion God and Lady Wisdom are identical. She takes on many features under which God offers himself, despite the variety of titles the Sage gives her (see 8:4; 9:9). The title he chooses here, '*fashioner of all*' (v. 22; also in 8:6; 14:2), is the feminine of the title he gives God in 13:1 and 14:18. It is a literary device to present her to his readers in the following passage (7:22—8:1).

Qualities of Lady Wisdom

The actual description of Lady Wisdom begins with a list of 21 properties of her '*spirit*'—a technique that would both recall to his readers the praises of the goddess Isis and refute the material pantheism of the Stoics. More important, this list identifies the '*spirit*' of Lady Wisdom with the divine Spirit which he spoke about briefly in 1:7 and with '*the Spirit of God*' that moved '*over the face of the waters*' (Gen 1:2). By this allusion he skillfully attributes the whole range of hellenistic science to God's creative power. Any effort to acquire her qualities apart from an attitude of humility is useless. Every experience of her is religious and results in thanksgiving.

The Sage draws heavily upon the religious and scientific vocabulary of Hellenism for these properties. His list includes these ten adjectives never mentioned elsewhere in the Greek translation of Jewish scriptures:

'*intelligent*' (vv. 22, 23), recalling a saying preserved in Plutarch that God is "an intelligent mind and body."

'*manifold*'—a term linked to magic and used to describe water as an element in the tract *Timaeus Locrus*.

'*mobile*' (or agile; see 13:11)—linked to the emotions.

'*unpolluted*' (or perhaps, "stable enough not to disintegrate").

'*loving the good*'—a religious epithet going back to Aristotle that gives personal status to Lady Wisdom.

'*irresistible*'—a term found in Epicurus to describe the ideal of human freedom.

'*beneficent*'—a common attribute for virtuous persons.

'*free from anxiety*'—already in 6:15 to describe the attitude of a person who fixes '*one's thought*' on Lady Wisdom. It is also associated with Isis.

'*all powerful*'—a favorite compound of the Sage; in fact, one that he seems to have coined (see 11:17; 18:15).

'*overseeing all*'—another compound that appears here also for the first time in Greek literature.

That the Sage had an overall plan in the qualities he chose to describe Lady Wisdom cannot be proved from this text. Their order seems to be arbitrary, except for the final quality which extends over the final two poetic lines or stichs. It affirms the superiority of Lady Wisdom's spirit over the pantheistic world spirit of the Stoics. As spirit, she possesses the same divine qualities that God himself poured out at creation to rule the universe and direct it in fulfilling his will.

Images of Lady Wisdom's Activity

From verse 24 the Sage no longer speaks about her spirit but directly about Lady Wisdom. He says about her what the Stoics said of the world spirit: '*she pervades and penetrates all things.*' She does so in a variety of ways, among which are scattered comments that betray the influence of a wide knowledge of hellenistic science and philosophy. The image describing her modes of presence is concrete: '*breath,*' '*emanation,*' '*reflection,*' '*mirror,*' and '*image*' (vv. 25-26). This list is offered as a set of synonyms to express the transcendence of both God and his wisdom. The terms cannot be analyzed in strict technical fashion but are an exercise of poetic imagery by the Sage to state in popular commonplaces his belief in Lady Wisdom's surpassing '*pureness,*' that is, a transcendence which enables her to deal with matter without losing her ability to transform the worshipers, to whom she gives the '*glory of the Almighty*'—God's visible power.

The term '*reflection*' appears here for the first time in Greek literature, but it became popular and is found in Heb 1:3 and in Philo. Although it can have both an active and passive meaning, most commentators prefer the active "radiance" to RSV's passive '*reflection.*' According to the preferred reading in 2:23, the Sage stated that God created humans in the '*image,*' of his own '*eternity.*' As '*image*' Lady Wisdom purifies this human '*image*' obscured by sin and restores it to the original purpose God had in creation.

As usual, the Sage's reflections provide readers with motives for remaining faithful to their ancestral religion, but here they are clothed in language familiar to persons acquainted with hellenistic religion (often unfamiliar to modern readers). He exalts Lady Wisdom by heaping up as many ways of expressing her power as possible by expanding and explaining the 21 qualities listed above. Viewed in this way, verse 24 is a commentary on her paradoxical qualities of being '*unique, manifold, subtle.*' She partakes of the nature of God himself who, though one, is everywhere and all-powerful, unchanging and yet '*renews all things.*' As Winston notes, the five bold metaphors show that Lady Wisdom receives and communicates God's glory and goodness by exhaling, emanating, radiating, mirroring, imaging. Her work thus fulfills the purpose of creation as stated in 1:14—to keep all things '*wholesome.*' But her special concern is to care for humans, for '*she passes into holy souls and makes them friends of God and prophets*' (v. 27). This is another way to proclaim her power to '*obtain friendship with God*' for those who seek her (7:14). The Sage will spell out how she carried out that mission throughout sacred history in the litany of praise that is practically an aretalogy (ch. 10).

The idea that to be just is to be a friend of God goes back as far as Plato and appears often in Greek philosophy. Of the biblical heroes that will be described, only Moses is explicitly called a '*prophet*' (11:1). Lady Wisdom's role in effecting union with God is repeated in negative language; without her no one can enjoy God's love. The RSV changes this into a comparison in translating, '*God loves nothing so much as the man who lives with wisdom*' (v. 28). The Sage will reaffirm the unique power of Lady Wisdom in 9:6: without being united to her no one can be acceptable to God. These strong statements about the absolute necessity of divine initiative for entering into friendship with God help to lay the groundwork for Christian theological speculation on grace.

The idea of a *daimon* dwelling in mortals is found in Greek classical literature since Plato. The ninth letter of Ps-Heraclitus speaks out about god dwelling in humans through virtue. But the Sage introduces this imagery into biblical language to celebrate the influence of Lady Wisdom. His comment about her being '*more beautiful than the sun*' is a hellenistic cliché, found also in the praises of Isis. This second reference to '*constellations of the stars*' (v. 29; see 7:19) falls more into the realm of aesthetics than science. It serves as a transition into an allusion to popular astral mysticism: belief that each soul has a kindred star. Wisdom is '*superior*' even to the light of the universe, for cosmic light '*is succeeded by the night,*' but she transcends all human limitations. The word translated '*superior*' has been modified in one manuscript to the comparative of the first adjective describing Lady Wisdom—more '*radiant*' (6:12)—but the RSV reading is preferable. Greek astrologers believed that shining stars had an effect on producing the births of illustrious persons. The Sage takes the image further and puts the blessing of Lady Wisdom into a '*superior*' realm, in which she gives believers victory over '*evil*' or '*night*' (v. 30).

The first verse of chapter 8 belongs to this paragraph. It marks the climax of the description of all that Lady Wisdom has done in creation. She is administrator of its vast expanse. The terminology of '*orders*' is the way the Stoics spoke about what most philosophers and Jewish tradition called 'providence' (8:1; see 14:3; 17:2). She reaches '*mightily*' and '*orders*' the universe in the same way that God is pictured as doing (see 12:18; 15:1). This description of Lady

Wisdom thus ends by attributing to her the very cosmic activity of God.

Young Jewish students, familiar with philosophical speculation about theories of a world soul that went back as far as Plato, could relate to what the Sage is doing here. They would see the wisdom of his method for explaining God's power over creation. He was exalting biblical tradition as offering a more profound vision of reality and human destiny than the cosmic speculation of hellenistic philosophers. No need then to abandon their ancestral faith! This artistic update comes as an invitation to those standing at the threshold of adulthood. The Sage urges them to make the decision to cross the limen into spiritual maturity and adult responsibility as believing members of God's chosen people.

4. THE GIFTS OF LADY WISDOM
Wis 8:2-18

[2]I loved her and sought her from my youth,
and I desired to take her for my bride,
and I became enamoured of her beauty.
[3]She glorifies her noble birth by living with God,
and the Lord of all loves her.
[4]For she is an initiate in the knowledge of God,
and an associate in his works.
[5]If riches are a desirable possession in life,
what is richer than wisdom who effects all things?
[6]And if understanding is effective,
who more than she is fashioner of what exists?
[7]And if any one loves righteousness,
her labours are virtues;
for she teaches self-control and prudence,
justice and courage;
nothing in life is more profitable for men than these.
[8]And if any one longs for wide experience,
she knows the things of old, and infers the things to come;
she understands turns of speech and
the solutions of riddles;
she has foreknowledge of signs and wonders

and of the outcome of seasons and times.
[9]Therefore I determined to take her to live with me,
knowing that she would give me good counsel
and encouragement in cares and grief.
[10]Because of her I shall have glory among the multitudes
and honour in the presence of the elders,
though I am young.
[11]I shall be found keen in judgment,
and in the sight of rulers I shall be admired.
[12]When I am silent they will wait for me,
and when I speak they will give heed;
and when I speak at greater length
they will put their hands on their mouths.
[13]Because of her I shall have immortality,
and leave an everlasting remembrance
to those who come after me.
[14]I shall govern peoples,
and nations will be subject to me;
[15]dread monarchs will be afraid of me when
they hear of me;
among the people I shall show myself
capable, and courageous in war.
[16]When I enter my house, I shall find rest with her,
for companionship with her has no bitterness,
and life with her has no pain, but gladness and joy.
[17]When I considered these things inwardly,
and thought upon them in my mind,
that in kinship with wisdom there is immortality,
[18]and in friendship with her, pure delight,
and in the labours of her hands, unfailing wealth,
and in the experience of her company, understanding,
and renown in sharing her words,
I went about seeking how to get her for myself.

If the Sage wanted to give a purely conceptual demonstration of the superiority of divine revelation over contemporary Greek theosophy, he would have omitted this development because it adds no new teaching on the functions of Lady Wisdom. This long "autobiographical" account of his interaction with Lady Wisdom in the person of King Solomon provides an affective dimension to the "Book of Wisdom proper." It illustrates the apologetic concern of the Sage that prompted him to draw upon the popular cult literature of Isis. His real aim was to show his readers that their own traditions provided a better religious home than the contemporary philosophy of Alexandria.

The cult of Isis had been revived by Egyptian priests during the second century B.C. and spread rapidly. Extant inscriptions indicate how widely Isis was celebrated in hymn-like litanies. These were called aretalogies because they praised her *arete* or "wondrous powers" she used on behalf of her worshipers and of the whole human race. Aretalogies consisted of three parts: (1) attributes of Isis as wise and powerful; (2) descriptions of gifts and wonders she provided for those who worshiped her; and (3) titles showing her role in human progress. The Sage imitates the composition of these hymns in his praise of Lady Wisdom. He has already praised her for the special attributes she received from God (see 6:12-16; 7:15—8:1). In this section he describes what favors she has granted to him as her faithful client. Finally, he will show her role in shaping sacred history (ch. 10).

This development celebrates the ethical powers Lady Wisdom communicated to him in his role as King Solomon, patron of biblical wisdom. She can make these Jewish students kings also. If they develop the advantages of their religious tradition, they will reign and enjoy greater happiness than they could ever discover in hellenistic philosophy or religion. He deliberately appropriates for Lady Wisdom the "wondrous powers" of Isis because these readers were familiar with them. Many words in this section are technical terms from hellenistic culture and ethics but new to biblical literature. This bold approach on the part of the Sage is lost on modern readers, unfamiliar with the background. Hence, my comments will be aimed at showing how startling the Sage's description of his personal encounter with Lady Wisdom must have appeared to his original readers.

Despite his rejection of Hellenism as a worthy substitute

for divine revelation to provide a way to human destiny, the Sage's method is not to cut his students off from the treasures of Greek thought and culture. In fact, he encourages them to make use of all its advances in human history—on condition that they see human culture in terms of God's plan and learn that true wisdom is his gift alone. To be able to receive as gift, one must be a believer—as the Sage will illustrate in the seven comparisons he develops on the basis of the Exodus below in Part IV. His own experiences will prepare them for these lessons.

Reflecting on his youth, "King Solomon" says of Lady Wisdom, '*I loved her*' (v. 2), using the Greek verb that means "love as a friend"—the only time this verb appears in Wis. He '*sought her*' as he himself had urged his readers in his opening exhortation (1:1). He continues to describe his mystical encounter with her in sexual imagery. His intention was to lead her away as his '*bride,*' so '*enamoured of her beauty*' was he. This beauty, he implies, comes from the fact that Lady Wisdom was the spouse of God. The RSV translates '*living with God,*' but the Greek term speaks of a marriage relationship (v. 3; the term appears again in vv. 9 and 16, but nowhere else in the Bible, except as a variant reading). The '*and*' in verse 3 is emphatic, having the sense of "indeed." And the tense of the verb '*love*' is not present but aorist, that is, it points to a specific commitment on God's part to love Lady Wisdom with affectionate concern (v. 3; different from the friendship in v. 2).

The effect of this marriage is described in terms of two qualities Lady Wisdom now enjoys: 1) she is '*initiate*' of God's '*knowledge,*' that is, enjoying experience of his intimacy; 2) she is '*associate in his works*' (v. 4). This is the first time that both of these feminine forms appear in Greek literature. The Greek word is actually more specific: '*chooser,*' and defines her role in creation (stated in vv. 5-6). Leaving aside the disputed text of Prov 8:30, this is the only biblical text that attributes a role in creation to personified Wisdom. Since the Sage clearly presents her as personal, placing her above both '*riches*' and '*understanding,*' it is necessary to capitalize '*wisdom who effects all things*' (v. 5).

The repetition of '*if*' is stylistic; it is not to cast doubt on her power but to exalt her uniqueness in God's saving plan (vv. 5, 6, 7, 8).

The same term is translated first by '*understanding*' (v. 6) and then by '*prudence,*' as one of the four "cardinal" '*virtues*' (v. 7). That designation does not go back to the hellenistic philosophers themselves, although some of them did single out four key powers of human nature. The Sage attributes these '*virtues*' as well as all other perfections that humans could desire to Lady Wisdom, as '*fashioner of all that exists,*' (v. 6, repeating the noun from 7:22).

What the Sage celebrates here is not the intellectual transcendence of Lady Wisdom—which he praised in the previous section—but the religious and ethical qualities that she can transmit to believers and which make her a desirable companion. The condition for enjoying her companionship is the obedience to the Sage's opening command to the '*rulers of the earth,*' namely, to '*love righteousness*' (v. 7; see 1:1). The fruit of this association is the four key '*virtues*' of popular hellenistic piety: '*self-control and prudence, justice and courage.*' As a technical term, '*virtue*' is a feature of Greek anthropology, which looked on it as fruit of self-discipline in developing the four basic potencies that humans enjoy, namely intellect, will and the appetites for pleasure and for self-preservation. Greek philosophy taught that each of these potencies had to be developed by personal effort until it was fully actualized, and thus it became a virtue (v. 7; see 4:1; 5:3).

The fact that "Solomon" expresses Lady Wisdom's place in his ethical development in terminology characteristic of Greek anthropology shows his appreciation for a philosophical analysis of human nature and his pains to place the gains of human knowledge at the service of revealed faith. But he does not attribute these key '*virtues*' to purely human resources; he sees them as accomplishments of Lady Wisdom. This judgment flows from his thesis that human destiny is a gift of God, not an earthly achievement. '*Nothing in life is more profitable for men than*' these virtues because they encompass '*righteousness,*' which is '*immortal*' (v. 7;

see 1:15). Why? Because they are the '*labours*' of Lady Wisdom. The imagery remains sexual, for '*labours*' is best understood in the sense of labor pains, by which Lady Wisdom brings forth '*virtues*' as fruit of her womb. The Sage took her as bride; she presents him with their children, '*virtues*.'

Greek ethical philosophers like to draw a contrast between children born of physical union, who were often a source of worry to their parents, and virtues as "children" of the upright, who never brought anguish to their "parents."

Before closing his description of Lady Wisdom's gifts, the Sage expands to point out her contributions for educated and cultured humans (v. 8). Her gifts enable Jewish students to feel at home in their cosmopolitan setting. They are capable of discussing '*things of old*' and of anticipating '*things to come,*' and of dialoging with their sophisticated neighbors. They are fluent in Greek oratorical style and involved in all aspects of nature study. The common biblical phrase '*signs and wonders*' here does not refer to God's mighty actions but to the natural laws governing the universe.

Fruit of Union With Lady Wisdom

Having listed many advantages to be gained by entering into intimacy with Lady Wisdom, "King Solomon" spells out how she equipped him for his role as leader of the chosen people when he '*determined to take her to live with him,*' that is, to marry her (v. 9; see v. 3). Her presence assured him of both intellectual light, '*good counsel,*' and emotional '*encouragement*' (v. 9).

He does this by speaking to himself, or rather, by summarizing in seven indirect statements how he had motivated himself at that decisive moment when he chose to marry Lady Wisdom (vv. 9b-16a). He arranges these motives in two sets of three, centered around verse 12. The RSV prints verse 12 in four poetic lines or stichs instead of the three of the Greek text. These motives—recalling 1 Kgs 3 and covering the whole range of human wisdom—appear as a meditation on the biblical picture of Solomon as patron saint of wisdom. He was famous, of course, for solving '*riddles*' that is, difficult cases (v. 8; see 1 Kgs 5). Lady Wisdom gave him '*good counsel*' in every situation, good or difficult (v. 9); she brought him '*honour*' in the sight of both common people and '*elders*' (v. 10); she made him famous among world '*rulers*' for his remarkable legal decisions (v. 11).

Solomon was so famous for his wisdom that political leaders would await his judgments and '*put their hands on their mouths*' when he spoke (v. 12, using the same image as that of the princes in Job 29:9). Lady Wisdom also gave him '*immortality*,' here not in the strong sense of eternal life but simply as creating an outstanding impression by extraordinary activity (v. 13). The term '*immortality*' appears here in the meaning it had among contemporary Greek philosophers when applied to a city or hero. The repetition of '*because of her I shall have*' (vv. 10 and 13) is one of the literary signals the Sage gives to read this group of verses as a unity within the larger description of the gifts of Lady Wisdom.

In a sense her sixth gift was the communication of herself, because she made it possible for Solomon to '*govern peoples*' (v. 14). In Greek, '*govern*' is the same verb by which Lady Wisdom was described as the one who '*orders all things well*' at the climax of the previous section (8:1, a connection not apparent in English because of the different translation). On earth Solomon enjoys the same role that the just will possess '*in the time of their visitation,*' when they will '*govern nations*' (3:7-8). The climax of this series of gifts to Solomon is his power to bring peace by not only conducting wars prudently but by letting Lady Wisdom give his reign true '*rest*' (vv. 15b-16a, which should be taken as a couplet with complementary parallel lines).

As he nears the end of this "autobiographical" passage written in the first person, the Sage again shifts to a generalizing approach to speak about the gifts of Lady Wisdom, for he wishes to teach that her gifts are available to all without distinction. This he does in verse 16bc (or 16 bde in Greek).

He uses litotes or understatement in the first statement when he says that '*companionship with her has no bitterness,*' as is clear from the following: as source of '*gladness and joy,*' Lady Wisdom brings perfect contentment. The imagery remains sexual; she is still the bride offering an intimate experience of God's gracious presence to her lovers. The text emphasizes this imagery by repeating the technical term for marriage partner (v. 16; see above on v. 3) and by introducing an Epicurean word for sexual intercourse, translated in the RSV as '*find rest.*'

The closing eight poetic lines of these reflections by the idealized Solomon repeat observations from earlier verses. In the first seven of these stichs the preposition '*in*' is artistically placed in the Greek text (vv. 17-18). It is put in the second half of the first three lines, in the first half of the next three lines, and finally directly in the middle of the seventh line. Such artistry shows to what length the author was willing to go to appeal to the literary tastes of his readers.

Although the Sage may seem to modern readers to be simply repeating himself, he is skillfully handling vocabulary to allude to popular philosophical debates. At times he shifts meanings of words within his development. Thus, '*immortality*' in verse 17 is no longer the weak sense of being remembered by humans, but the eternal life that can be possessed only through Lady Wisdom. From the time of Plato the question of '*kinship*' with the deity was discussed by philosophers: was it possible or not? Some hellenistic philosophers claimed it was the prerogative of kings. By arguing that the God of revelation offers '*kinship*' with himself, the Sage helped to prepare for later Christian reflection on grace as a sharing in the divine nature (v. 17; see 2 Pet 1:4).

These final lines spell out this '*kinship*' in appropriate terms as '*pure delight...unfailing wealth...understanding...renown*' (v. 18). The RSV translates the description of '*understanding*' as '*the experience of her company.*' A more literal translation of '*experience*' is "joint exercise," from the root dealing with "gymnasium" (naked training place). In time its connotation had widened and it became almost a technical term in Stoic circles to describe the strong bond of community existing between a teacher and his admiring disciples, as between Zeno and Cleanthes. The bond of '*understanding*' displayed is the practical wisdom of prudence, the virtue perfecting human intelligence (see on 8:7).

Participating in gymnastics was considered a prerequisite for citizenship. Young Jews would even go to the length of having an operation to disguise their circumcision to be able to participate. Some commentators (like David Winston in the Anchor Bible) push the date of Wis down to the reign of the Emperor Claudius, who forbad Jews from participating in gymnastic contests in 41 C.E. and thus curtailed their access to citizenship. But the whole approach of the Sage is to encourage his students to pursue their ancestral traditions rather than to protest against being expelled from civil rights. Although he shows a willingness to be flexible, he operates in a conservative religious framework. The reasons he offers for not apostatizing are a sense of gratitude and a keen appreciation for God's care of his chosen people. These divine gifts to him through Lady Wisdom have made his life happy since the day he '*went about seeking how to get her*' for himself (v. 18). Now he wants to communicate the same desire to young scholars. This apologetic aim leads him to, as it were, start once more with another literary appeal that would influence them to remain true to their faith. This appeal takes the form of a personal prayer.

5. A PERSONAL PRAYER FOR WISDOM
Wis 8:19—9:18

> [19]As a child I was by nature well endowed,
> and a good soul fell to my lot;
> [20]or rather, being good, I entered an undefiled body.
> [21]But I perceived that I would not possess wisdom
> unless God gave her to me—
> and it was a mark of insight to know whose gift she was—
> so I appealed to the Lord and besought him,
> and with my whole heart I said:

9 "O God of my fathers and Lord of mercy,
who hast made all things by thy word,
[2]and by thy wisdom hast formed man,
to have dominion over the creatures thou hast made,
[3]and rule the world in holiness and righteousness,
and pronounce judgment in uprightness of soul,
[4]give me the wisdom that sits by thy throne,
and do not reject me from among thy servants.
[5]For I am thy slave and the son of thy maidservant,
a man who is weak and short-lived,
with little understanding of judgment and laws;
[6]for even if one is perfect among the sons of men,
yet without the wisdom that comes from thee he will be
regarded as nothing.
[7]Thou hast chosen me to be king of thy people
and to be judge over thy sons and daughters.
[8]Thou has given command to build a
temple on thy holy mountain,
and an altar in the city of thy habitation,
a copy of the holy tent which thou
didst prepare from the beginning.
[9]With thee is wisdom, who knows thy works
and was present when thou didst make the world,
and who understands what is pleasing in thy sight
and what is right according to thy commandments.
[10]Send her forth from the holy heavens,
and from the throne of thy glory send her,
that she may be with me and toil,
and that I may learn what is pleasing to thee.
[11]For she knows and understands all things,
and she will guide me wisely in my actions
and guard me with her glory.
[12]Then my works will be acceptable,
and I shall judge thy people justly,
and shall be worthy of the throne of my father.
[13]For what man can learn the counsel of God?
Or who can discern what the Lord wills?
[14]For the reasoning of mortals is worthless,
and our designs are likely to fail,

[15]for a perishable body weighs down the soul,
and this earthly tent burdens the thoughtful mind.
[16]We can hardly guess at what is on earth,
and what is at hand we find with labour;
but who has traced out what is in the heavens?
[17]Who has learned thy counsel, unless thou hast given wisdom
and sent thy holy Spirit from on high?
[18]And thus the paths of those on earth were set right,
and men were taught what pleases thee,
and were saved by wisdom."

Looked at solely from the angle of content, this "Book of Lady Wisdom" appears repetitious. But the Sage is not writing primarily to inform. He shapes his material for the purpose of influencing his readers by the artistic power of religious insights. Readers familiar with the aretalogies or litanies of Isis would appreciate his skillful adaptation of their structure and techniques to achieve an aretalogy in honor of Lady Wisdom. This second part of Wis embodies the three parts of an aretalogy: 1) a lyical expression of praise: 2) a catalogue of her wondrous deeds on behalf of her worshipers, and 3) a list of titles proclaiming her benefits for humanity.

In this prayer begging God to give him Lady Wisdom, "Solomon" carries out the second part of an aretalogy: a listing of her wonderful deeds in his life as a worshiper. His prayer is tied together by a literary inclusion through the repetition of the words '*men*' and '*wisdom*' (vv. 2 and 18). The prayer covers all the gifts she made available to him personally. The function of this shift from a list of common benefits is to affirm that all human endowments are gifts of God's love and mercy. The short "autobiographical" introduction to this prayer orients readers to this view of reality. At its conclusion "Solomon" locates the critical moment of his life when he cried out, '*O God of my fathers and Lord of mercy*' (9:1).

The situation evoking this prayer is decisive for understanding the text. Its vocabulary with apparent allusions to

Plato have caused some commentators to interpret verses 19-20 as referring to a pre-existing soul's being plucked from its heavenly home to be imprisoned in a mortal body. But the Greek phrase employed is not the ordinary idiom for '*entered*' (v. 20). It is better rendered as "I arrived at the condition of having" an '*undefiled body*.' A careful study of both text and context shows that it speaks of the liminal stage of growth: "Solomon" is on the verge of assuming adult status. Now he must choose the path he is going to take within the community. The prayer celebrates his decision to open himself to Lady Wisdom and '*to take her for my bride*' (v. 2). Failure to note this has led many to explain these verses as referring to the pre-existence of the soul.

"Solomon" attributes to Lady Wisdom his organic ethical growth in all areas of existence, '*body*' and '*soul*.' He had already described his birth at length to establish his community with all other human beings (7:1-6). Despite being a king, he too needs divine grace to fulfill his destiny. He does not go back to the start of life but shows that ongoing personal choice must appropriate the gifts that assure final destiny. He had attained an '*undefiled body*' because Lady Wisdom already '*taught me*' (8:20; see 7:22). By responding to her he enjoyed the benefits of moral fulness, the so-called cardinal virtues (8:7). But he still must complete the picture of how Lady Wisdom continues to function for the community of believers.

Within the context of salvation history, "Solomon" is going to picture God as Savior—an image that appears first at the end of this prayer and that will remain prominent in the book. The body-soul relationship presented here depends ultimately upon Aristotle's teaching on matter and form and on hellenistic medical theories about body and soul as being complementary principles of humans (see 15:3). His particular concern, however, is with his role as '*king*' of the chosen people (9:7). This mission accounts for the term '*lot*' (8:19), a kind of technical term from hellenistic inscriptions honoring kings. He proclaims that God's plan for him is to be noble in '*soul*.' But then he corrects himself to specify that in virtue of his '*being good*,' he gained mastery over himself and arrived at the point of having '*an undefiled body*' (vv. 19-20).

"Solomon" goes on to correct himself once more, this time with the ambiguous Greek term translated '*possess*' (v. 21). Its double sense cannot be easily captured in English. The RSV makes a clear choice by adding the complement '*wisdom*,' not found in Greek. He appears to repeat his insistence that only God can give wisdom (see 7:15) by adding '*I would not possess wisdom unless God gave her to me.*' Yet, the Greek text is apparently deliberately ambiguous. The usual meaning of thc term here is "self-possessed," especially in the realm of chastity, another virtue extolled in the kingship tracts. Hence, "Solomon" seems to be contrasting himself with the arrogance of pagan kings who pretended to acquire virtue by their own efforts and to lead others to acquire it. With this humble avowal he speaks to God '*with all my heart*' (v. 2).

This long prayer is a sophisticated literary composition taking its inspiration from the famous prayer of Solomon at Gibeon, to which it makes allusion and from which it borrows themes (see 1 Kgs 3:6-9 and 2 Chr 1:8-10, as well as the comments of M. Gilbert in *Biblica* [1969] pp. 301-303). This prayer is artistically organized in a concentric structure of ABA', with verses 1-6 being balanced by verses 13-18. The great variety of literary figures shows that only careful study can extract its richness. It must have been a welcome challenge to the original readers.

The pleas to have Lady Wisdom that are found in verses 4, 10ab and 17b function in parallel; all refer to God's giving her to his children. The originality of the request is that "Solomon" asks to have Lady Wisdom as his bride in a way parallel to how God has her as his "throne partner" (v. 4; the technical term is discussed on 6:14). He also begs God to make her his "helper" so '*that I may learn what is pleasing to thee*' (v. 10). This is necessary because no one can know God's '*counsel*' without enjoying the companionship of his '*wisdom. . .and holy spirit from on high*' (v. 17).

This prayer marks a turning point in the theological unfolding of Wis because it represents a change in focus from Lady Wisdom's role in creation, by which God '*formed man*' (v. 2), to her role in salvation, for all '*were saved by wisdom*' (v. 18). The Sage sees all reality as integrated by God's saving plan and wishes his readers to organize their own lives by means of God's wisdom as revealed in his saving power.

Explanation of the Prayer

The first strophe of the prayer (vv. 1-6) is addressed to the traditional '*God of the fathers*' as '*Lord of mercy*' (a title never found elsewhere in the Bible), who is creator of '*all things by thy word.*' The Sage attributes to Lady Wisdom an active role in creation: '*by thy wisdom has formed man*' (v. 2; Wisdom should be capitalized). She has a further relationship to humans, who '*have dominion over*' this creation. In this first stanza "Solomon" does not refer to himself as king but simply as a human being, one person in the race that was given by God the task to '*rule the world in holiness and righteousness*' (v. 3). The word for '*rule*' (repeated in 12:15 of God's activity) is never found elsewhere in the Bible but was common in hellenistic rhetoric and law, and appears in kingship tracts. Earlier, the Sage had attributed creation directly to God (2:23). Now he assigns a special role in it to Lady Wisdom, whom he again calls God's "throne partner" (v. 4, paraphrased in the RSV as '*that sits by thy throne*'; see on 6:14). He presents her not as a goddess but as a quality of God in his relationship to creation and especially to humans.

This image is significant because it shows that God's saving will is not confined to his chosen people alone, although God gives them special graces to achieve their destiny. Salvation history is a mirror in which later generations can learn their place in the universe and reach out in God-like liberality toward all human striving. The figure of Lady Wisdom is a reminder to the students that the '*God of my fathers*' alone can bring both Jew and Gentile to their final destiny. As the article of Gilbert cited above concludes, the Sage offers an optimistic view of human history and encourages his readers to enter into the long line of heroes who responded totally to their vocation despite human weakness. The God who puts on '*holiness*' as an invincible '*shield*' (5:19) has empowered mortals to rule his creation although they are '*weak and short-lived*' (v. 5).

The Sage does not let human weakness destroy his trust in the '*Lord of mercy*' (v. 1). He ends his first stanza with the same phrase found in his reflection on the emptiness of adultery; its fruits '*will be held of no account*' (3:17). Here, this same phrase, now applied to the person without wisdom, is translated, '*he will be regarded as nothing*' (v. 6).

In the second and central stanza (vv. 7-12), "Solomon" assumes his identity as king to speak of the three tasks God imposed upon him, namely, to be king, to be judge, and to build the Temple with its altar in Jerusalem. With careful artistry he mentions these tasks at the beginning and the end of the stanza (vv. 7-8 balanced by v. 12). Just as the Jerusalem Temple was to be a '*copy of the holy tent*' that God prepared for his people in the desert, so the king's '*works*' are to be a copy of God's '*works*' in creating all with his throne partner, Lady Wisdom (vv. 8-9, 12). The term '*copy,*' which goes back to Plato's use of the imitation theme and was popular with the hellenistic Jewish writer Philo, is found only here in the Bible. It was common in the pagan religious literature that saw mortals as a '*copy*' of the divine.

This prayer reminds God that Lady Wisdom '*was present when thou didst make the world*' and so can communicate true understanding of both physical objects and God's '*commandments*' (v. 9). This insight leads him to a second petition: that God may send Lady Wisdom '*that she may be with me*' (v. 10, in the center of the stanza). She will '*toil*' for Solomon, just as she toiled with God in creation, to '*guide*' him wisely in his mission as king (vv. 10-11). The text recalls what was said earlier, namely, that '*he who rises early to seek her will have no difficulty*' (6:14, where the Greek text says that she '*will not toil*'). The message of this stanza goes beyond its conceptual content for it is communicated with repeated allusions to images familiar to its original readers. The Sage's passing allusions to events in salvation history prepare his readers for the coming chapters, in which he will use events surrounding the Exodus to communicate trust in God.

The final stanza of this prayer (vv. 13-18, serving as A' in the concentric structure) celebrates the role of Lady Wisdom in the unfolding of human destiny, but now employing philosophical terminology. The approach is both polemic and preparatory for the attack on philosophical piety in chapter 13. The phrase about the '*perishable body*' as '*this earthly tent*' that '*weighs down the soul*' recalls Plato (v. 15; see *Phaedo* 81c). It is a good example of the Sage's ability to express his personal faith in a way that draws upon insights from Greek culture even when he is warning his young Jewish students against this "secular humanism." The allusion recalls the introductory remarks to the prayer about his own privilege of receiving '*an undefiled body*' (8:20). In both cases the Sage's trust grows out of his faith in God as master of creation and goal of human destiny.

This stanza contrasts the strict limitations inherent in human weakness with the endless possibilities opened up by God's grace communicated through Lady Wisdom. She and she alone overcomes the '*worthless*' reasoning of '*mortals*' (v. 14). Despite the vocabulary, it is not certain that the Sage actually read Plato's dialogues. His ideas had become commonplace, and the Sage could have become acquainted with them in a variety of ways. He was not a professional philosopher preaching an abstract anthropology but a teacher concerned with practical choices he had to present to his students. He does not speculate on the '*soul*' as having independent existence. In fact, by making use of Hebrew parallel style, he equates '*body*' with '*earthly tent*' and '*soul*' with '*thoughtful mind*' (v. 15). The term translated as '*thoughtful*' is a compound never recorded earlier; it is probably the Sage's own creation to give an Aeschylean tone to his prayer.

A shift to the third person in the question beginning in verse 13 makes it appear that "Solomon" has finished the prayer and is speaking directly to his readers. But his return to addressing God in verse 17 shows that this is still part of the prayer. The questions are rhetorical and are spoken in the hearing of God. They lead up to the final plea that voices the alienation of all humans who rely solely on their own devices. They cannot know, much less do '*what God wills.*' Why? '*For the reasoning of mortals is worthless*' without Lady Wisdom's '*counsel*' (vv. 14, 17). Verses 13-16 are a meditation on human weakness, a favorite theme of the Sage. But it takes place in God's presence and prepares for the final pleas to God for help.

As noted above, Gilbert shows that verse 17 is an implicit petition for the support of Lady Wisdom (v. 17, parallel to vv. 4 and 10). But here the Sage identifies her with God's '*holy spirit from on high.*' He had mentioned God's "holy spirit of discipline" (1:5, translated by RSV as '*a holy and disciplined spirit*') as a property that God gives to worshipers. With this divine presence the situation of mortals is not hopeless. God's graciousness heals the wounds of human alienation. This sudden revelation confirms my comment that Lady Wisdom is a personification of God's saving grace at work in the world and especially through the helps he gave his chosen people (see on v. 3). '*The paths of those on earth were set right*' by God's universal saving will (v. 18). This distinction between levels of appropriating God's will anticipates Paul's contrast between letter and spirit (see 2 Cor 6:6).

This belief in God's saving will generates the message of the rest of Wis. The Sage will now unfold God's saving activity in the world to invite his readers to renew their loyalty to the God of revelation. He views the past as prelude announcing that they too will be '*saved by wisdom*' (v. 18, that is, by Lady Wisdom). The closing lines of his prayer introduce the final part of the aretalogy in chapter 10—a list of the benefits of Lady Wisdom for the salvation of humanity, rather than for the benefit of human culture as in the praises of Isis. These lines also look forward to the final part of Wis, the seven comparisons that update the plague narratives to make of them a '*copy*' of the ways by which God protects his own people and punishes their enemies.

6. ODE TO LADY WISDOM'S ROLE IN SALVATION HISTORY
Wis 10:1-21

10 Wisdom[a] protected the first-formed
father of the world,
when he alone had been created;
she delivered him from his transgression,
[2]and gave him strength to rule all things.
[3]But when an unrighteous man departed from
her in his anger,
he perished because in rage he slew his brother.
[4]When the earth was flooded because of him,
wisdom again saved it,
steering the righteous man by a paltry piece of wood.
[5]Wisdom[b] also, when the nations in wicked agreement
had been confounded,
recognized the righteous man and preserved him blameless before God,
and kept him strong in the face of his compassion
for his child.
[6]Wisdom[b] rescued a righteous man
when the ungodly were perishing;
he escaped the fire that descended on the Five Cities.[c]
[7]Evidence of their wickedness still remains:
a continually smoking wasteland,
plants bearing fruit that does not ripen,
and a pillar of salt standing as a monument
to an unbelieving soul.
[8]For because they passed wisdom by,
they not only were hindered from recognizing the good,
but also left for mankind a reminder of their folly,
so that their failures could never go unnoticed.

[9]Wisdom rescued from troubles those who served her.
[10]When a righteous man fled from his brother's wrath,
she guided him on straight paths;
she showed him the kingdom of God,
and gave him knowledge of angels;[d]
she prospered him in his labours,

and increased the fruit of his toil.
[11]When his oppressors were covetous,
she stood by him and made him rich.
[12]She protected him from his enemies,
and kept him safe from those who lay in wait for him;
in his arduous contest she gave him the victory,
so that he might learn that godliness is more
powerful than anything.

[13]When a righteous man was sold,
wisdom[e] did not desert him,
but delivered him from sin.
She descended with him into the dungeon,
[14]and when he was in prison she did not leave him,
until she brought him the sceptre of a kingdom
and authority over his masters.
Those who accused him she showed to be false,
and she gave him everlasting honour.

[15]A holy people and blameless race
wisdom[e] delivered from a nation of oppressors.
[16]She entered the soul of a servant of the Lord,
and withstood dread kings with wonders and signs.
[17]She gave to holy men the reward of their labours;
she guided them along a marvellous way,
and became a shelter to them by day,
and a starry flame through the night.
[18]She brought them over the Red Sea,
and led them through deep waters;
[19]but she drowned their enemies,
and cast them up from the depth of the sea.
[20]Therefore the righteous plundered the ungodly;
they sang hymns, O Lord, to thy holy name,
and praised with one accord thy defending hand,
[21]because wisdom opened the mouth of the dumb,
and made the tongues of babes speak clearly.

[a]Gk *She* [b]Gk *She* [c]Or *Pentapolis* [d]Or *of holy things* [e]Gk *She*

The Sage completes Part II of his work—a long protreptic or exhortation—with a magnificent ode to Lady Wisdom. This ode fulfills the third and final task of an aretalogy in praise of Isis: to recite her benefits on behalf of human society. There is a difference, however, because this ode deals with her gifts to the heroes of God's chosen people. The function is similar, in that the Sage sees these gifts as directed to the ultimate good of all humanity, which is salvation (see 9:18).

To communicate to his readers fuller awareness of God's favors and to arouse responsibility to witness to them is the Sage's goal throughout this exhortation. This ode illustrates how he carries out that goal. In describing Lady Wisdom's influence on seven holy Israelites and concluding with the whole nation at the time of the Exodus, the Sage gives these figures representative roles. A willingness to learn from tradition is crucial for keeping it alive. This ode celebrates how the Israelite tradition offers salvation to all who believe.

Its outstanding literary feature is the dramatic use of anaphora or repetition of a key word at the beginning of successive clauses. Its six sections begin with an emphatic '*she*' to designate Lady Wisdom (vv. 1, 5, 6, 10, 13, 15; see RSV marginal notes). Translations like the RSV regularly insert the noun '*wisdom*' for the convenience of modern readers, but this practice obscures the majestic anaphora of the Greek text as well as the organic connection between chapters 9 and 10. In fact, the ode employs the noun '*wisdom*' only twice before the final couplet that brings the "Book of Lady Wisdom" to a close.

Some commentators consider this chapter as a later addition; for example, to make the first half of Wis the same length as the second half. Yet, while this ode to the working of Lady Wisdom in salvation history could stand alone, both uniformity of style with chapter 9 and the fact that it is necessary to complete the aretalogy are decisive in maintaining that it is an integral part of the Sage's original plan. Even the insertion of one person who ignored Lady Wisdom to his own destruction, namely Cain (v. 3), serves to announce the series of contrasts that form the final part of his work. They explain God's conduct toward those who withstood his chosen people.

The scenes dealt with in this ode are all taken from the Bible. To understand them requires the kind of knowledge that young Jewish students would possess—including the ability to identify the eight persons (none of whose names are given in the Greek text) and the incidents alluded to. But even here the Sage incorporates vocabulary from hellenistic sources—showing once more his aim of presenting Jewish traditions in language familiar to cosmopolitan Alexandrians. Technical vocabulary from Greek culture in this ode points to the specialized audience the Sage addresses. Since most of his subtle allusions are not familiar to modern Christians, today's reader loses the message of urgency that this ode originally conveyed.

The following comments call attention to some of these allusions to help modern readers experience the impact that the ode made upon the original audience.

1) Adam (vv. 1-2). Giving a poetic summary of the fall, the Sage describes Adam by a compound adjective that he had already used in 7:1, '*first-born.*' No mention is made either of Eve's fall or of her presence, but Adam is said to have been created *monos,* translated '*alone*' (v. 1). But in this context *monos* means helpless, a meaning going back as far as Homer (see John 8:29; 16:32). Adam was given the command '*to rule all things,*' but this responsibility was not limited to him (see 9:2-3).

As a footnote to Adam's triumph, thanks to Lady Wisdom, the Sage notes that Cain was overcome by '*his anger*' (v. 3). It is not clear why he inserts this negative example, unless to prepare for Part IV. C.L.W. Grimm offers another reason. This would have been the place to praise Enoch, but since he had already been referred to in 4:10-14, the Sage substitutes Cain.

2) Noah (v. 4). Only here and in the general statements in verses 8-9 does the Sage explicitly mention Lady Wisdom in this ode. Beginning with this scene he calls each hero '*righteous*' thus linking the activity of Lady Wisdom with upright

conduct. Since the style of this item differs from that of all the others in the ode, it is possible that Noah was inserted to anticipate the later reference to him in the attack on idolatry. That text designates God himself as the one who '*guided*' Noah (14:6). The verb for God's action is the same in both of these scenes, but here it is translated '*steering.*' Noah's ark is poetically designated as a '*raft,*' and its rudder as a '*paltry piece of wood*' (14:5).

3) Abraham (v. 5). It is not his call but rather Abraham's heroic obedience in being willing to sacrifice his son Isaac that the Sage offers as an example of Lady Wisdom's guidance (Gen 22:1-9). This provides an example of her role in teaching '*what pleases*' God (9:18).

4) Lot (vv. 6-9). As a city dweller Lot provides a good example of how precarious is the situation of the Sage's audience. The fate of Lot's enemies offers an image of the inevitable punishment of pagan oppressors. Genesis 19:24 mentions only two cities as being destroyed, although five are listed in Gen 14:2. The Sage calls them by the Greek term found in Herodotus but never used in the Bible—the Pentapolis. He links this area with legendary accounts of the territory around the Dead Sea. The Jewish historian Josephus also mentions the '*pillar of salt*' as still standing (v. 7). The technique of contrast introduced here will be exploited in the seven contrasts between the way God treats those who worship him and their enemies in Part IV. A literary inclusion on the verb '*rescued*' closes this incident (vv. 6 and 9).

5) Jacob (vv. 10-12). Lady Wisdom's guiding protection for Jacob provides a summary of what the Sage teaches she can do for those who trust in God. Nowhere in the book of Genesis is Jacob linked to the '*kingdom of God,*' an expression that became common only in the gospels. The parallelism equates the kingdom with '*knowledge of angels*' (literally of the '*holy ones,*' mentioned in 5:5, but translated there as '*saints*' or, according to the RSV margin, '*of holy things*'). The former translation sees an allusion to Jacob's dream of the ladder with angels ascending and descending (Gen 18:12). The alternate rendering, '*holy things,*' puts the expression in parallel with '*kingdom of God*' and makes it

refer to Jacob's education into '*godliness.*' Lady Wisdom '*stood by him,*' affording exactly the same kind of protection that God offers his people in the final statement of the entire book (19:22). Lady Wisdom functions as teacher toward Jacob by showing him the unique power of '*godliness,*' a quality that the Sage urges his readers to cultivate to obtain victory over their opponents.

6) Joseph (vv. 13-14). These verses offer a masterful summary of Joseph's career without repeating the vocabulary of the book of Genesis. This appeal to contemporary terminology includes the metaphorical use of '*sceptre*' for authority. The '*sin*' from which Lady Wisdom '*delivered*' Joseph was not any personal fault but the sinful situation to which he was exposed—just like the readers of Wis.

Final Instructions and Warnings

7) Chosen People and Moses (vv. 15-21). This final example mingles both triumph and reproach. The Sage pictures what God did for his people but in a way that both warns and encourages his readers. First, he recalls the lament in Isaiah 63:13-14 of the postexilic community overwhelmed by their enemies. But then he turns and in an apostrophe or direct address reminds God of his '*holy name*' and '*defending hand*' that the chosen people praised when he freed them from Egypt. In keeping with his introduction of contemporary vocabulary in parallel with traditional biblical terminology, the Sage calls the '*miraculous*' clouds of Exodus 13:21-22 both '*shelter*' during the day (from Psalm 105:39; 104:39 LXX) and '*starry flame*' by night (v. 17), a phrase repeated in 17:5 but found nowhere else in Scripture.

He mentions a second proper name, again using the Greek name of '*Red Sea*' rather than the Hebrew "Reed Sea" (v. 18). The statement that '*the righteous plundered the ungodly*' probably refers to events before the Jewish departure. When the Egyptians gave '*jewelry of silver and gold and clothing*' for the asking (Ex 12:35-36), they did so under duress, because the Sage uses the same verb for '*plundered*' that appears in Exodus 12:36 (v. 20). In his elaborate comparisons later in the book, the Sage will freely shift details and embellish the biblical narratives to score points more effectively.

The remark that the '*righteous... sang hymns*' (v. 20) is a passing reference to the liturgy celebrated in connection with the Exodus. This liturgy will be described more fully in connection with the plague in 18:6-9. With this apocalyptic picture of the Exodus, the Sage brings his "Book of Lady Wisdom" to a dramatic close. Her final gift was that she '*made the tongues of babes speak clearly*' (v. 20). This phrase incorporates the key word '*clearly*' from Isaiah 35:6, which describes the wonders of messianic times. The Sage sees these saving experiences of the Jews as concrete proofs of God's ability to save his people in their present need.

He will now go on to argue at great length that these saving interventions create a need for choice among readers. These Jewish students must opt for faith in God if they hope to experience his saving power. Otherwise they will join the forces of God's enemies and be excluded from the reward of his eternal presence. God creates humans for endless life with himself, and they reach that destiny only with his help, by faithfully doing '*what pleases*' him in their personal life (9:18). This method of describing Israel's rescue from the Egyptians shows that the Sage already has in mind the literary form of comparison or *syncrisis* that he will employ in Part IV. There, however, he will not use the figure of Lady Wisdom but speak of God as acting directly to bless and to punish.

After the general introduction to the seven comparisons (11:1-3), the Sage places the first syncrisis, contrasting how God treated his chosen people and their enemies during the Exodus period. In each situation compared, God uses the same element of creation to show favor to his people and to punish their enemies. These comparisons complement well the final part of this aretalogy; hence the flow of the text. And yet, they need to be viewed in the wider horizon of God's wise providence toward the whole of his creation. For this reason, after the first comparison the Sage interrupts Part IV and inserts the third major part of Wis, which can be called either a meditation on divine providence or the "Book of Divine Wisdom and Human Folly" (11:15—16:1a).

PART III: THE BOOK OF DIVINE WISDOM AND THE FOLLY OF IDOLATRY (11:15—16:1)

Introduction

More than any other part of Wis, Part III reveals the Sage as a teacher, as one familiar with literary procedure and as a person acquainted with historical trends that teachers learn over years of presenting lessons. Having appealed to his students for loyalty to their tradition and to faith in God's activity in history, he now turns to portray the enemy—the world that is hostile to the '*God of my fathers*' (9:1). He undertakes a diatribe against idolatry in all of its forms. This diatribe, carefully planned and orchestrated, is the most overtly apologetic part of Wis. It focuses on the kinds of idolatry actually practiced in the ancient world and reveals their folly. The examples and the way they are developed help trace this writing to Alexandria. The Sage's great attention to the worship of animals makes sense in light of Egypt's religious history.

Just as in portraying the work of Lady Wisdom in the world the Sage pointed to concrete instances of her influence, so now he attacks specific abuses fostered by forms of idolatry that flourished in the hellenistic world. In addition—again revealing the concerns of a teacher—in the center of his development he provides a brief account of the origin of idolatry and the reason for its spread (14:9—15:6). By uncovering the selfish motives of those who popularized idolatry, the Sage strengthens his case for loyalty to the revealed Jewish religious tradition.

This diatribe defending God's providence and exposing the folly of idolatry comes immediately after the first of the seven comparisons that form Part IV of Wis. The intercalation of parts is no accident. It puts the condemnation of idolatry into close connection with the celebration of God's involvement in the history of his chosen people. This arrangement told readers that, only if they kept the total picture of God's saving plan before them, would they escape being deceived by the allure of Hellenism from their traditional faith.

Plan of Part III

This part of Wis illustrates how the Sage developed his theses by means of contrasts and how he inserted digressions that add a dimension to his teaching. His main purpose is to show the folly of idolatry in as many ways as possible. In so doing he also exalts the wisdom of God's providence and reminds his readers that God punishes those who misuse his gifts. The following is an overview of the development:

A. (11:15—12:27) Meditation on Divine Providence
 1) (11:15—12:2) God's restraint in dealing with the Canaanites.
 2) (12:3-27) Four monologues on God's providence in history.

B. (13:1—14:8 + 15:7—16:1) Condemnation of four forms of idolatry, in climactic order:
 1) (13:1-9) Eon or nature worship.
 2) (13:10—14:8) Worship of wooden idols (+ C below).
 3) (15:7-13) Worship of clay idols.
 4) (15:14-19) Worship of animals.

C. (14:9—15:6) A stylized history of the origin and spread of idolatry (inserted in the middle of section B).

The execution of this plan is not always as smooth as this outline suggests because the Sage develops his points as a teacher rather than as a professional writer. He cannot refrain from inserting remarks that anticipate further developments or refer back to earlier pieces in the form of flashbacks. Thus, he anticipates his series of dialogues with God about how he exercises his providence (12:3-27) by his comment in 11:16 '*that one is punished by the very things by which he sins.*' This principle guides the development of the whole of Part III in contrast to the underlying thrust of Part IV, that God uses the same element of nature to reward his friends and punish their enemies. Over and above the inner unity of chapters 13-15, this part forms a unity that should be interpreted as a whole.

In his attack on natural philosophical religion (13:1-9), the Sage comes closest to displaying scientific knowledge of philosophy. He shows that, while he values its insights, he considers all human knowledge as incomplete and incapable of bringing humans to their true destiny. In his concern to uphold the unique place of God in human salvation, his arguments at times seem almost caricatures. His efforts at moral persuasion are not the only explanation of his excesses. He adopts the bombastic style of pagan philosophical attacks on idolatry in authors like Heraclitus and Horace. He signals that he does not attempt to give an exact historical account of his opponents' position by describing the sinful Canaanites in terms associated with both Greek tragedy and the cult of Dionysus (12:3-11).

The strong emotion displayed in attacking the various forms of idolatry indicates that the Sage wrote from a sense of urgency. He wanted his students to recognize that their own religion was best. Without asking them to withdraw from human culture, he wants them to exercise that divine '*kindness*' with which God deals with all humans (12:19). This attitude of '*kindness*' (the RSV translation of *philanthropia,* literally "love of mankind") was the Stoic name for that sympathetic outreach of the divine toward all, and a quality that the Sage admired (see 11:23, 26; 12:8, 18-19; 14:13; 15:1).

This third part of Wis abounds in literary allusions and stylistic features that would appeal to students acquainted with hellenistic rhetoric—like irony, litotes or understatement, and climax. The types of idolatry are arranged effectively in climactic order. Beginning with philosophical nature worship, the Sage calls those who espouse it '*foolish*' (13:1). Those who worship metal or wooden idols are '*miserable*' (13:10, better translated as "doomed"). Thirdly, he attaches more malice to the one who fashions idols of clay, '*for this man, more than all others, knows that he sins*' (15:3). Finally, the climax is reached in calling those who worship animals '*most foolish, and more miserable than an infant*' (15:14).

Role of Part III in the Book

This part of Wis plays an important role in the unfolding of the Sage's thesis; it is not simply a tangent. Its length is greater than that of the "Book of Lady Wisdom." It incorporates several "flashbacks," the type of literary cross-references which link what might look like unrelated developments into a dynamic unity in this great exhortation.

Far from going off on a tangent, Part III is a digression only in the sense that ancient Greek historians used parallel developments within their writings to incorporate material found in modern footnotes and appendixes. It is really an example of hellenistic Jewish missionary literature. It serves to exalt the God of Israel as unique creator and ruler, to point out the evils of idolatry for individuals and groups, and to reinforce the Jewish minority in its loyalty to the vision of reality revealed in their Scripture.

In addition, certain features within the text serve to show that the Sage is not writing against any actual persecutor of the Jews. He develops traditional arguments against idolatry in the sophisticated setting of scholastic polemic. Thus, the three-fold attack on animal worship is organized to form an inclusion that frames both the first half and then the entirety of Part III (11:15-26, with 12:23-27 and then with 15:18—16:1). The whole presentation reads more like an academic exercise than a response to a political attack against Alexandrian Jews. The Sage maintains the atmosphere of a classroom. Only well educated readers would appreciate the learned allusions and profit from them in their personal religious growth.

Before he became rector of the Pontifical Biblical Institute in Rome, M. Gilbert produced a careful study of Wis 13-15. He developed his own insights as well as critiquing earlier studies. His minute analyses demonstrate the superior literary skill of the Sage. My comments have leaned upon him, but are much briefer. In two points I differ from his conclusions: 1) I see these two chapters as being part of a larger unity that extends from 11:15 to 16:1a, and 2) I focus more attention on the social situation that influenced the Sage's development. See M. Gilbert, *La critique des dieux dans le Livre de la Sagesse* (Rome, 1973).

1. APOLOGIA FOR DIVINE PROVIDENCE
Wis 11:15—12:2

[15]In return for their foolish and wicked thoughts,
which led them astray to worship irrational
serpents and worthless animals,
thou didst send upon them a multitude of irrational
creatures to punish them,
[16]that they might learn that one is punished by the very
things by which he sins.
[17]For thy all-powerful hand,
which created the world out of formless matter,
did not lack the means to send upon them a multitude of
bears, or bold lions,
[18]or newly created unknown beasts full of rage,
or such as breathe out fiery breath,
or belch forth a thick pall of smoke,
or flash terrible sparks from their eyes;
[19]not only could their damage exterminate men,[a]
but the mere sight of them could kill by fright.

[20]Even apart from these, men[b] could fall at a single breath
when pursued by justice
and scattered by the breath of thy power.
But thou hast arranged all things by measure and number
and weight.
[21]For it is always in thy power to show great strength,
and who can withstand the might of thy arm?
[22]Because the whole world before thee is like a speck that
tips the scales,
and like a drop of morning dew that falls
upon the ground.
[23]But thou art merciful to all, for thou canst do all things,
and thou dost overlook men's sins,
that they may repent.
[24]For thou lovest all things that exist,
and hast loathing for none of the things which
thou has made,
for thou wouldst not have made anything if thou hadst
hated it.
[25]How would anything have endured if thou hadst not
willed it?
Or how would anything not called forth
by thee have been preserved?
[26]Thou sparest all things, for they are thine,
O Lord who lovest the living.
12 For thy immortal spirit is in all things.
[2]Therefore thou dost correct little by
little those who trespass,
and dost remind and warn them of the things wherein
they sin,
that they may be freed from wickedness
and put their trust in thee, O Lord.

[a] Gk *them*
[b] Gk *they*

The Sage abruptly interrupts his reflections that contrast God's use of the same element of nature to bless his people and to punish their enemies. He shifts to more general reflections on God's providence. His apparent false start in

11:4-11 is deliberate, however, because it invites readers to link Parts III and IV—as does the fact that both begin with a direct address of God (11:4 and 15). Before readers can appreciate how God guides salvation history, they must have a grasp of his all-embracing providence, including his response to the widespread rejection of his kingship by the practice of idolatry.

The particular form of idolatry that evokes the Sage's harshest criticism is worship of animals—an Egyptian practice that was ridiculed by many ancient philosophers. He deals with it by way of a double inclusion, treating it at the beginning of Part III (11:15-26) and at the end of both its halves (12:23-27; 15:18—16:1). In all three passages he stresses how God punishes this form of idolatry by means of animals. This is an example of the law of talion, a principle that appears repeatedly in this development on divine wisdom and human folly, namely: '*one is punished by the very things by which he sins*' (v. 16).

This approach points strongly to the Egyptian origin of Wis. No other group of readers would have such a keen interest in animal worship. His readers would see images of animal deities all around them, such as '*serpents*' (v. 15; better translated in the wider meaning of "reptiles" or "creeping animals"). The attacks on this form of idolatry would evoke a response in Jewish students living in Egypt and prepare for a powerful diatribe against the folly of idolatry. Before beginning his attacks on its other forms, the Sage offers positive considerations on God's overarching providence. He lays down certain principles that will help readers evaluate their situation and recognize God's blessing upon them.

A further reason for beginning this part of his work with criticism of animal worship is that it illustrates the close union between '*foolish and wicked thoughts*' that is, the mutual influence of ignorance and malice in sin (v. 15). The RSV translation places the two causes on equal terms, but the Greek text implies that the foolishness of sinners springs from their malice. A more literal translation is: "in place of foolish reflections of their wickedness." The Sage repeats vocabulary from 1:5, which says that God's spirit will depart '*from foolish hearts*'—a reminder of the moral demands of God's providence. Just as malice breeds ignorance, so wisdom begets uprightness.

Having introduced his topic, the Sage immediately states a special case of the principle of talion, namely, that God punishes the sinner '*by the very things by which he sins*' (v. 16; again in 12:2, 27; 16:1). This form of God's poetic justice is a favorite theme of the Sage, who states it in a variety of ways throughout Wis (see 1:16; 3:10; 18:4; 19:13). It is stated often also in hellenistic Judaism and is repeated with great enthusiasm in this attack on the worship of animals.

The Sage addresses this law of talion, of course, not to the ancient Canaanites but to his contemporaries, for whom he emphasizes God's punishments. The verb for '*sin*' appears seven times in Wis, all in Part III (11:16; 12:2, 11; 14:31; 15:2bis, 13). It forms a literary inclusion that unifies this series of philosophical considerations on God's providence (11:16 and 12:2)—a section that consists of 33 stichs or poetic lines. The piece is so structured that in its exact middle line the Sage addresses God with the well-known principle of hellenistic jurisprudence, '*But thou hast arranged all things by measure and number and weight*' (v. 20). This principle divides these reflections into two distinct parts.

The God Who Inspires Fear (11:17-20)

This first half paints a terrifying, apocalyptic picture of God whose '*all-powerful hand*' brought the entire universe into being when he '*created the world out of formless matter*' (v. 17). The Sage draws upon a technical term from Aristotelian cosmology, '*matter,*' to describe this created activity. Greek philosophers never reasoned to creation in the strict sense of the word, that is, the bringing of beings into existence from no anterior being. For them matter was eternal. Aristotle was the first to develop a philosophical system that posited matter and form as incomplete and complementary principles of physical beings. Hence the term hylomorphism, a term coined by combining the Greek words for matter and form. By imposing shape upon matter, form generated individual physical beings. The Sage finds this terminology compatible with the biblical teaching on God as absolute creator. It proved a good tool for integrating Greek philosophy into the picture of God taught in Jewish Scriptures.

To carry out this polemic against animal worship, the Sage extols the creative power of God's '*all-powerful hand*' over not only the animals that the Egyptians worshiped but even over mythical '*uncreated beasts*' that would inspire dread. This passage recalls God's apocalyptic intervention throughout creation on behalf of the just, whom he rewards with everlasting life (see 5:17-23). The Sage's vocabulary departs from biblical terminology as he borrows from and imitates Greek poetic writings. For example, the tragic poets spoke of creatures that '*breathe out fiery breath*' and '*flash terrible sparks from their eyes*' (v. 18). Yet he keeps the figure of "winnowing" that the prophets applied to God, although the RSV translation of '*belch forth*' and '*scatter*' obscure the image (vv. 18, 20). The figure does not fit into the imagery of animal activity, showing that the word by this time had lost its original connotation.

It is doubtful whether any translation could convey completely the emotive impact of this passage, and yet that is its principal function. The Sage is not pretending to communicate information about a situation but to arouse terror and awe in his readers. The list of events reaches its climax in a double personification of God's '*justice*' and '*power*' (v. 20; both should be capitalized) — titles given earlier: '*justice*' in 1:8 (see 14:3 and 18:11) and '*power*' in 1:3 and in another apocalyptic scene in 5:23. The term for '*justice*' is not the same one used to designate the saving justice of God that is '*immortal*' (1:15). Rather it is *Dikē*, the personified forces of avenging justice found in pagan philosophy and poetry. Later Jewish tradition also makes '*power*' a designation of God (see Matt 26:64).

The Sage's terrifying apocalyptic description comes to a surprise ending with a sober statement on God's universal justice in terms of hellenistic practice. At times the Bible brings two of these quantities together, but the union of '*measure and number and weight*' is characteristic of legal texts (v. 20). Thus this maxim lends an additional dimension to the Sage's address to his readers as '*judges to the ends of the earth*' (6:1). Again he is reaching out to Greek expertise for new ways to express God's providence. Coming at the exact center of the introduction to this diatribe against idolatry, this praise of God's ruling power provides a fitting transition to a more positive apologia of divine providence.

In Praise of God's Providence (11:21—12:2)

The tone of this development is philosophical and logical. Note the four-fold repetition of '*for*' and the final '*therefore.*' The Sage states the profound principles of the divine rule over creation. He provides a context in which his attacks on all forms of idolatry will be more forceful. This portrait of an all-powerful and yet merciful God—able to evaluate ethical situations and supply the needs of his creatures—marks a sharp contrast to the arbitrary and amoral conduct of pagan deities. The Sage will show later that God gives stability to his people (15:1-6), but other peoples display the weakness of the gods they create for themselves.

Continuing to address God, he reminds him that his '*power*' is absolute: '*who can withstand the might of thy arm?*' (v. 21). This technique of apostrophe or direct address to the subject of his exhortation rather than to his audience is especially effective in dealing with this quality of God. It captures the depth of the religious experience that the Sage wants his readers to enjoy, but which is not possible except as a gift of the God who maintains both transcendent and immanent presence. God is transcendent because the whole world before him is the '*speck that tips the scales and like a drop of morning dew*' (v. 22). Yet he dwells within human hearts so that all '*may repent.*'

The link between God's mercy and his omnipotence is dealt with here in terms of how God achieves the goals of his creation. His mercy and love are expressions of '*power,*' not of weakness. They provide insight into his purpose in creating, namely, the good of his creatures. God does not weaken himself in creating humans and in lavishing gifts upon them. In fact, creation is the supreme act of mercy, a communication of divine gifts to mortals, the arena in which God displays his power in the form of mercy.

Above, the Sage had addressed his prayer to God under the title of '*Lord of mercy*' (9:1). In Part I he described God's mercy to his elect (3:9; 4:15) or to the '*lowliest*' (6:6). Now he universalizes and speaks of God's concern for every human being as his creature. God fulfills the ideal of the hellenistic kingship tracts, which is that the ruler display a truly humane attitude toward everyone, precisely as being members of the human race. The apologetics of this part of Wis embody the same philosophy. It is clear that the Sage proposes to offer an alternative to the way his contemporaries used human intelligence.

These reflections clarify some of the cryptic statements in the opening prologue of Wis, as when the Sage stated paradoxically, '*wisdom is a kindly spirit and will not free a blasphemer from the guilt of his words*' (1:6). The very nature of God as just and as having unselfish love and concern for every human being, animal and other created things prevents him from '*loathing*' any of his creatures (v. 24). God's creative power is necessarily an expression of dynamic love because hate would never lead him to bring anything into existence.

This insight into God's creative activity also clarifies the puzzling statement that '*the generative forces of the world are wholesome and there is no destructive poison in them*' (1:14). Now it is clear that the Sage was talking about God's creative love as exercised in his plan for the entire universe. In both places he is forced to deal with the reality of sin. He attributes it to human agents who can mar the work of creation but who cannot find their destiny outside of God's compassion. God does not turn his back on his plan; each creature has its role in the total unfolding of creation. In God's plan even animals have a place which is guaranteed by his wanting them '*preserved*' (v. 25).

The verb '*called forth by thee*' (v. 25) is unusual; evidently it is equivalent to being created, although that meaning does not appear for it in the Greek Bible (LXX). When animals were worshiped by human beings as divine, they are used in a way contrary to God's plan; but the sin belongs not to them but to '*men*' (v. 23). God does not destroy these '*men*' but invites them to '*repent*' so that they may enter into the plan of his saving will, which is to '*spare all things*' as his own (v. 26). In making this statement the Sage addresses God with another title new to the Bible, '*O Lord who lovest the living.*' This paraphrase of two Greek words is necessary to convey the sense in English. The noun means '*lord*' in the sense of master, and designates God in 6:7; 8:3; 13:3, 9. The adjective, an extremely rare compound, means literally "loving souls." Here the motive is that God sees his own '*immortal spirit*' in all living creatures.

Instead of '*immortal*' the adjective in Greek is "incorruptible," corresponding to the noun '*incorruption,*' found in 2:23; 6:18,19. The Sage once again draws upon the theosophical vocabulary of his day to express the absolute dependency of all creatures on God's active presence to sustain them in existence (12:1). He mingles humans and animals together so that from this verse alone the nature of divine incorruption is not evident. But he clarifies any misunderstanding by adding the next verse, directed to humans who enjoy the gift of '*incorruption,*' by which they can live with God forever (how is explained in 6:18-21).

This practice of alluding to other parts of the work—the literary technique of "flashbacks"—occurs over 40 times in Wis. It is one of the strongest arguments for the book's unity. It also points to the Sage as a teacher who developed this intricate book over an extended period of time, frequently in dialogue with his own continued reflection and growth.

A final reference to humans as vulnerable to sin serves to bring these thoughts on divine providence back to the task of personal responsibility (12:2). In contrast to the dramatic intervention of God in the apocalyptic passages, the Sage now pictures the mercy of God as moving to '*correct little by little*' (12:2). God moves gently to '*remind and warn them,*' two verbs never linked to God elsewhere in the Bible. The Sage applies prevailing legal language to God's interventions so that readers can interpret their own situation.

The final response he advocates is '*trust*' in God (12:2), the first of the four times he uses this verb—often translated as "believe." Trust is a response that the Hebrew Bible—and even more often the New Testament—proposes as necessary for any personal relationship with God. The Sage never suggests that believers are exempt from sin, but views them as open to receive God's compassion and mercy.

He relies on this openness to encourage his readers to choose the path of conversion and to '*repent*' of their sins (v. 23). The prophets often called on Israel to turn from sin, and Ezekiel states that God wants conversion (33:11). Yet, this is the first appearance of the word '*repent*' in the Bible—a word that becomes so important in the gospel tradition. The word appears in Prov 14:15LXX and in Sir 44:16, but these passages differ from the Hebrew text. '*Repent*' stresses responsible activity, an emphasis that seems to have risen in Jewish eschatological sects with mystical orientation. Their members cultivated repentance as a necessary condition for sharing in the reign of God that they were eagerly expecting.

2. FOUR MONOLOGUES ON GOD'S PROVIDENCE
Wis 12:3-27

> [3]Those who dwelt of old in thy holy land
> [4]Thou didst hate for their detestable practices,
> their works of sorcery and unholy rites,
> [5]their merciless slaughter of children,
> and their sacrificial feasting on human flesh and blood.
> These initiates from the midst of a heathen cult,
> [6]these parents who murder helpless lives,
> thou didst will to destroy by the hands of our fathers,
> [7]that the land most precious of all to thee
> might receive a worthy colony of the servants of God.
> [8]But even these thou didst spare, since they were but men,
> and didst send wasps as forerunners of thy army,

to destroy them little by little,
[9]though thou wast not unable to give the ungodly into the hands of the righteous in battle,
or destroy them at one blow by dread wild beasts or thy stern word.
[10]But judging them little by little thou gavest them a chance to repent,
though thou wast not unaware that their origin was evil
and their wickedness inborn,
and that their way of thinking would never change.
[11]For they were an accursed race from the beginning,
and it was not through fear of any one that thou didst leave them unpunished for their sins.

[12]For who will say, "What hast thou done?"
Or who will resist thy judgment?
Who will accuse thee for the destruction of nations which thou didst make?
Or who will come before thee to plead as an advocate for unrighteous men?
[13]For neither is there any god besides thee,
whose care is for all men,
to whom thou shouldst prove that
thou has not judged unjustly;
[14]nor can any king or monarch confront thee about those whom thou hast punished.
[15]Thou art righteous and rulest all things righteously,
deeming it alien to thy power
to condemn him who does not deserve to be punished.
[16]For thy strength is the source of righteousness,
and thy sovereignty over all causes thee to spare all.
[17]For thou dost show thy strength when men doubt the completeness of thy power,
and dost rebuke any insolence among those who know it.
[18]Thou who art sovereign in strength
dost judge with mildness,
and with great forbearance thou dost govern us;
for thou hast power to act whenever thou dost choose.

[19]Through such works thou hast taught thy people

that the righteous man must be kind,
and thou has filled thy sons with good hope,
because thou givest repentance for sins.
[20]For if thou didst punish with such
great care and indulgence[a]
the enemies of thy servants[b] and those deserving death,
granting them time and opportunity to give
up their wickedness,
[21]with what strictness thou has judged thy sons,
to whose fathers thou gavest oaths and covenants full of
good promises!
[22]So while chastening us thou scourgest our enemies ten
thousand times more,
so that we may meditate upon thy goodness
when we judge,
and when we are judged we may expect mercy.

[23]Therefore those who in folly of life lived unrighteously
thou didst torment through their own abominations.
[24]For they went far astray on the paths of error,
accepting as gods those animals which even their
enemies despised;
they were deceived like foolish babes.
[25]Therefore, as to thoughtless children,
thou didst send thy judgment to mock them.
[26]But those who have not heeded the warning
of light rebukes,
will experience the deserved judgment of God.
[27]For when in their suffering they became incensed
at those creatures which they had thought to be gods,
being punished by means of them,
they saw and recognized as the true God him whom they
had before refused to know.
Therefore the utmost condemnation came upon them.

[a] Some ancient authorities omit *and indulgence;*
others read *and entreaty* [b] Or *children*

Taking the example of the Canaanites as a type or model, the Sage introduces a series of four separate developments in the form of short monologues that speak to God about the working of his providence toward his chosen people (vv. 3-11; 12-18; 19-22; 23-27). Throughout this passage he continues to address God and does not speak directly to his readers again until he begins the second half of Part III in 13:1.

The pieces of this section are difficult to understand fully because the Sage is doing several things at the same time: describing, summarizing, poking fun and passing judgment. In a few places the text is not clear; many textual variations exist because scribes tried to clarify the manuscripts. The construction does not seem to be as carefully worked out as that of earlier parts. Yet, the general flow of the Sage's apologia of God's dealing with both his worshipers and their enemies is clear. The teacher in him comes through the text strongly. He appears as a person preoccupied with justifying God's activity vis-a-vis his people.

These examples may have been test cases that the Sage has preserved from actual classes. All of them are rooted in the Jewish Scriptures and never drift off into fantasy. Yet, these monologues freely modify details of the biblical text, add details and introduce philosophical reflections—all calculated to touch the lives of the students. The following comments on these developments focus on motives evident in each.

Why God Eliminated the Canaanites Gradually (12:3-11)

The question that arises for a modern reader is why the Sage introduces such reflections on God's way of punishing the ancient Canaanites into his exhortation. He cites their incorrigible malice: '*their origin was evil and their wickedness inborn*' (v. 10). Yet their punishment does not seem to result from a special intervention of God. And the Sage does not invoke the principle of talion given above to explain God's action, namely, '*one is punished by the very things by which he sins*' (11:16).

Nonetheless, the Sage presents these reflections as a confirmation of his statements about divine providence. The

RSV omits the particle serving as connective in the Greek text, *kai gar* (v. 3). It does not form a logical bond but rather creates a phatic link, that is, it invites readers to keep in touch with the situations being described. Its aim is to evoke a response on their part rather than to offer logical explanations. The text aims at arousing in the readers personal feelings about the way God's providence dealt with their historical enemies. The success of the exhortation depends on communicating to them a source of gratitude and sense of awe before God's power and mercy (12:23-24).

The mood created is important because it will influence the readers' stance toward their contemporaries who practice mystery cults. These young scholars must not be misled when God fails to eliminate all who foster '*detestable practices*' (v. 4). The language of these descriptions resembles Greek tragedy and describes the Canaanites in terms that apply to leaders of the mystery cults. The word translated '*rites*' is the term that designates practices of Greek mystery cults below (v. 4; see 14:15, 23). And the adjective that appears in the RSV as '*sorcery*' is common in texts used in rites of magic cults.

The obscurity of verse 5 has produced such a variety of readings that no extant manuscript gives an acceptable reading. The Sage attributes to ancient Canaanite cults the long list of sins not on the basis of historical research but simply by applying contemporary opinions about mystery cults (vv. 4-6). Winston gathers evidence for various opinions in his Anchor Bible edition (pp. 239-240). Despite their sins, God did not wipe out the Canaanites immediately; rather, '*thou didst spare*' them as '*men*' (v. 8). Instead of frightening animals mentioned (11:17-18), God sent only '*wasps*' against them. Strangely, the Sage chooses an insect never mentioned in the Bible rather than the '*hornets*' of the book of Exodus (23:28LXX).

Recalling God's ability to wipe out all pagans, he pictures Israel's slow conquest as founding a '*colony*' in the '*land most precious of all to thee*' (vv. 7, 9; see 11:17). This expression is a paraphrase for '*holy land*' employed by the Jews of the diaspora (v. 3). God's mercy toward the Canaanites in giving '*them a chance to repent*' is more striking in view of the harsh language in which the Sage describes them in the triple example of litotes or understatement, and especially in view of his belief that '*their way of thinking would never change*' (vv. 9-11). Such language is geared toward evoking an emotional response. Hence judgments such as, '*their origin was evil and their wickedness inborn*' (v. 10), must be understood in the context of these complaints being addressed to the creator who '*lovest all things that exist*' (11:24). God knows that their evil comes from the accumulated impact of generations of sinful living.

The Sage closes this set of reflections with an ambiguous statement that God left the Canaanites '*unpunished for their sins*' (v. 11). In Greek the term '*unpunished*' also means '*amnesty*,' a word that fits the mood of this development. Thus, the Sage leaves the situation unresolved as he moves along in his efforts to get a handle on the mysterious workings of God's providence.

Monologue on How God Uses His Strength (12:12-18)

This short apostrophe to God opens with four rhetorical questions, the first of which is similar to the protest of the wicked in the Greek translation of Job 22:17LXX. The entire paragraph contains a concentration of legal terms: '*judgment*,' '*accuse*' (or prosecute), '*advocate*' (v. 12, with a play on words in Greek between the words '*advocate*' and '*unrighteous*'), '*condemn*' (v. 15), '*judge in mildness*' (v. 18).

These reflections concentrate on how God uses his '*strength*' (vv. 16, 17, 18). Although he could overwhelm all opposition, the Sage reminds him, '*thou art righteous and rulest all things righteously*' (v. 15). The image he paints of God is much like that of the model ruler of the hellenistic kingship tracts who considers it unfitting his status '*to condemn him who does not deserve to be punished*' (v. 15). But a new element is added in the assertion that God's '*strength is the source of righteousness*' (v. 16; the implications will be spelled out in 15:3). In a statement similar to 11:23, the Sage affirms that God's '*sovereignty over all causes him to spare all*' (v. 16). Only toward those who '*doubt the completeness of thy power*' does God make this power be felt with severity (v. 17).

The picture of God provides a "flashback" to the scene of God being forgiving toward the '*lowliest*' (vv. 15-16 with 6:7-8). The quality of '*mildness*' that God displays toward '*us*' is the same quality that the arrogant wanted to test in the innocent just man (2:10; there the term is translated '*forbearance*' which appears here for a different Greek word!). This second monologue ends on an ambiguous note also. The Sage wonders at the tension between God's infinite '*power to act*' and his '*forbearance,*' a link to the fourth monologue below. A sense of mystery of their God as one who cannot be analyzed by human intelligence was a necessary quality of the faith needed by the Jewish community as it faced human resistance.

Monologue on God's Justice (12:19-22)

This third variation on the theme of God's justice deals with it as the model for God's '*people*' in general and for '*the righteous man*' in particular; he must be '*kind*' (v. 19, or "humane"—the same adjective that appears in 1:6 and 7:23). The Sage spells out what was implicit in the previous reflection, namely, that he is seeking to understand how God '*taught thy people*' and '*filled thy sons with good hope*' through '*repentance*' (v. 19). God's providence is known from his '*works*' (v. 19; a term found also in 8:4; 9:9; 13:1, 7; 14:5); these '*works*' manifest the concrete unfolding of the divine plan.

At times the Sage adds a special twist that makes his reasoning hard to follow. These puzzles have led to textual variants like the ones noted in verse 20 in the RSV. The difficulty is to grasp the point of the comparison between the '*strictness*' by which God has '*judged thy sons*' and the '*care*' with which '*thou didst punish*' their enemies, namely, '*ten thousand times more*' (vv. 20-22). How does such divine conduct prepare the Jews to exercise and to '*expect mercy*'? The Sage wants his pupils to be realistic; God has always exacted punishment from his people as well as from their enemies (v. 22; see 11:9-10). Like all his gifts, even God's punishments promise blessings of freedom for believers (see v. 2). The warning of this passage must not be missed. It shows believers that they too must walk in the faith of their ancestors if they hope to benefit by God's mercy.

Monologue on God's Punishments (12:23-27)

The Sage rounds out this series of reflections with one on the conduct of the ancient Egyptians towards the Jews at the time of the Exodus—linking their conduct to the folly of animal worship to form a conceptual bond with the introduction to this "Book of Divine Wisdom and the Folly of Idolatry" (see 11:15). This apostrophe has a tight structure and serves as a fitting introduction to the long attack on idolatry in chapters 13-15.

The Sage begins by comparing the relationship between ignorance (living '*in folly*') and malice (living '*unrighteously*'; v. 23). This time he seems to see ignorance or '*folly*' as the underlying cause of sin. Yet the two lifestyles reinforce each other because sin soon makes its devotees go '*far astray on the paths of error*' and become '*deceived like foolish babes*' (v. 24). The Sage's concern is not to describe the ancient Egyptians but to teach his Jewish readers, for he shifts to the future tense to assert that those who fail to learn from God's '*light rebukes*' (ones adapted to their immaturity) '*will experience the deserved judgment of God*' (v. 26).

This series of monologues directed toward God close with a reference to the principle of talion, because the Egyptians were punished in the plagues by the animals they worshiped. That punishment seemed to bring God's enemies to faith, for they were forced to '*recognize*' the Lord as '*the true God.*' (v. 27). But theirs was a cold, intellectual decision rather than faith in the biblical sense as loving obedience that expresses itself in conversion. It brings not salvation but '*the utmost condemnation*' (v. 27).

Once more the Sage leaves the choice to his readers as to

whether they will live in trust of the '*God of my fathers*' (9:1) or imitate the pagans who '*refuse to know*' him, that is to worship him as loving Father (v. 27; see 16:16). The meaning of the verb '*refuse*' comes from the Greek idiom to express unbelief as positive rejection of obedience to God in response to his revelation. This verb sets the stage for the second half of Part III—on the folly of idolatry—in which the Sage will illustrate its malice by a brief history of its origin and forms.

3. DIATRIBE AGAINST NATURE OR EON WORSHIP Wis 13:1-9

13 For all men who were ignorant of God were foolish by nature;
and they were unable from the good things that are seen to know him who exists,
nor did they recognize the craftsman
while paying heed to his works;
[2]but they supposed that either fire or wind or swift air,
or the circle of the stars, or turbulent water,
or the luminaries of heaven were
the gods that rule the world.
[3]If through delight in the beauty of these things
men assumed them to be gods,
let them know how much better than these is their Lord,
for the author of beauty created them.
[4]And if men were amazed at their power and working,
let them perceive from them how much more powerful is he who formed them.
[5]For from the greatness and beauty of created things
comes a corresponding perception of their Creator.
[6]Yet these men are little to be blamed,
for perhaps they go astray
while seeking God and desiring to find him.
[7]For as they live among his works they keep searching,
and they trust in what they see, because the things that are seen are beautiful.

[8]Yet again, not even they are to be excused;
[9]for if they had the power to know so much
that they could investigate the world,
how did they fail to find sooner the Lord of these things?

Picking up on the theme of how the ancient Egyptians recognized the God of Israel as '*the true God,*' the Sage devotes the next three chapters to a critique of pagan theodicy. In the highly structured development that I outlined in the introduction to this part of Wis, he works toward a climax in his condemnation of animal worship. This opening paragraph, carefully conceived and artistically composed, is enclosed in a striking inclusion formed by the phrases '*unable. . .to know him who exists*' and '*power to know so much*' of God's work (vv. 1 and 9).

In this striking development the Sage joins a philosophical argument against the worshipers of the universe and its stars to traditional language about religion and worship. It forms an important step in his apologia for traditional biblical faith. The Sage indicts philosophical religion as false because it does not lead to the goal of blessed immortality but leaves its followers '*foolish.*' The opening of the RSV fails to communicate the intended contrast with the biblical form of a beatitude like '*happy the man. . .*'(see Ps 1:1). By contrast, the text proclaims, "foolish are all men" (v. 1).

In keeping with his earlier assertion that without Lady Wisdom, '*the reasoning of mortals is worthless*' (9:14; see 10:8), the Sage directs his attack against those pagans who '*were ignorant of God.*' "Ignorance of God" was a technical term in hellenistic religious writing to mean impiety. This ambiguous expression conveys a belief that ignorance and malice reinforce each other. The Sage designates God first as '*him who exists,*' a phrase that translates the name by which God revealed himself to Moses on Mount Sinai (Exod 3:14LXX). He chooses this title because it is also the masculine form of the Greek philosophical term in the Platonic tradition for the deity: "that which exists." In this choice is embodied a key element of this criticism of religion based on purely human intelligence: it never arrived at the God who freely reveals himself.

The Sage's way of beginning this diatribe alerts his readers that he is not composing an abstract philosophical essay. He deals with the historical situation of Jewish students living in daily contact with images of a deity in competition with their ancestral God. Adopting the approach of arguing for the existence of God on the basis of causality, he equates God as '*him who exists*' with '*the craftsman*' whose works are seen in the universe (v. 1; the same term designates a human '*craftsman*' in 14:18). Here he is aware that Greek philosophy never arrived at the notion of creation in the strict sense; it never discovered the totally transcendent deity upon whom the universe was totally dependent.

Although he adopts philosophical terms, the Sage's approach and goal are religious: to justify the power of faith as founding a relationship with the personal creator. The malice and ignorance of pagans prevent them from coming '*to know him who exists.*' The Sage is being ironic in his attack on pagan religion because he has just affirmed that by God's punishments in the Exodus the Egyptians '*recognized as the true God him who they had before refused to know*' (12:27). He is contrasting the difference between a philosophical argument and a personal relationship to the God who has revealed himself as humanity's savior. This approach is apologetic, aimed at convincing his readers to trust in the gifts of Lady Wisdom they have received from God. Because pagan thinkers did not put to full use the qualities of the '*nature*' God gave them (v. 1), they fell short in opening their lives to the ultimate destiny he alone can give. His Jewish readers would do well to learn from such errors that God's gifts must be utilized.

In place of the unique '*craftsman,*' pagan philosophers have substituted either the basic elements or heavenly bodies. They '*supposed*' or '*assumed them to be gods*' (vv. 2-3). These expressions come from a hellenistic terminology never found in the biblical tradition. The unexpected omission of the element earth is explained as an anticipation of the Sage's attack on those who worship earth in the form of idols made of wood or clay (13:10—14:8 and 15:7-13). This mention of elements implies that God can be sought on a variety of levels. On a more material level, popular piety identified '*air*' with Zeus and the realm of spirits. On a philosophical level, the Stoics held that the world soul was refined '*fire*.' All ancients considered the '*stars*' as living; astral piety proclaimed kinship between souls and individual stars.

The RSV translation of verse 2 should put '*gods*' in apposition to all the objects named. The last two items are better rendered as "lights of the universe, moderators of heaven." The Sage does not use these phrases in any technical sense but in the popular imagery of his time. He passes judgment upon philosophical religion in two parallel opinions (vv. 3 and 4-5). Both consist of a statement in the form of an '*if*' clause that is followed by an imperative beginning with '*let them*.' And both conclude with a clause introduced by '*for*.'

The Sage's criticisms are:

1) the beauty of the stars and elements should have led pagans to recognize that their '*craftsman*,' namely, the Lord, as '*much better . . ., for the author of beauty created them*' (v. 3).

2) the '*power and working*' of stars and elements should have led to '*a corresponding perception of their Creator*' (vv. 4-5).

This expression of his condemnation in the form of balanced arguments is a further indication that the Sage was concerned to produce an artistic piece capable of motivating readers by its form as well as its content. He accentuates the parallel by including in the final clause of both a title of God never found elsewhere in the Bible or in pagan literature: '*author of beauty*' (v. 3) and a word surprisingly translated as '*Creator*' (v. 5; literally, "Fashioner of natures"). On the whole, the RSV misses the dynamism of this diatribe. It also fails to convey the philosophical implications of how God as '*Creator*' is known '*from the greatness and beauty*' of creatures, namely, "by analogy." "Analogy" is a technical term the Epicureans used for empirical knowledge as opposed to the a priori knowledge favored by Stoic philosophers. Both the word and the concept are absent from biblical talk about coming to know God.

In verses 6-7, familiarity with the diatribe style would alert original readers that the Sage is introducing an objection by an imaginary opponent. This objector acts as a foil to heighten the tension. He takes the side of those who worship natural elements and finds in their conduct '*little to be blamed.*' Unfortunately, modern editors do not indicate this imaginary dialogue and give no hint of the controversy. The Sage's procedure mirrors the kind of temptation facing young Jewish students and voices their doubts about how far they should adapt to contemporary cosmopolitan society.

Two particles at the beginning of the first two stichs or poetic lines of verse 6 show the urgency that the Sage places on keeping in contact with his audience. Both of these are elements of phatic communication, that is, the non-conceptual dimension of a speech act that maintains contact between the participants. These are: the particle *kai gar,* an almost untranslatable expression to heighten the emotive force of the phrase (see on 12:3), and the adverb *tacha,* 'perhaps,' used in philosophical tracts to signal a questionable statement. The rest of this objection contains typical religious vocabulary that the Sage introduced in Part I: '*seeking God*' (1:1; 6:12); '*search out*' (6:7); '*find*' (6:14); '*pardoned*' (6:6, 8).

In verses 8-9, the Sage responds to this imaginary opponent by a strong refusal to compromise with any form of nature worship. The opening phrase '*yet again*' of the RSV fails to indicate that this is a continuation of the dialogue. It would be better rendered, "on the contrary." The same term occurs in the narrative of the temptation of Jesus when he counters the devil's quote of Scripture (Matt 4:7).

Judgment against Nature Worship

The entire exchange ends with the third conditional sentence of the passage. It puts the burden of justifying their position on the opponents. Allusions to widespread religious speculation of that period are lost on modern readers. The Sage is concerned with refuting a form of pantheism that offered pious persons the satisfying feeling of being in harmony with the universe. Although he is sympathetic to an appeal to the beauty of nature, he formulates solid reasons for refusing to compromise. His skill in handling the arguments of those attracted to this form of piety stresses that in the long run it is '*foolish*' (v. 1). Thus, he concludes that its devotees fall prey to self-deception by their intelligence.

The first part of the final sentence sets the tone: if they think they '*know so much*'! Then the final two lines summarize the Sage's criticism, which centers around two key words:

1) '*investigate.*' This verb translates a technical term from hellenistic philosophy for a thorough search of a significant area of human existence—a meaning not found in the Greek translation of the Hebrew Bible (LXX).

2) '*world.*' The Greek word here is not *cosmos*, the term for the orderly universe, but *eon*. "Eon" is often found in the stereotyped phrase meaning "for ever." But it was also a philosophical term designating a special quality of duration connected with human beings: they have a unique dimension of life. Along this line of reasoning, "eon" also designated the limitless duration of the universe. As such Eon was personified and celebrated as one, unchanging divinity, having no beginning, middle or end (compare the statement about Lady Wisdom in 7:18, 27).

No single English term captures the features attributed to this personification. He was celebrated in hellenistic texts by such titles as "begettor of the cosmos" and portrayed as one of the emanations that link the deity to matter. Eon became a crucial concept in those philosophies that denied any direct contact between the divine and matter. This is the concept that is translated here as '*world.*' The Sage combats a form of religious contemplation whose goal was to "become Eon." The search for Eon as a product of human resources rivaled the search for Lady Wisdom, God's "throne partner." The Sage rejects this form of worship because it sets up finite existence as a rival to the one God who alone is '*Lord of these things*' (v. 9).

Only readers who knew this background could appreciate the literary skill of the Sage in this short argument. He has condensed years of teaching and study in this tight piece of reasoning. He unfolds this warning with such poetic skill because he knew his topic well and was deeply committed to his faith in the one '*Lord*' and '*Creator*' of the universe (vv. 3-5).

The centrality of this piece and of the remainder of the diatribe against all forms of idolatry will become clearer with the reading of the seven comparisons in Part IV about how God blessed his people and punished their enemies. The response of the chosen people contrasts favorably to the sterile contemplation of all the '*foolish by nature*' pagans who refused to make the transition from '*things that are seen*' to a living knowledge of God (v. 1).

Despite its aura of respectability, philosophical religion that chooses to rest upon human intelligence alone must be classed under the '*foolish and wicked thoughts*' the Sage warned his readers against (11:15). If pursued to their logical conclusion, such ignorance leads to self-destruction.

4. TIRADE AGAINST WORSHIPERS OF WOODEN IDOLS
Wis 13:10—14:8

> [10]But miserable, with their hopes set on dead things, are the men who give the name "gods" to the works of men's hands,
> gold and silver fashioned with skill,
> and likeness of animals,
> or a useless stone, the work of an ancient hand.
> [11]A skilled woodcutter may saw down a tree easy to handle
> and skilfully strip off all its bark,
> and then with pleasing workmanship

make a useful vessel that serves life's needs,
[12]and burn the castoff pieces of his work
to prepare his food, and eat his fill.
[13]But a castoff piece from among them,
useful for nothing,
a stick crooked and full of knots,
he takes and carves with care in his leisure,
and shapes it with skill gained in idleness;
he forms it like the image of a man,
[14]or makes it like some worthless animal,
giving it a coat of red paint and colouring its surface red
and covering every blemish in it with paint;
[15]then he makes for it a niche that befits it,
and sets it in the wall, and fastens it there with iron.
[16]So he takes thought for it, that it may not fall,
because he knows that it cannot help itself,
for it is only an image and has need of help.
[17]When he prays about possessions and his
marriage and children,
he is not ashamed to address a lifeless thing.
[18]For health he appeals to a thing that is weak;
for life he prays to a thing that is dead;
for aid he entreats a thing that is utterly inexperienced;
for a prosperous journey, a thing that
cannot take a step;
[19]for money-making and work and success with his hands
he asks strength of a thing whose hands have no strength.

14 Again, one preparing to sail and about to voyage over
raging waves calls upon a piece of wood more fragile
than the ship which carries him.
[2]For it was desire for gain that planned that vessel,
and wisdom was the craftsman who built it;
[3]but it is thy providence, O Father,
that steers its course,
because thou has given it a path in the sea,
and a safe way through the waves,
[4]showing that thou canst save from every danger,
so that even if a man lacks skill, he may put to sea.

[5]It is thy will that the works of thy wisdom should not be without effect;
therefore men trust their lives even to the smallest piece of wood,
and passing through the billows on a raft they come safely to land.
[6]For even in the beginning, when arrogant giants were perishing,
the hope of the world took refuge on a raft,
and guided by thy hand left to the world the seed of a new generation.
[7]For blessed is the wood by which righteousness comes.

[8]But the idol made with hands is accursed,
and so is he who made it;
because he did the work, and the perishable thing was named a god.

The Sage moves to a second and more blameworthy form of idolatry, which he describes in two parallel pictures. The first portrays the idolatry of those '*who give the name "gods" to the works of human hands,*' namely, those who cater to human superstition by making idols (13:11-19). And the second blames those who for a sea voyage put their trust in idols rather than in God's wise providence (14:1-8).

The purpose of the opening verse is to insert these pictures into the overarching movement of this book of "the Folly of Idolatry." Unfortunately the modern reader has no way of knowing the biblical allusions embodied in the opening term '*miserable*' without some help from biblical scholars. It is formed from the noun common in Greek LXX vocabulary to mean "doom." Paul used it in the anguished cry of the person despairing of salvation (Rom 7:24). Earlier the Sage had described '*whoever despises wisdom and instruction*' as '*miserable*' (3:1).

By the technique of flashback the Sage links this description of idol makers to his statement that the '*hope*' of the '*ungodly*' in '*disregarding the righteous*' was vain (3:10-11). He sees idol makers as doing precisely this. They set '*their hopes on dead things*'—an expression that identifies the idols with the gods they represent. As such, these idolaters provide an example of persons who '*bring on destruction by the works of their hands*' (1:12) in giving the '*name "gods" to the works of men's hands*' (v. 10).

Much of the imagery for the first picture comes from the biblical attacks on idolatry—specifically from the polemic against idolatry in Isaiah 44:9-20. The Sage, however, has composed this piece with great literary skill and produced a devastating critique of idol worship by skillful imagery. Although he mentions metal and stone idols in his introductory verse, he deals only with wooden idols in both these descriptions.

This detailed diatribe of 27 stichs or poetic lines consists of only three sentences. The first is a conditional sentence with two series of clauses describing the activities of an idol maker: first as craftsman and then as an idler making an idol from scraps (see v. 13). Next comes a short ironic statement to show that idols are truly '*dead things.*' The third sentence concludes with another series of ironic contrasts showing that those who set '*their hopes*' on idols are '*miserable*' (vv. 16-19).

The Sage adds little to the condemnation of idolatry already found in Isaiah. His contribution is in the vividness with which he paints the folly of this form of superstition. His goal is to motivate his readers to remain faithful to their traditional monotheism. Modern readers may think that intelligent Jews would be in no danger of practicing idol worship, but the Sage knows that human reason can be influenced by all sorts of petty motives. He pointed out some of them in chapter 2. Persons who abandon moral integrity lose the vision and energy to choose God and his will.

The two pictures show craftsmen starting out with good intentions. Yet they end by using God's creatures foolishly. Perhaps the reason why the Sage painted these specific examples was that they make a striking contrast to the seven comparisons with which he concludes his book. In them he pictures God as using the same creatures to bless and to punish. In these two examples he points to craftsmen who use the same creature of God to make a useful vessel and then to '*form*' the same wood into an idol that '*cannot help itself*'—much less others (v. 16). Ironically the '*woodcutter*' does this with a kind of tree '*easy to handle*' an adjective describing Lady Wisdom (v. 11; see 7:22).

Once the craftsman has used the wood wisely, what is left is '*useful for nothing*' (v. 13). That puts the wood into the same category of those who reject God's will (see 3:17; 4:5; 9:6). This description contrasts the difference between the situation of God and of mortals. Through his wisdom God communicates transcendent value to mortals although they may foolishly turn from him. Human craftsmen are limited to turning God's gifts into '*useful*' or '*worthless*' products. '*A skilled woodcutter*' takes the same tree and makes both '*a useful vessel*' and at the same time carves '*some worthless animal*' that ensnares others (v. 14). The fault is not in the wood; even the wood that saved Noah was '*useless*' (v. 10:4).

To show how useless an idol is, the Sage draws upon satires on idols found among pagan writers (v. 16). He adds to the irony by offering an extended list of seven petitions addressed to the idol in a parody of pagan prayers. These petitions contain five words never found in the Greek LXX Bible and conclude with a striking play on words underlying the terms translated '*strength*' and '*no strength*' (v. 19).

God's Protecting Providence (14:1-8)

The Sage's love of balance leads him to add a second attack related to wooden ships and idols. It is the tale of a craftsman who skillfully builds a ship and yet prays to the idol carved on its bow. On a deeper level the real builder is Lady Wisdom, as proclaimed by the feminine form of '*craftsman*' (v. 2; see the masculine in 7:22 and 8:6). The Sage does not pursue this example but returns to her saving intervention in the rescue of Noah (vv. 6-7), whom he had mentioned only briefly in describing how Lady Wisdom saved the ancient patriarchs (10:4). A flashback connects the two scenes by repeating the same Greek word about piloting the ark (*'guided'* in 14:6, translated *'steering'* in 10:4). In both cases *'wisdom'* was the one who *'saved'* the travelers (10:4 and 14:4). This double allusion to Lady Wisdom—her only mention outside of Part II—links her to this critique of idolatry.

Because of the great richness of allusion and denseness of ideas in this passage, Gilbert spent 30 pages analyzing this passage. He places primary emphasis on verse 7 as a general affirmation of the goodness of God's creatures. The *'wood'* that is *'blessed'* as a source of *'righteousness'* is not solely the ark of Noah but all wood, for it shares in God's blessings on creation. He ends his division treating Noah with verse 6 and considers verse 7 as a general statement binding both examples about wood together. By contrast, verse 8 states the divine curse that falls upon all makers of idols. It forms an inclusion with the mention of metal and stone idols, *'works of men's hands'* (vv. 8 and 13:10). Gilbert includes verses 9-10 in this passage although he recognizes their transitional nature. I prefer to treat them as the introduction to the Sage's long series of reflections on the origin and spread of idolatry.

Our disagreement is over how the Sage conceived the structure of this paragraph (14:1-8), and about what role he assigned to it in the unfolding of this part of the book on the "Folly of Idolatry." It is a problem of determining the literary form of this paragraph. It begins as a narrative. It tells about an entrepreneur seeking wealth by making use of the *'wisdom'* of a *'craftsman'* who planned a *'vessel.'* Ironically, he trusts his success to an idol! But suddenly the Sage interrupts this tale and shifts to the technique of apostrophe—used in the monologues at the beginning of Part III (11:15—12:27). This time he invokes God with a title common in Greek pagan prayers but never found in any prayer of the Hebrew Bible, *'Father'* (v. 3).

In this prayer the Sage envisions all creation as a vessel that God, the universal *'Father,'* steers by his *'providence.'*

He radicalizes his polemic against idolatry by contrasting the inefficacy of idols with concrete examples of God's power. First, God '*gave a path even in the sea*' (v. 3; no '*it*' should be inserted). The Sage is speaking of how God rescued his people during the Exodus by taking them through the Red Sea. He alludes to Psalm 76:20LXX, '*thy path in the sea.*' Next, he completes his reference to the Exodus with a reminder to God: you desire '*that the works of thy wisdom should not be without effect*' (v. 5). But this also recalls to his readers the string of examples about the saving power of Lady Wisdom (10:1-21).

The Sage then introduces another example of God's care in the story of Noah (vv. 5-6). It shows the enduring '*effect*' of God's '*providence*' that preserves humanity in each '*new generation.*' The term is the same as that translated as the '*generative forces*' that God made '*wholesome*' (1:14)—beginning a flashback to the prologue. Next, the Sage completes this paragraph with a general statement clothed in a different literary form—a blessing. He declares '*blessed*' the '*wood*' which God's providence provides to carry humanity to '*righteousness*' (v. 7, completing the flashback by referring to this term in 1:15). This complex development closes with a statement that both '*the idol*' and '*he who made it*' are '*accursed*' because it bears the name '*god*' (v. 8). This statement acts as an inclusion with the same practice condemned above at the start of this tirade against wooden idols (13:10).

This long analysis was necessary to show that this paragraph is a critical summary of the Sage's case against idol worship. He condemns it as a denial of trust in the almighty power of God. No wonder he is so anxious to protect his students from the slavery of an institution that flourished in their pagan surroundings!

5. THE ORIGIN AND SPREAD OF IDOLATRY
Wis 14:9—15:6

> [9]For equally hateful to God are the ungodly
> man and his ungodliness,

[10]for what was done will be punished
together with him who did it.
[11]Therefore there will be a visitation
also upon the heathen idols,
because, though part of what God created,
they became an abomination,
and became traps for the souls of men
and a snare to the feet of the foolish.

[12]For the idea of making idols was the
beginning of fornication,
and the invention of them was the corruption of life,
[13]for neither have they existed from the beginning
nor will they exist for ever.
[14]For through the vanity of men they entered the world,
and therefore their speedy end has been planned.
[15]For a father, consumed with grief at
an untimely bereavement,
made an image of his child, who had
been suddenly taken from him;
and he now honoured as a god what
was once a dead human being,
and handed on to his dependents
secret rites and initiations.
[16]Then the ungodly custom, grown
strong with time, was kept as a law,
and at the command of monarchs
graven images were worshipped.
[17]When men could not honour monarchs[a] in their
presence, since they lived at a distance,
they imagined their appearance far away,
and made a visibile image of the king
whom they honoured,
so that by their zeal they might flatter
the absent one as though present.
[18]Then the ambition of the craftsman impelled
even those who did not know the king
to intensify their worship.
[19]For he, perhaps wishing to please his ruler,

skilfully forced the likeness to take more beautiful form,
[20]and the multitude, attracted by the charm of his work,
now regarded as an object of worship the one whom shortly before they
had honoured as a man.
[21]And this became a hidden trap for mankind,
because men, in bondage to misfortune
or to royal authority,
bestowed on objects of stone or wood the name that ought not to be shared.
[22]Afterward it was not enough for them
to err about the knowledge of God,
but they live in great strife due to ignorance,
and they call such great evils peace.
[23]For whether they kill children in their initiations, or celebrate secret mysteries,
or hold frenzied revels with strange customs,
[24]they no longer keep either their lives or their marriages pure,
but they either treacherously kill one another,
or grieve one another by adultery,
[25]and all is a raging riot of blood and murder,
theft and deceit, corruption, faithlessness,
tumult, perjury,
[26]confusion over what is good, forgetfulness of favours,
pollution of souls, sex perversion,
disorder in marriage, adultery, and debauchery.
[27]For the worship of idols not to be named
is the beginning and cause and end of every evil.
[28]For their worshippers[b] either rave in exultation,
or prophesy lies,
or live unrighteously, or readily commit perjury;
[29]for because they trust in lifeless idols
they swear wicked oaths and expect to suffer no harm.
[30]But just penalties will overtake them on two counts:
because they thought wickedly of God
in devoting themselves to idols,
and because in deceit they swore unrighteously

through contempt for holiness.
[31]For it is not the power of the things by which men swear,[c]
but the just penalty for those who sin,
that always pursues the transgression of the unrighteous.

15 But thou, our God, art kind and true,
patient, and ruling all things[d] in mercy.
[2]For even if we sin we are thine, knowing thy power;
but we will not sin, because we know
that we are accounted thine.
[3]For to know thee is complete righteousness,
and to know thy power is the root of immortality.
[4]For neither has the evil intent of human art misled us,
nor the fruitless toil of painters,
a figure stained with varied colours,
[5]whose appearance arouses yearning in fools,
so that they desire[e] the lifeless form of a dead image.
[6]Lovers of evil things and fit for such objects of hope[f]
are those who either make or desire or worship them.

[a]Gk *them*
[b]Gk *they*
[c]Or *of the oaths men swear*
[d]Or *ruling the universe*
[e]Gk *and he desires*
[f]Gk *such hopes*

Commentators are divided about how to deal with this section. Gilbert's careful study points out many of the literary features the Sage uses and so enriches appreciation of the artistry involved. Special attention must be paid to flashbacks linking this development to Parts I and II. They deliberately repeat expressions that link the spread of idolatry to earlier reflections on God's work in the world.

Difficulties in interpreting these paragraphs arise from elements I have noted earlier: internal structure, the role this section plays in the Sage's overall thesis, the exact meaning of specific terms, and a deliberate quest for paradox. In addition is the problem of defining the limits of this section. My decision to fix 14:9 as the start of a new development is based on recognizing the literary marker that the Sage provides. He employs an archaic verb never found elsewhere in the Bible to form an inclusion (14:10 and 15:6). The verb—a technical term for offering sacrifices—means to "perform rites." The RSV misses this key literary feature by translating it first as '*do*' and second as '*make*.'

What the Sage does here is to compose a true literary digression in the strict classical sense of a long excursus or footnote. In it he explains the origin and disastrous effects of idolatry upon humanity. He elaborates upon the dynamic interaction between ignorance of God and human malice that is operative in idolatry. So he interrupts his diatribe on the four forms of idolatry to explain how such an evil institution started, why it exists and where it gets its power. In this light, 14:9-10 forms a kind of title or "thematic announcement" of the subject to be treated, namely, the double sin of fostering idolatry and of participating in it.

In keeping with his fondness for contrast, the Sage closes this digression with a prayer of gratitude to God for protecting his people from all forms of idolatry (15:1-6). The whole passage thus forms an integral part of his polemic against hellenistic religion and of his apologia for traditional faith in the God of revelation.

This approach toward the origin of idolatry is similar to that attributed to the shadowy historian Euhemerus, who traced it to the creation of gods by humans wishing to honor heroes and benefactors of humanity after their death. Because such literature exists now only in fragments, it is impossible to determine how close a link exists between Euhemerus and the Sage. But the theory fits into this description of how humans began '*to error about the knowledge of God*' (v. 22). The borrowing of terminology from edicts erected by kings also links this section to the growing cult of hellenistic rulers.

The Sage warms up to his task by introductory remarks about the evil of '*idols*' as inviting a divine '*visitation*'—a traditional biblical term to designate a divine intervention, either to bless or to punish (v. 11). In Wis '*visitation*' always has eschatological overtones, and is always favorable except here and in 19:15. The Greek translation of Jeremiah 10:15

(departing from the Hebrew) calls God's final punishment upon idols a '*visitation.*' Of course, condemnation of idols is common in the Bible. What is different here is that the Sage appropriates motives for his critique from hellenistic philosophy.

In an artistic grouping of Greek words that have the same final sound, the text offers three reasons why God will punish idols. They have become '*an abomination*' and '*traps*' and '*a snare*' (v. 11). The style shows that this is not a technical court judgment but a conscious effort to present a plea in a form constructed according to the canons of Greek style. Yet the Sage is also making an important disclosure on the basis of the universal spread of idolatry: all '*men*' have been ensnared and have been made '*foolish.*' He comes back to this thesis often. It is a variation of his theme that without '*the wisdom that comes from*' God, mortals '*will be regarded as nothing*' in terms of their true destiny (see 9:6).

The Sage states this judgment as a general principle: '*the idea of making idols was the beginning of fornication*' (v. 12). Jewish readers could not fail to see this as the reverse of the maxim, '*The fear of the Lord is the beginning of understanding*' (Prov 1:7). In this anti-maxim '*fornication*' is the biblical equivalent of idolatry, as lusting after pagan gods. Lest this condition seem irreversible, the Sage adds a clarification: this disastrous situation is the result of human sin, '*the vanity of men*' (v. 14). God will bring an end to it.

These introductory remarks also serve to link this digression to the statement in Part I: '*through the devil's envy death entered the world*' (2:24). Now he completes the picture by saying that '*through the vanity of men*' idols '*entered the world*'—thus revealing how pagans chose death as their god. '*Vanity*'—a word coined by Epicurus—means "illusion," and so is an appropriate word for the Sage's polemic. Only the saving '*visitation*' of God can end the reign of death and the '*corruption*' that idolatry brings (v. 12). These examples complete earlier remarks on justice and evil. Now the Sage affirms that God is not going to let the '*vanity*' of idolatry created by human beings be the last word. With a rebuke to the human '*idea*' about making idols (v. 12), he states that the '*speedy end*' of idols '*has been planned,*' that is, by God (v. 14).

He now offers two parallel examples of how idolatry was inaugurated:

1) by a '*father*' mourning for a beloved child who died '*suddenly.*' In grief he set up among '*his dependents secret rites and initiations*' (vv. 15-16a). Some commentators have tried to single out the person involved. In keeping with Euhemerus' theory, however, which puts the origin of idolatry back into the deep past, it is better to see this as a vague reference to an obscure '*custom*' that eventually acquired the power of '*law.*' The example is not meant to be an accurate historical account of the first idol, but places responsibility for them in human hands.

2) by rulers, civil servants and artists seeking to maintain their power to flatter those in authority (vv. 16b-21). Since the evil snowballed, the Sage introduces it as a companion situation to explain the spread of idolatry. In keeping with the subject matter, the Sage draws upon wording of public inscriptions erected to honor rulers and benefactors. In hellenistic inscriptions '*ambition*' was one of the most praised qualities of public officials (v. 18).

Significant for helping to fix the date of Wis is the term '*worship.*' It was an ancient Ionian word that never appears in any religious inscription before the time of Augustus. The Sage picked up this term, popular in religious texts in the early Roman period, to pass judgment on human greed and '*ambition*' as contrary to the '*command*' of the king of all creation (v. 16). The irony of the implied contrast between the ephemeral hellenistic rulers and the God of the universe would impress Jewish students.

To describe the man-made gods, the Sage borrows another term from the recently introduced cult of rulers, now regarded as '*objects of worship*' (v. 20). He concludes his example by pointing out the folly and evil of making humans divine: it '*became a hidden trap for mankind.*' The expression, '*the name that ought not to be shared,*' is ambiguous (v. 21). It can apply both to the name of God as ineffable and to idols, incapable of sharing anything with humans. Yet humans turned to them because of '*misfortune*' or the commands of '*royal authority*' (v. 21).

With the following description of the evils brought about by idolatry, the Sage starts to formulate his condemnation of all idolatry because of the moral evils it brought. He ends it with a warning that it will be punished by the Lord (vv. 22-31). His highly emotional charge maintains that the original decision of humans to inaugurate idolatry, which was '*to err about the knowledge of God*,' has by his time brought humanity into a state of '*great evils*' (v. 22). But humans are so blind that they call their situation '*peace*.' Compare the famous line of Tacitus, "They make a desert and call it peace." Similar sentiments are found in other hellenistic writers, such as Ps-Heraclitus, "Though evils they made the city a desert."

Vices Fostered by Idolatry

The Sage lists twenty-two vices (vv. 23-27, the same number as there are letters in the Hebrew alphabet. Several "alphabetical" (technically abecedarian) psalms have the same number of verses. Sin turns the world of God's peace into '*a raging riot . . . tumult . . . confusion*.' These vices spell out what it means to live '*in ignorance*' (v. 22). The Sage's audience would recognize the term '*ignorance*' as a technical term in the Platonic and Stoic traditions (see 13:1; 17:13). To root all sin in idolatry he begins this catalogue with vices linked to '*initiations*' and '*secret mysteries*,' terms found above (v. 23; see v. 15, translated '*rites*'). These '*mysteries*' recall the Canaanite crimes (12:3-7) and contrast with the saving '*secrets*' of Lady Wisdom (6:22; translating the same term). The bulk of these vices were already condemned in Jewish Scripture. Yet this list includes the following terms absent from the Greek Bible (LXX): '*treacherously kill, adultery, faithlessness, perjury, forgetfulness of favours, perversion, disorder, debauchery*' (vv. 24-26).

After this catalogue the Sage enlarges his introductory assertion that '*making idols*' was the '*beginning*' of '*corruption of life.*' For he now says, '*the worship of idols . . . is the beginning and cause and end of every evil*' (v. 27; see v. 12). He confirms this charge by the example of participants in orgiastic mystery cults who lapse into ethical madness under the influence of these cults. But they will not go unpunished! With this final warning the Sage brings this part of his major digression to a conclusion with a condemnation of false oaths. The verb '*swear*' occurs three times (vv. 29, 30, 31). The ease with which they swear false oaths shows how shallow is their opinion of them.

He also includes a flashback to the opening warning of the book. He had told the '*rulers of the earth*' to '*think of the Lord with uprightness*' (1:1). Now he blames idol worshipers '*because they thought wickedly of God*' (v. 30; these are the only two times this particular word for '*think*' appears in Wis). He then restates the principle of talion, characteristic of Part III: sin brings its own punishment. But here he does so with rhetorical flourish. First, in the negative: that it is not the '*power*' of the idols that punishes (v. 31). Then, by personifying God's Vengeance as intervening—although the RSV translation has the abstract '*just penalty*'—for Vengeance '*always pursues the transgression of the unrighteous*' (v. 31; see 1:8 and 11:20).

The Sage could have ended his digression here because he has provided the background for his attack on idolatry. But he adds a short monologue to God (15:1-6). This shift in the form of communication has an effect on his message. It recalls his earlier prayers and the depth of communion he experienced with God, who destined his children for '*immortality*' (v. 3). This prayer overflows with nostalgia. It has four flashbacks: 15:1 to 8:1: how God rules all; 15:3 to 1:14-15: the link between '*righteousness*' and '*immortality*'; 15:4-5 to 1:3-4: on '*deceitful*' evil; 15:6 to 8:2: on '*lovers*' of good and evil. The Sage pauses to relish the thought of the Father who has lovingly preserved his people as a means of communicating his traditional faith.

He increases the contrast between pagan sinfulness and the chosen people's experience of belonging to God by using the plural '*we*' rather than the individual "I." The attributes of God that he mentions are the covenant qualities. God is '*kind and true, patient, and ruling all things in mercy*' (v. 1; see Exod 34:6). The Sage does not quote even this famous description of the covenant God in wooden fashion. Instead of using the Greek word that describes the Lord as '*faithful,*' he calls him '*true*'—to contrast him with unreal idols. And he repeats Stoic vocabulary from the praises of Lady Wisdom, now to nourish hope in God as '*ruling all things*' (v. 1; see 8:1).

As God's chosen people they act not in ignorance (see 13:1) but '*knowing thy power,*' that is, accepting and obeying the Lord's dominion over the universe. The Sage becomes spokesman before God for his readers and puts on their lips the promise, '*we will not sin*' (v. 2). He prays out of the Jewish sense of faith as obedience: '*to know thee . . . to know thy power*' is to receive the possibility of '*complete righteousness*' (v. 3). Only this '*righteousness*' can bring them to the destiny that God has in store for his children. Its source is God's '*power.*' Why? Because God does not have to be afraid of any created rival, he can remain perfectly just and beneficent. Hence, '*to know*' God as having supreme '*power*' over the universe is the '*root of immortality*' (v. 3; recalling 1:14-15). The Sage does not repeat here what he explained at length in Part II, namely, that this saving experience of God is pure grace, free gift. Rather, he spells out the need of obedience on the part of his people by warning against the foolishness of idolatry.

Just as his reflections on the origin of idolatry shed light on his treatment in Part I about what true justice is, so his boasting about how the Jews did not paint idols '*with varied colours*' clarifies his criticism of the role of artists in the spread of idolatry (v. 4; literally "paint with shadows" like scene painters who portrayed perspective). He refers to a particular feature of idol making, the practice of painting them to make them more attractive—a further proof of '*evil intent*' (v. 4). How dangerous was their influence appears in the brief allusion to the legend of Pygmalion, who fell in love with '*the lifeless form of a dead image*' he had created (v. 5).

His final reference to idols brings the Sage back to the point where he can continue the attacks on the four forms of idolatry that he interrupted in 14:8. This long digression closes with the inclusion mentioned above about those who "perform rites" with idols, and with a repetition of the maxim that sin brings its own punishment. '*Lovers*' of idols will have a '*hope*' that is as '*lifeless*' as their foolish creations. They will experience emptiness and vanity no matter what part they play in the cult of idols (v. 6). This final warning serves to reinforce the statement that the '*hope*' of the ungodly who rebelled against the Lord is vain (see 3:10-11).

6. CONDEMNATION OF SELLERS OF CLAY IDOLS Wis 15:7-13

[7]For when a potter kneads the soft earth
and laboriously moulds each vessel for our service,
he fashions out of the same clay
both the vessels that serve clean uses
and those for contrary uses, making all in like manner;
but which shall be the use of each of these
the worker in clay decides.
[8]With the misspent toil, he forms a
futile god from the same clay—
this man who was made of earth a short time before
and after a little while goes to the
earth from which he was taken,
when he is required to return the soul that was lent him.
[9]But he is not concerned that he is destined to die
or that his life is brief,
but he competes with workers in gold and silver,
and imitates workers in copper;
and he counts it his glory that he moulds counterfeit gods.
[10]His heart is ashes, his hope is cheaper than dirt,

and his life is of less worth than clay,
[11]because he failed to know the one who formed him
and inspired him with an active soul
and breathed into him a living spirit.
[12]But he considered our existence an idle game,
and life a festival held for profit,
for he says one must get money however one can, even by base means.
[13]For this man, more than all others, knows that he sins
when he makes from earthy matter fragile vessels and graven images.

The Sage returns to condemning various kinds of idolatry but now with a shift of focus. He presents the case of a manufacturer of all kinds of '*vessels*' (vv. 7 and 13, forming an inclusion). '*With misspent toil*' he makes clay amulets—almost as a hobby or a way to kill time (v. 8). The Sage's condemnation focuses on the thoughtlessness and greed of the potter.

The language is some of the strongest in Wis. In fact, Gilbert calls it an "explosion" of suppressed anger. Its insertion illustrates the practical bent of the Sage, who did not set out to give an abstract discourse on idolatry but in the spirit of a diatribe to warn his readers against its disastrous effects on human morals. He once again begins with the particle *kai gar* that serves as what modern linguists call phatic communication. It keeps contact with the readers and invites them to experience the full impact of the text—here, scorn and disgust for greedy dealers in clay amulets.

Evidently the Sage already had this section in mind when he omitted the element "earth" from objects worshiped (13:1-9). He reserved idols of this lowly element for special condemnation. Hence, this paragraph serves as the third step in the four-fold attack on idolatry in this "Book of Divine Wisdom and the Folly of Idolatry." The greedy potter does not worship his '*fragile vessels and graven images,*' but the Sage condemns him '*more than all others*' because he '*knows that he sins*' (v. 13). Instead of worshiping the God who '*breathed into him a living spirit,*' he puts his '*glory*' into making '*counterfeit gods*' and lives only '*for profit...however he can*' (vv. 9-12).

Underlying this criticism is Pythagorean speculation that human life is a '*festival*' (v. 12). In it people choose one of three goals that generate the basic "forms of life." They search either for glory or for gain or for enjoying the spectacle, that is, wisdom. Models for these three forms are the soldier, the merchant and the philosopher. Later philosophers added a fourth form of life, living for pleasure. The Sage takes this opportunity to paint an ironic contrast between the human potter and God as the true craftsman forming all humanity.

Abusing the talents he has received, the potter fashions '*with misspent toil*' a '*god*,' which is '*futile*' (v. 8; the same term is used for those who worship nature in 13:1). His worthlessness is evident in his failing to consider that he has soon '*to return the soul that was lent him*' (v. 8). The Sage links this description to his previous warnings: first, that God's wisdom will not enter into a body indebted to sin (v. 8, alluding to 1:4); and second, that one is a fool to consider death as the end and righteousness as '*counterfeit*' (v. 9, recalling 2:16).

This portrait borrows from pagan writers who mocked the custom of honoring idols made out of the same material that serves for '*clean uses and...for contrary uses*' (v. 7). The Sage also includes biblical allusions. For example, at death a human returns to earth '*from which he was taken*' (v. 8; see Gen 3:19). The Greek translation of Isaiah 44:20LXX describes a potter whose '*heart is ashes*' (v. 10). From Isaiah the Sage also borrows the verb '*forms*' (four times in this paragraph). But even when he alludes to the image of God creating when he '*breathed*' into clay '*a living spirit*' (v. 11; see Gen 2:7), the Sage alters the vocabulary into Stoic terminology of "lifegiving breath," a technical expression in Alexandrian physicians.

This short diatribe adds one new motive for condemning idolatry: it encourages exploitation of others '*even by base means*' (v. 12). So those who make a living by trafficking in '*graven images*' are as guilty as their worshipers (v. 13). In a striking way the life of the greedy potter illustrates the law of talion that permeates Part III. His calculated coldness turns '*his heart*' to '*ashes*' and makes '*his life of less worth than clay*' (v. 10). Readers can infer that a similar fate awaits members of the chosen people who grow cold in their loyalty to the Lord.

7. CONDEMNATION OF ANIMAL WORSHIP
Wis 15:14—16:1

[14]But most foolish, and more miserable than an infant,
are all the enemies who oppressed thy people.
[15]For they thought that all their heathen idols were gods,
though these have neither the use of their eyes to see with,
nor nostrils with which to draw breath,
nor ears with which to hear,
nor fingers to feel with,
and their feet are of no use for walking.
[16]For a man made them,
and one whose spirit is borrowed formed them;
for no man can form a god which is like himself.
[17]He is mortal, and what he makes with
lawless hands is dead,
for he is better than the objects he worships,
since he has life, but they never have.
[18]The enemies of thy people worship
even the most hateful animals,
which are worse than all others, when
judged by their lack of intelligence;
[19]and even as animals they are not so beautiful in appearance that one would desire them,
but they have escaped both the praise
of God and his blessing.
16 Therefore those men were deservedly punished
through such creatures,
and were tormented by a multitude of animals.

In this climax to his diatribe against idolatry the Sage returns to the opponents he spoke about at the end of the opening half of Part III (12:22-27). He focuses on the Egyptians as '*enemies who oppressed thy people*' (v. 14). Once more he compares them to '*infants*' (v. 14, translated as '*babes*' in 12:24)—a Greek idiom for those who lack wisdom. His shift back to direct address to God—as he did at the conclusion of his long digression on the origin of idolatry (15:1-6)—heightens the tone of his appeal. Prayerful attention to God's presence is the strongest protection against the deception of idolatry. More important than abstract arguments against idolatry is the profound religious spirit that comes through this literary exhortation.

Those who opposed the God of Israel and '*oppressed thy people*' were '*most foolish,*' the most inexcusable of idolaters (v. 14). He hints that they failed to learn the lessons of why God punished them because they still reckoned '*all their heathen idols. . .gods*' (v. 15; see 12:27). In this context the Sage paraphrases the mockery of idols found in Ps 113:12-15LXX (Hebrew Ps 115:4-7). As usual, he updates the vocabulary and adopts a more literary style. One striking change is the omission of any reference to idols as unable to speak. Possibly he thinks of those hellenistic temples in which ventriloquists gave oracles through idols with moveable mouths. So he ignores this practice but concludes that all idols are '*dead*' (vv. 15-17).

His preference is for hellenistic scientific vocabulary to replace biblical terms, as in the words translated '*draw breath*' and '*feel*' (v. 15). Ultimately he concludes that idols are helpless because '*a man made them*' (v. 16). They mirror the contingency of every human being, whose '*spirit is borrowed*'—a phrase that recalls what he said about the maker of clay amulets who forgot that his soul was '*lent him*' (v. 8).

In this final apostrophe of his "Book of Divine Wisdom and the Folly of Idolatry," the Sage pulls together a variety of its literary images. In contrast to the infinite divine Creator who puts his '*immortal spirit in all things*' (12:1), what a mortal tries to create '*with lawless hands is dead*' (v. 17). The long review of the origin of idolatry showed that it could turn a mortal into '*an object of worship*' (14:20). Now the Sage applies the same expression to show that a worshiper of idols debases his own dignity and makes himself worse than '*the objects he worships*' (v. 17).

When the Sage warns that '*no man can form a god which is like himself*' (v. 16), he recalls to his readers their dignity because God made them '*in the image of his own eternity*' (2:23). All his warnings against idolatry are pleas to keep open to cultivate the divine '*spirit*' lent to them (v. 16).

One final variation on the principle of talion is latent in the pride of those who '*worship even the most hateful animals*' (v. 18). Like them, all sinners will be '*deservedly punished through such creatures*' (16:1), that is, the creatures they abuse. For their sin the Egyptians merit the name of being '*most foolish*' (v. 14). They practiced a kind of idolatry that shocked pagan hellenistic writers: the worship of '*even the most hateful animals,*' those which in divine providence '*escaped both the praise of God and his blessing*' (vv. 18-19; see v. 13, with an allusion to the serpent of Gen 3:14). The Sage opened his long diatribe with a form of idolatry that had at least some mitigating circumstances—worship of nature (13:1-9). He closes with a form that is indefensible.

As a restatement of the principle of talion, the first verse of chapter 16 makes the conclusion of Part III. The '*therefore*' indicates that the Egyptians merited their punishment, and the second poetic stich states what it was. They '*were tormented by a multitude of animals.*' The adjective "creeping" is unaccountably omitted in the RSV, but it is in the Greek text to form an inclusion with the same term in the opening verse of Part III (11:15, translated there as '*serpents*').

This long literary digression prepares readers to hear an updated version of the lessons of the Exodus, which the Sage has skillfully arranged in the form of seven contrasts. He already gave the first one (11:1-14); now he will complete his project that forms Part IV of his work (16:2—19:22).

Part IV: The Book of History (11:1-14 + 16:2—19:22)

Introduction

This final part of Wis is at once the clearest and the most complicated, the easiest and the hardest to understand. In its overall conception, it is the clearest part because it is a clearcut series of seven contrasts between what happened to the Jews and to their enemies during the period surrounding the Exodus from Egypt, the central event in Israel's religious history. The Sage presents these contrasts as concrete illustrations of how the principles proclaimed in the first two parts of Wis found application in Israel's liberation from Egypt. Each contrast shows how God employed the same element of his creation to '*show kindness to thy people*' and to punish their foes (16:2).

Yet these contrasts often prove difficult to follow because of two complicating factors: (1) The Sage pictures God as using the same created elements to bless his chosen people and to punish their enemies. This literary method involves playing with several variants at the same time. Since he seldom uses proper names, readers can become lost in a maze of pronouns, especially when the descriptions shift back and forth between Jews and Egyptians. (2) He freely modifies details in the biblical accounts and adds from oral traditions or simply creates new contrasts by juxtaposing originally distinct events. For modern readers unfamiliar with Jewish oral traditions, such descriptions can easily be confusing.

For these two reasons this final part of Wis is often frustrating reading, especially for those trying to reconstruct literal accounts of events. The understanding is further complicated by the impression that the Sage did not revise his descriptions before this book was published. The lack of clarity has led to many textual variants and editors often disagree about which manuscript to follow.

Some critics find this part excessively long. Yet the contrasts exhibit attractive features. To give some examples: (1) They are all written in the second person singular. They are addressed to God, not exactly as a prayer but as a kind of liturgical recital to remind him of his part in Israel's history. (2) They include frequent allusions to the liturgical practices of Israel—a quality that shows the practical nature of Wis. (3) They contain many literary "flashbacks" that recall statements in earlier parts of the book. This technique binds the entire work together into a dynamic unit despite its wide-ranging subject matter and diversity of presentation. The flashbacks prove a strong argument against seeing any part as a separate unity.

Literary Form

This part of Wis, composed as a series of contrasts, is technically a "syncrisis." This genre is not found in the Hebrew Bible but existed in Attic orators and hellenistic historians. However, the Sage used it creatively and integrated it into his apologetic goal, which was to stir up fidelity to traditional faith among intelligent Jewish readers by making them proud of their ancestral God and his saving care. His method is to draw practical lessons by a skillful juxtaposing of details that portray God's providence at work. To do so he rearranges elements of biblical narratives without trying to preserve exact details. He also introduces features of Greek writing, like speculation on the harmony of elements in the universe (16:16-17:1).

The freedom with which the Sage handles the biblical text and subordinates it to his final goal is decisive against calling this part of Wis a "midrash," that is, an updated commentary on specific biblical texts. This judgment will become clearer in the following commentaries on individual scenes, for I shall point out various techniques employed to make the Exodus from Egypt—the key moment of God's providential liberation of Israel—the springboard for renewed trust in him. He alone can use all '*nature*' as an ordered cosmos for the benefit of his people (see 19:20).

Especially noteworthy for hellenistic influence is the treatment of the psychology of fear in the fourth contrast (17:2-21). In part it was inspired by the "descents into Hades" found in Greek literature as far back as the *Odyssey*. But the entire syncrisis is a fitting close to the Sage's apologetic aim explained in the general introduction.

1. CONTRASTS RESUMED: GOD MAKES ANIMALS SATISFY OR CAUSE HUNGER
WIS 16:2-4

> [2]Instead of this punishment thou didst
> show kindness to thy people,
> and thou didst prepare quails to eat,
> a delicacy to satisfy the desire of appetite;
> [3]in order that those men, when they desired food,
> might lose the least remnant of appetite
> because of the odious creatures sent to them,
> while thy people, after suffering want a short time,
> might partake of delicacies.
> [4]For it was necessary that upon those oppressors inexorable want should come,
> while to these it was merely shown how their enemies
> were being tormented.

The close relationship between Part III and Part IV of Wis is evident from the ease with which the Sage moves back from the one to the other. He has just presented the Egyptians as indulging in the worst form of idolatry. Now he presents God's manner of dealing with them as the foil to celebrate his care for his chosen people. But the two developments are distinct. They illustrate separate approaches to God's activity in history. Part III demonstrated the principle of talion: humans are punished in the very way they sin. But this short paragraph is set up as a contrast in which animals demonstrate God's way of dealing with two different groups of people. On the one hand, he was able to '*satisfy the desire*' of his people for nourishing food by providing '*quails to eat*' (v. 2; see Exod 16:13). But he also sent '*odious creatures*' to deprive the Egyptians of their appetite.

As in the first syncrisis (11:5-14), to create a contrast the Sage has to introduce an incident from a different biblical scene, for the Egyptians did not enter the desert with the Jews. Nor does the account of the plagues record any scene showing God sending '*odious creatures*' to deprive Egyptians of '*the last remnant of appetite*' (v. 3). The closest punishment is the result of the frogs in the second plague (Exod 7:26—8:3).

The freedom with which the Sage adapts biblical accounts throughout these contrasts to his idiosyncratic interpretation shows that he is not concerned about historical accuracy of events or surface details. He structures his contrasts with a view of extolling God's power and providence. Because this comparison is so short and the allusion unclear, many variants exist in the Greek manuscripts. Such variants often result from efforts of scribes to clarify a text they do not understand. Here the Sage himself provides a key to his meaning in the final couplet (v. 4). '*It was necessary*' that these '*oppressors*' suffer '*want.*' In other words, God was the real cause of the event. His saving providence is at work to teach his people as in 12:19 and 16:28.

God's providence touches the '*oppressors*' as enemies of his people (v. 4; see 10:14 for the same term used of Joseph's '*masters,*' whom he was able to dominate with the help of Lady Wisdom). Upon them came '*inexorable want*' (v. 4). The attribute may seem excessive, but '*inexorable*' appears in pagan religious poetry to convey the boundless persistence of the gods in caring for their own clients.

This short contrast reminds readers that throughout sacred history '*their enemies were being tormented*' (v. 4). The Sage alerts them to the reality of God's protection of his people even in their greatest dangers. This and the following examples will encourage fidelity to the God of the heroes celebrated above. Only such loyalty insures that they too will enjoy eternal happiness. The assurance that they receive from being '*shown*' God's power to punish is already part of their reward (contrast 18:19).

2. THIRD CONTRAST: GOD MAKES POISONOUS ANIMALS HEAL AND WOUND
Wis 16:5-15

[5]For when the terrible rage of wild
beasts came upon thy people
and they were being destroyed by the
bites of writhing serpents,
thy wrath did not continue to the end;
[6]they were troubled for a little while as a warning,
and received a token of deliverance to
remind them of thy law's command.
[7]For he who turned toward it was saved, not by what he
saw, but by thee, the Saviour of all.
[8]And by this also thou didst convince our enemies
that it is thou who deliverest from every evil.
[9]For they were killed by the bites of locusts and flies,
and no healing was found for them,
because they deserved to be punished by such things;
[10]but thy sons were not conquered even
by the teeth of venomous serpents,
for thy mercy came to their help and healed them.
[11]To remind them of thy oracles they were bitten,
and then were quickly delivered,
lest they should fall into deep forgetfulness
and become unresponsive to thy kindness.

[12]For neither herb nor poultice cured them,
but it was thy word, O Lord, which heals all men.
[13]For thou has power over life and death;
thou dost lead men down to the gates
of Hades and back again.
[14]A man in his wickedness kills another,
but he cannot bring back the departed spirit,
nor set free the imprisoned soul.
[15]To escape from thy hand is impossible.

The Sage makes this third comparison an intimate outpouring to his '*Lord*' (v. 12), beginning with the particle of phatic communion, *kai gar*. Here it is best translated by a phrase like, "yes, and" (vv. 5 and 12, rather than the '*for*' of the RSV). It must be distinguished from the logical connective '*for,*' which occurs five times in this contrast (vv. 7, 9, 10, 11, 13). The repetition of '*for*' indicates that the Sage wants to stress the connection between the events he narrates.

The scene described is another occasion when the Israelites complained against God, although the Sage does not mention this unflattering detail as the cause of the fiery '*serpents*' (v. 5; see Num 21:5-9). In keeping with the apologetic tone of these contrasts, he does not include any criticism of the chosen people. His focus is on the efficacy of God's favor to insure success for his people. While keeping the word for '*serpents*' from the biblical story, he opts for contemporary style. He avoids proper names and refers to the chosen people simply as '*they*' or '*them*'—a feature that the RSV modifies for clarity by supplying appropriate nouns throughout the contrasts.

The Sage's intention is to build on the biblical story and to make it—like the bronze serpent God ordered Moses to make—a '*token*' of God's '*deliverance*' (v. 6). The Greek word that is translated '*token*' also means "symbol," a word that gives a better indication of the Sage's method. '*Token*' is a common term in secular Greek. In fact, Demosthenes has the same phrase found here in the sense of "guarantee of deliverance." The Sage also flashes back to the recognition scene at the final judgment when the evildoers stand '*shaken*' at the unexpected '*salvation*' of the '*righteous*' (5:2). The same kind of contrast prevails between the brief suffering of the just and the final punishment of the wicked.

He prepares to make the event a '*token*' by stating explicitly that God sent punishment '*for a little while as a warning*' (v. 6). '*Warning*' is a rare term, related to the verb employed to describe how God used to '*warn*' his people throughout history (12:2). The Sage does not have to state what this '*token*' was because he addresses students familiar with the Hebrew Bible. He hastens to add, however, that it was not the '*token*' itself or the seeing that saved one '*who turned toward it,*' but rather God, '*the Saviour of all,*' a title never given to the Lord in the Hebrew Bible (v. 7).

The choice of this title '*Saviour of all*' reflects the tension under which the Sage operates. He speaks to God about how he rescued his people long ago, yet he is offering that intervention as a '*token*' of God's desire to be worshiped by all humanity. By adding the warning that the '*token*' itself did not save the Jews of the Exodus, he separates this incident from the idolatry he criticized in Part III. Furthermore, by repeating vocabulary from 5:2, he creates a flashback to the judgment scene and makes the plagues symbols of final salvation. What God did for his people through Lady Wisdom (see chapter 10), he is now pictured as doing directly: '*it is thou who deliverest from every evil*' (v. 8).

In keeping with the style of a syncrisis, the Sage contrasts the healing by describing how God used animals to punish. But to do this he combines two plagues and substitutes '*flies*' for the "dogflies" of the text of Exodus (v. 9; Exod 8:17). The eighth plague spoke about locusts eating all the vegetation of Egypt but did not '*kill*' its people (v. 9; see Exod 10:12-15). However, the pharaoh did call the effects of the locust plague '*death*' (Exod 10:17). The Sage shows different levels of death as he makes Egyptians symbols of God's enemies. They were obdurate like the Canaanites who '*murdered helpless lives*' (12:6; in Greek the term "soul" appears in both 12:6 and 16:9 to mean '*lives*'). These complicated explanations indicate that the Sage was not writing to convince outsiders to protect the political rights of the Jews. Rather he was concerned about creating a literary product that would speak to his fellow believers.

The theme of remembering, an important tool for encouraging his readers, appears twice in this short contrast: (1) The way God intervened, by forcing Moses to construct a '*token,*' provides a visible sign to '*remind them of thy law's command*' (v. 6; a parallel between the tablets of the law and the bronze serpent seems intended). (2) After a second description of how the '*mercy*' of God '*healed*' his '*sons*' from '*the teeth of venomous serpents,*' the Sage employs both '*remind*' and '*forgetfulness*' (vv. 10-11, again substituting scientific terminology for the biblical vocabulary). Rather than invite them to remember the "law," he substitutes the term '*oracles,*' more in keeping with the image of falling into '*forgetfulness,*' that is into *lethe,* the mythical river of Hades, here personified (v. 13; as in 1:14).

This way of reading the text is further recommended by the following clarifying phrase: '*became unresponsive to thy kindness.*' According to the RSV note this text is obscure, but it fits the Greek idea that '*kindness*' demands response. Xenophon said that friends of Virtue do not lie in Lethe. Throughout this book the Sage urges his readers to look at God's benefits and to take courage. Now he uses a Greek image to warn them against '*forgetfulness*' of God's gifts. He will repeat this image of the River Lethe in 17:3 (where RSV keeps '*forgetfulness*').

The Sage begins to expand on the events of salvation history from a psychological perspective in order to apply them to contemporary situations in much the same way as hellenistic interpreters were updating the stories of Homer with ethical significance. Thus he finishes this prayer with a general expression of trust in God's '*power*' to rescue from punishment and to give eternal reward. Like the syncrisis itself, this appendix begins with the phatic *kai gar*—throwing emphasis on the vocative '*O Lord*' with a believing "yes" (v. 13).

Just as the '*token*' did not heal the Jews in the desert,

neither did '*herb nor poultice*' (v. 12). Only God's '*word . . . heals all men*' (v. 12), that is, God's will, expressed in '*thy law's command*' and '*thy oracles*' (vv. 6, 11). The healing that the Sage speaks about is necessary for eternal destiny. This appendix, then, justifies the title of God as '*the Saviour of all*' in this polemic context (v. 7). God wants even the enemies of his people to enter his saving presence: '*for thou lovest all that exists*' (11:24).

In this context '*life and death*' take on the meaning of spiritual states (v. 13). The Sage employs the classical expression going back to the *Iliad* in the parallel stich: '*gates of Hades*' (v. 13; elsewhere in the LXX only in Isa 38:10; 3 Macc 5:51; see Matt 16:18). The Greek text of 1 Kgs 2:6 has the same wording as the second stich of verse 13 except for the omission of '*gates*' (see also Ps 29:4LXX). The Sage had already said that a human cannot create a living being (15:17). Now he reminds God that while a '*man in his wickedness kills another. . .he cannot bring back the departed spirit,*' that is, '*the imprisoned soul*' from Hades (v. 14).

The contrast concludes with a flashback that refutes the opening soliloquy by the ungodly that death ends all because '*no one has been known to return from Hades*' (2:1). On the contrary! The Lord has '*power over life and death*' and will '*set free*' those who remain faithful. This prayer ends by stating the truth that God is in control of all creation: nothing can '*escape from thy hand*' (v. 15). This verse forms the conclusion of the prayer. In fact, verses 13b and 15a are united in Tobit 13:2.

3. FOURTH CONTRAST: GOD USES NATURE TO STARVE OR NOURISH
Wis 16:16—17:1

> [16]for the ungodly, refusing to know thee,
> were scourged by the strength of thy arm,
> pursued by unusual rains and hail and relentless storms,
> and utterly consumed by fire.

[17]For—most incredible of all—in the
water, which quenches all things,
the fire had still greater effect,
for the universe defends the righteous.
[18]At one time the flame was restrained,
so that it might not consume the creatures
sent against the ungodly,
but that seeing this they might know
that they were being pursued by the
judgment of God;
[19]and at another time even in the midst of water it burned
more intensely than fire,
to destroy the crops of the unrighteous land.
[20]Instead of these things thou didst give thy people
the food of angels,
and without their toil thou didst supply them from
heaven with bread ready to eat,
providing every pleasure and suited to every taste.
[21]For thy sustenance manifested thy sweetness toward
thy children;
and the bread, ministering[a] to the desire
of the one who took it,
was changed to suit every one's liking.
[22]Snow and ice withstood fire without melting,
so that they might know that the crops of their enemies
were being destroyed by the fire that blazed in the hail
and flashed in the showers of rain;
[23]whereas the fire, in order that
the righteous might be fed,
even forgot its native power.
[24]For the creation, serving thee who hast made it,
exerts itself to punish the unrighteous,
and in kindness relaxes on behalf of those who
trust in thee.

[25]Therefore at that time also, changed into all forms,
it served thy all-nourishing bounty,
according to the desire of those who had need,
[26]so that thy sons, whom thou didst love,

O Lord, might learn
that it is not the production of crops that feeds man,
but that thy word preserves those who trust in thee.
[27]For what was not destroyed by fire was melted when
simply warmed by a fleeting ray of the sun,
[28]to make it known that one must rise before the sun to give
thee thanks,
and must pray to thee at the dawning of the light;
[29]for the hope of an ungrateful man will
melt like wintry frost,
and flow away like waste water.
17Great are thy judgments and hard to describe;
therefore uninstructed souls have gone astray.

[a]Gk *and it, ministering*

This central contrast begins with that divine intervention after the Exodus when God fed his people with manna in the desert. Once more, to develop a syncrisis the Sage must widen his portrayal of this intervention. He expands to picture how God organized nature in general and especially the element of '*fire*' (v. 16; '*fire*' appears five times in this section) to bless and to punish. The Sage alludes to his earlier notice that told how the Egyptians were forced to recognize God when he '*punished*' them with animals (12:27). The Sage begins with the picture of God as having '*scourged*' them for refusing to acknowledge him (v. 16; again in 18:13).

By attempting to bring together disparate themes while he is developing a contrast, the Sage creates several obscurities that have led to textual variants. As he gets further into these contrasts, he writes with less precision; evidently he assumes that his readers are familiar with the allusions in the narratives and able to fill in details. Modern readers, less familiar with biblical stories and Jewish tradition, have great difficulty in following the accounts, especially when the Sage creates his own version. In this scene he adds the element of '*unusual rains*,' and understands '*fire*' not only as the lightning of Exodus 9:24-26 but also as a '*flame*' (vv.

16-18). He explains that God staged all these '*incredible*' events to serve as a '*judgment*' upon '*the unrighteous land*' (vv. 17-19) and as instruction for the Egyptians.

Only then does he turn to explain how God directed the same elements to aid his people (vv. 20-28). By concentrating on the element of '*fire,*' the Sage takes a pychological approach to the purpose of the plagues. Fire was an element prominent in contemporary hellenistic philosophical theory. For example, Philodemus gave it a role in the punishment of the wicked. The apocalyptic dimension that played a key role in the punishment of the '*ungodly*' in Part I (5:17-23) also reappears in the description of the '*flame*' that burned '*in the midst of water*' (v. 19). The Sage may want to allude to a theory of hellenistic science that held a fiery mass within the earth.

Instead of picturing the elements as helping the chosen people directly, the Sage introduces a new factor into this contrast—the manna. It complicates the development but also affirms God's transcendent providence as what sustained his people during their journey through the desert (see Exod 16:14-21). The Sage derives his term for manna from the Greek translation of the didactic psalm that describes Israel's history. It translates the Hebrew phrase '*bread of the strong*' as '*food of angels*' (v. 20, referring to Ps 78:25; LXX 79:25).

In the course of elaborating on the biblical narrative, the Sage also draws ethical guidance from God's way of '*providing*' for his people. When he says that the manna provided '*every pleasure*'—in the sense that it had power to be '*suited to every taste*' (v. 20)—he explains this in terms of God's powerful presence. Its '*sweetness*' (from the "honey" taste of Exod 16:31) becomes a symbol of spiritual blessings '*toward thy children*' (v. 21). As the RSV note indicates, the Greek text does not contain the word '*bread*' in verse 21; so the '*ministering*' refers back grammatically to God's '*sustenance,*' but logically to his '*sweetness.*' God's gifts make his power present. The Sage keeps the tone positive by omitting any reference to the people's later complaints against the manna (Num 11:6; 21:5).

At the end of the contrast the Sage returns to the manna and its power to resist the *'fire'* used to cook it (v. 27, picking up on v. 23). Yet it melted in the *'fleeting ray of the sun'* each morning (v. 27). From this he draws a moral: the duty of praising God for his gifts (vv. 27-28). By providing this food before daylight, God invites his people to dwell in an attitude of *'thanks'* even before *'the dawning of the light,'*—a liturgical reference to the early hour of morning *'thanks'* (v. 28). The Sage goes to great pains in this subtle comparison to complete his teaching about human immortality. The manna was not desirable for itself but only as a gift of God's care, a symbol or *'token'* of true salvation (see 16:6). Its quality of *'providing every pleasure'* alludes to the Epicurean understanding of the life of the gods as one of total pleasure (v. 21). Only God's gift can bring mortals to share the enduring *'pleasure'* of divine life.

In this section various plays on words flow in an almost chain-of-consciousness rapidity as the Sage multiplies motives to encourage his readers to take advantage of God's care and to avoid the lot of *'an ungrateful man'* whose *'hope- . . . will melt like wintry frost'* (v. 29). This image is a flashback to the fate of Israel's enemies at the last judgment. Their *'hope'* too is like *'hoarfrost'* (5:14, translating the same Greek term). Unfortunately the RSV does not capture many of the aesthetic and literary dimensions of the passage. The Sage implies that humans are divided into only two groups: those who thank and praise God (hence the liturgical overtones) and those who do not. God will guide the first group to their true destiny with himself, but the second will be lost as surely as the *'waste water'* (v. 29).

Between these two parts that show nature supporting the work of the manna, the Sage inserts reflections about how God *'punishes the unrighteous'* through *'creation'* (vv. 22-26). To round out this cosmic activity of God through *'creation,'* he introduces items from the plague of hail (Exod 9:22-25), but shifts details to serve his didactic aim. *'Snow'* is not mentioned in the plague narrative itself, although the term does appear in the sign God gave Moses in turning his hand *'leprous, as white as snow'* (v. 22; Exod 4:6). And it is not the '*hail*' that is called '*ice*' in the Hebrew, but rather the manna itself in the Greek translation of Num 11:7, for the Hebrew "bdellium."

Mixing his images, the Sage imagines God as playing on creation as a musical instrument, striking it to punish the '*unrighteous*' and releasing its cords '*in kindness*' to aid '*those who trust in thee*' (v. 24). Thus, right here in the middle of the seven contrasts he states the principle that guides this and all the others. That is, all the events surrounding the Exodus are '*tokens*' or symbols teaching readers that God's power is at work in '*creation*' for them (16:24-26; see 16:11-12; 18:22). As a teacher he gives specific applications of this principle in these seven contrasts.

Critics point out that the Sage becomes repetitious in them and suggest that he may have written this part of his book after he had lost some of his earlier poetic incisiveness. But this wordiness could also point to a lack of opportunity to revise this section of his protreptic. Or the Sage may have felt the need to insist that the powers of nature, which pagans often divinized, adhere to it, as '*creation*,' that is, as manifestations of God's '*all-nourishing bounty*' (v. 25). The comparisons serve to continue his polemic against all forms of idolatry.

The Sage never completely resolves the tension between relating to God '*who lovest all things that exist*' (11:24) and the God whose special care is with '*thy sons, whom thou didst love*' and teach (v. 26). It is clear that he feels this tension himself and expresses it in the couplet that closes this fourth contrast. God's '*judgments*' are '*hard to describe*' and confusing to '*uninstructed souls*' (17:1). This verse conveys both his wonder at God's mysterious workings and his willingness to reflect upon them. The compound '*hard to describe*,' coined by him, embodies the spirit he wishes to communicate to his students so that they will not turn away from their responsibility as believers to God or to each other, but continue to learn from their tradition and to act as God's children.

4. FIFTH CONTRAST: GOD PUNISHES BY DARKNESS AND BLESSES BY LIGHT
Wis 17:2—18:4

[2]For when lawless men supposed that they held the holy
nation in their power,
they themselves lay as captives of darkness
and prisoners of long night,
shut in under their roofs, exiles — the Egyptians
from eternal providence.
[3]For thinking that in their secret sins
they were unobserved
behind a dark curtain of forgetfulness,
they were scattered, terribly alarmed,
and appalled by spectres.
[4]For not even the inner chamber that held them protected
them from fear,
but terrifying sounds rang out around them,
and dismal phantoms with gloomy faces appeared.
[5]And no power of fire was able to give light,
nor did the brilliant flames of the stars
avail to illumine that hateful night.
[6]Nothing was shining through to them except dreadful,
self-kindled fire,
and in terror they deemed the things which they saw
to be worse than that unseen appearance.
[7]The delusions of their magic art lay humbled,
and their boasted wisdom was scornfully rebuked.
[8]For those who promised to drive off
the fears and disorders of a sick soul
were sick themselves with ridiculous fear.
[9]For even if nothing disturbing frightened them,
yet, scared by the passing of beasts
and the hissing of serpents,
[10]they perished in trembling fear,
refusing to look even at the air, though
it nowhere could be avoided.
[11]For wickedness is a cowardly thing,
condemned by its own testimony;

distressed by conscience, it has always
exaggerated the difficulties.
[12]For fear is nothing but surrender of the helps that come
from reason;
[13]and the inner expectation of help, being weak,
prefers ignorance of what causes the torment.
[14]But throughout the night, which was really powerless,
and which beset them from the recesses
of powerless Hades,
they all slept the same sleep,
[15]and now were driven by monstrous spectres,
and now were paralyzed by their souls' surrender,
for sudden and unexpected fear overwhelmed them.
[16]And whoever was there fell down,
and thus was kept shut up in a prison not made of iron;
[17]for whether he was a farmer or a shepherd
or a workman who toiled in the wilderness,
he was seized, and endured the inescapable fate;
for with one chain of darkness they all were bound.
[18]Whether there came a whistling wind,
or a melodious sound of birds in widespreading branches,
or the rhythm of violently rushing water,
[19]or the harsh crash of rocks hurled down,
or the unseen running of leaping animals,
or the sound of the most savage roaring beasts,
or an echo thrown back from a hollow of the mountains,
it paralyzed them with terror.
[20]For the whole world was illumined with brilliant light,
and was engaged in unhindered work,
[21]while over those men alone heavy night was spread,
an image of the darkness that was
destined to receive them;
but still heavier than darkness were they to themselves.

18 But for thy holy ones there was very great light.
Their enemies heard their voices but did not
see their forms,
and counted them happy for not having suffered,
[2]and were thankful that thy holy ones,

though previously wrong, were doing them no injury;
and they begged their pardon for having been at variance with them.
[3]Therefore thou didst provide a flaming pillar of fire
as a guide for thy people's unknown journey,
and a harmless sun for their glorious wandering.
[4]For their enemies deserved to be deprived of light and imprisoned in darkness,
those who had kept thy sons imprisoned,
through whom the imperishable light of the law was to be given to the world.

This contrast illustrates the skill of the Sage in adapting literary techniques of Hellenism to convey insights into God's protection of his people. At this time Homer was a textbook for learning Greek literature. Yet his stories about the foibles of the gods were often an embarrassment to sophisticated readers. So commentators began to update the homeric myths by transforming them into psychological admonitions. They interpreted the crude stories about the faults of the gods and ancient heroes as symbolic of human vices and the punishments they bring upon sinners.

In a similar vein certain writers of the Jewish diaspora felt that a literal understanding of Mosaic texts was inadequate and unworthy of inspiration—as Philo's allegorical interpretations show. The Sage does not adopt that method. Instead, he draws from details of the narratives about the Exodus insights into universal moral truths. To do so in this contrast, he draws upon a familiar technique of pagan literature—the so-called "descents into Hades." Examples of this genre extend from the *Odyssey* to the *Aeneid.* These descent stories provided a fertile source of literary and scientific material that could be easily integrated into an exaltation of God's '*eternal providence*' over the events of human destiny (v. 2). The Sage's frequent use of the conjunction '*for*'—often as a loose connective typical of the diatribe—illustrates his efforts to persuade readers in a style familiar to them.

The longer section of this syncrisis is a description of how God caused darkness to instill paralyzing fear into the enemies of his people (vv. 2-21). The large number of words not found in the Greek LXX Bible—35 in this passage—as well as the prosaic descriptive style are appropriate because the Sage here speaks of '*fear*' in the philosophical sense. He is not dealing with the biblical "fear of the Lord," but with a human emotion. He defines this fear in the verse line that comes at the exact center of this 55-line description of its origin and effects. This structuring exemplifies the Greek love of balance. By contrast, the whole plague of darkness is covered in the biblical narrative by three short verses (Exod 10:21-23).

The entire comparison is neatly set off with a double inclusion: the first formed by two rarely used terms for '*enclosed*' (missed in the RSV, which translates the same term as '*shut in*' and '*imprisoned*'); the second is a play on words between '*lawless*' and '*law*' (17:2 and 18:4). The embellishments of the Sage do not fall under the biblical technique of updating a text called "midrash," but represent a method of giving free play to the imagination to convert a biblical scene into a source of religious insight and prayer. This whole presentation finds in visual images symbols of spiritual and emotional experiences.

The Sage begins on a note of irony. The '*lawless*' Egyptians, pictured as foolishly thinking they '*held the holy nation in their power,*' recall the '*most foolish*' idol worshiper '*who oppressed thy people*' (v. 2; see 15:14). God's intervention reveals them as the real '*prisoners*' because they are '*exiles from eternal providence*' (v. 2). Their predicament is described in poetic terminology foreign to the Greek LXX Bible. Again the personification of Lethe, the river of forgetfulness, should be kept as a proper noun (instead of '*forgetfulness*' in v. 3; see on 16:11). The unusual expressions have spawned a variety of manuscript readings. Instead of '*they were scattered,*' which does not fit the context of being imprisoned, many manuscripts read, "They were surrounded by darkness" (v. 3).

The efforts of the Egyptians to find sanctuary by seeking

refuge in the '*inner chamber*' of their homes or shrines only makes their situation worse. The Sage repeats the term '*inner chamber*' (vv. 4, 14; these are the only biblical uses). Instead of being '*protected*' there, they are terrified by the '*sounds*' and '*phantoms*' of this unnatural darkness (v. 4). Since this darkness was the effect of God's '*power,*' no recourse to nature was able to relieve the Egyptians (v. 5).

The Grip of Fear

The Sage reaches heights of lyric beauty as he goes on to give a graphic description of how the grip of fear fires the Egyptians' imagination (vv. 6-11). Self-fed fright makes them think that the reality is even worse than what they experience. Their imagination lights up inner vision like an all-consuming bonfire as their darkness becomes a '*self-kindled fire.*' Alluding to the contests between Aaron and the magicians, the Sage suggests that the Egyptians tried to escape from this darkness by resorting to '*their magic art*' (v. 7). The role of this verse is to warn readers against failing to heed God's '*rebuke*' by acting as if they are wiser than God. '*Rebuke*' is a technical word in Philo for the inner divine witness, equivalent to '*conscience*' mentioned below (v. 11). The vocabulary chosen creates a flashback to the power and resourcefulness of Lady Wisdom who assists her followers in every need (see 8:6).

Using an image that has become popular in modern times, the Sage calls this kind of self-centered arrogance the act of '*a sick soul,*' a term found in Plutarch's tract *On Superstition.* Continuing to draw upon the vast resources of hellenistic psychological language, he describes how imagination takes over when '*nothing disturbing*' is actually present. Ironically the very '*beasts*' and '*serpents*' the Egyptians worshiped now destroy them with '*trembling fear*' (v. 11; see 11:15). They flee from reality by refusing '*to look even at the air*'—a term to be understood in this context in its ancient sense of haze or mist, as Winston demonstrates in the Anchor Bible (v. 10).

Verse 11 reads like a generalizing conclusion about '*wickedness.*' However, this comment seems out of place in a development on fear, and the RSV notes that the first poetic stich is "uncertain and probably corrupt." Its translation is a conjecture to make sense out of this uncertainty. The second line of verse 11 explains how ill-will is the basis of ignorance—a tension that surfaces several times in Wis (see 1:16; 2:10-11, 21; 11:15: 12:23). '*Wickedness*' flows from the confusion of moral '*conscience,*' a term found here in the Bible for the first time in its technical anthropological sense as developed in hellenistic ethics. The word continued to keep its wider meaning of "consciousness."

The word translated as '*distressed*' is the same one translated '*holds together*' in describing the Spirit (v. 11 and 1:7). The specific function of '*conscience*' is to bring together all elements involved in making a moral judgment. When '*wickedness*' enters the process, it has a corrupting effect. Hence, an appropriate translation would be: "wickedness constrains conscience"—producing an unbalanced situation that disturbs the order of God's creation. Or, in keeping with the imagery of the passage, '*conscience*' is kept prisoner by '*wickedness.*'

One of the most evident signs of the constraint of wickedness is the '*fear*' that the Sage describes so vividly. He climaxes his description with a definition: '*fear is nothing but the surrender of helps that come from reason*' (v. 12). He then goes on to expand: fear is a double evil. On the one hand, it is irrational, a misuse of God's gift of '*reason.*' On the other hand, it drives one to '*prefer ignorance*' rather than face up to the demands of reality (v. 13). Biblical authors seldom resort to definitions, which are common in Greek thinkers. So this verse is a good example of reaching out to Greek learning to show how philosophical method can be put at the service of faith.

Not only are hellenistic techniques employed but the wording of this definition recalls that Zeno called fear "the expectation of evil." In fact, the explanation uses Zeno's word '*expectation*' as well as other terms found in contemporary scientific literature: '*reason*' from philosophy, and the technical term for '*helps*' from medicine (vv. 12-13). From this elaboration of his definition until the end of his long contrast, the Sage composes another parallel description of fear exactly the same length as the one preceding the definition. In balanced fashion it completes his description of the psychological effects of fear on the Egyptians (vv. 13-21).

The description focuses on the mysterious '*inner*' darkness of the mind that paralyzes sinners with '*ignorance*' in the moral sense, that is, the nightmares arising from fear. The explanation abounds in plays on words and artistic word order (hyperbaton). The two sources of dreams—'*night*' and '*Hades*' are '*powerless*' because they cannot resist God as he uses them to punish his enemies with '*sleep*' (v. 14). The term for '*recesses*' of Hades is the same in Greek as for the '*inner chambers*' to which the Egyptians fled for protection (vv. 4 and 14). From Hades came '*monstrous spectres*'—evidently nightmares—which alternated with periods when they were paralyzed by the '*surrender*' that fear causes (v. 15). Again the terminology comes from pagan writers; for example, Diodorus Siculus speaks of '*unexpected fear*.' Fear locked the Egyptians in '*a prison not made of iron*,' a poetic phrase never found elsewhere in the Bible.

The universal scope of this prison is suggested by listing the classes of people affected: '*farmer...shepherd...workman*.' Winston suggests wisely that the Greek word translated '*wilderness*' should be "tranquility" (v. 17; the confusion is the result of reversing two letters). Once seized, each of these persons '*endured the inescapable fate*,' a pagan concept, because "fate" was their word for inescapable destiny (v. 17; see 19:4). It sums up both the situation of God's enemies—a state of absolute hopelessness—in contrast to the confidence of believers.

This reflection on the plague of darkness presents it as a symbol of the religious truth stated in Part I: the hope of the upright, '*full of immortality*,' is the direct opposite of the '*vain*' hope of sinners (3:4, 11), a hope that is like '*frost*' that melts and fades away (5:14 and 16:29). Sinners are held bound by a '*chain*' of darkness as in a '*prison*' (vv. 16-17). These images are heaped up for the apologetic purpose of keeping young Jews faithful to the God of revelation.

To complete his symbolism the Sage enumerates seven natural phenomena that '*paralyzed them with terror.*' He maintains a balance not only in the number of lines of the two parts of this description of fear but also in vocabulary. Thus, the adjective describing the '*whistling wind*' is from the same root as the '*hissing serpents*' (vv. 9 and 18); the term for the '*sound*' of birds is the same as the '*sounds*' that terrified the Egyptians (vv. 4 and 18). Both halves mention '*unseen*' phenomena (vv. 6 and 19). The Greek has additional artistic features lost in translation, like assonance and plays on words. The Sage closes with a return to the '*brilliant*' quality that illumined the whole world but could not penetrate the Egyptian consciousness (vv. 5 and 20). The verb used in the negative sense of hindering their discernment also describes the positive power of God to allow '*unhindered work*' for his people (vv. 11 and 20).

In case readers miss the contrast of creation as both enslaving and liberating, the Sage states it explicitly at the end of this long description. Ultimately, it is not creation as an activity of God that punishes sinners, but their own inner darkness nourished by sin (v. 21). This final verse provides a necessary corrective to the principle that creation '*exerts itself to punish the unrighteous*' (16:24, with the same verb translated here as '*spread*'). All God's works are '*saving,*' but sinners turn them into instruments of punishment for themselves.

Light for God's Chosen

After this long development on darkness, in which God's name is not mentioned, this fifth contrast closes with a short meditation on '*light.*' It is eleven lines long, exactly one-fifth of the corresponding treatment of darkness. God provides a '*great light*' and '*pillar of fire*' for '*thy holy ones*' (18:4). The reference to God by means of the pronoun '*thy*' and the repetition of '*light*' form an inclusion to set this prayerful dialogue apart. Yet these two sections form one contrast because the Sage referred to those enjoying God's '*light*' at the end of the first part, and to the '*darkness*' of his people's enemies at the close of the second development (17:20 and 18:4).

This is the first time that the Sage calls God's people his '*holy ones*' since the chapter on the saving activity of Lady Wisdom (10:15, 17). To have them move around freely in the midst of the Egyptians is another adaptation of the biblical account to his goals. The original narrative pictured the Israelites as dwelling apart from the Egyptians (Exod 10:23). But the Sage concentrates on the conduct of the Egyptians:

1) they '*accounted*' the Jews '*happy*,' that is, they pronounced beatitudes or blessings over them when they were forced to acknowledge God's intervention on their behalf. This action recalls how the wicked in Part I mocked the just for calling '*the last end of the righteous happy*' but were later forced to admit the truth of their claim (2:16).

2) they '*were thankful*' that in leaving Egypt the Jews were '*doing them no injury*' (v. 2).

3) they '*begged*...*pardon*' of the Jews for '*having been at variance with them*' (v. 2, although the RSV notes that the meaning is uncertain). The Greek has "beg" rather than '*begged pardon.*' The text seems to be deliberately ambiguous. It goes on to explain that the '*great light*' functioned in two ways. First, it was '*a flaming pillar of fire*' that God sent to '*guide*' his people's '*journey*' through the desert—just as he guided Lady Wisdom (v. 3; see 7:15). Second, the light was by day '*a harmless sun,*' because it did not '*smite them*' on their '*glorious wandering*'—a poetic description of the Exodus.

The Sage brings this long comparison to an end by telling God that he had rightly '*imprisoned*' the Egyptians '*in darkness*' for their crime of imprisoning the people destined to give the '*imperishable light of the law to the world*' (v. 4). '*Imperishable*' (the same adjective that describes God's '*spirit*' in 12:1) is formed from the theologically important abstract '*incorruption*' (2:23, translated '*immortal*' in 6:18, 19). As explained above, '*incorruption*' is a key aspect of the Sage's explanation of how God confers eternal life upon the souls of his holy ones. God made the Mosaic Law the medium for communicating this gift. That Law nourished divine friendship and opened believers to receive God's gift of '*incorruption*' that brought them to their eternal destiny.

The Sage will rcturn to the subject of the Law and its importance in the next contrast (18:6-9). Here he states that the Law was meant for all the '*world.*' In so doing he implies that his readers are missionaries for the spread of God's offer of eternal life to their cultured associates. He also makes this description of God's power to protect his people a flashback to his lament over the wicked whose malice prevented the '*light*' of righteousness from shining upon them (5:6-7).

5. SIXTH CONTRAST: GOD'S WORD BRINGS DEATH AND SAVES
Wis 18:5-25

> [5]When they had resolved to kill the
> babes of thy holy ones,
> and one child had been exposed and rescued,
> thou didst in punishment take away
> a multitude of their children;
> and thou didst destroy them all
> together by a mighty flood.
> [6]That night was made known beforehand to our fathers,
> so that they might rejoice in sure knowledge of the oaths
> in which they trusted.
> [7]The deliverance of the righteous and
> the destruction of their enemies
> were expected by thy people.
> [8]For by the same means by which thou

didst punish our enemies thou
didst call us to thyself and glorify us.
[9]For in secret the holy children of good
men offered sacrifices,
and with one accord agreed to the divine law,
that the saints would share alike the same things,
both blessings and dangers;
and already they were singing the praises of the fathers.
[10]But the discordant cry of their enemies echoed back,
and their piteous lament for their children
was spread abroad.
[11]The slave was punished with the same
penalty as the master,
and the common man suffered the same loss as the king,
[12]and they all together, by the one form of death,
had corpses too many to count.
For the living were not sufficient even to bury them,
since in one instant their most valued
children had been destroyed.
[13]For though they had disbelieved everything
because of their magic arts,
yet, when their first-born were destroyed,
they acknowledged thy people to be God's son.
[14]For while gentle silence enveloped all things,
and night in its swift course was now half gone,
[15]thy all-powerful word leaped from heaven, from the
royal throne,
into the midst of the land that was doomed,
a stern warrior [16]carrying the sharp sword of thy authentic command,
and stood and filled all things with death,
and touched heaven while standing on the earth.
[17]Then at once apparitions in dreadful
dreams greatly troubled them,
and unexpected fears assailed them;
[18]and one here and another there, hurled down half
dead,
made known why they were dying;

[19]for the dreams which disturbed them
forewarned them of this,
so that they might not perish without
knowing why they suffered.

[20]The experience of death touched also the righteous,
and a plague came upon the multitude in the desert,
but the wrath did not long continue.
[21]For a blameless man was quick to
act as their champion;
he brought forward the shield of his ministry,
prayer and propitiation by incense;
he withstood the anger and put an end to the disaster,
showing that he was thy servant.
[22]He conquered the wrath[a] not by strength of body,
and not by force of arms,
but by his word he subdued the punisher,
appealing to the oaths and covenants given to our fathers.
[23]For when the dead had already fallen
on one another in heaps,
he intervened and held back the wrath,
and cut off its way to the living.
[24]For upon his long robe the whole world was depicted,
and the glories of the fathers were engraved on the four
rows of stones,
and thy majesty on the diadem upon his head.
[25]To these the destroyer yielded, these he feared;
for merely to test the wrath was enough.

[a]Gk *multitude*

Repeating the designation of the Jews as '*thy holy ones,*' the Sage begins this sixth contrast without using any proper names. In speaking to the God of '*our fathers,*' he does not need any further designation of the Egyptians than '*they*' (vv. 5-6). He picks up terminology from the first contrast when he speaks of their resolve '*to kill the babes,*' two words previously used to form the new compound "infant-slayers" (v. 5; see 11:7). The background of the final plague is provided by describing the exposure and rescue of Moses in elegant Greek phrasing. Again the omission of names presumes wide biblical learning on the part of original readers. That crime against Moses provoked God's '*punishment*' of taking away not only the first born of the Egyptians but '*them all together*' (v. 5, repeated in v. 12).

The text adds further background data in the form of a description of the Passover celebrated by the Jews on the eve of their departure from Egypt (vv. 6-9). This paragraph can be called a digression in the sense of its being a footnote explaining God's plan. It reflects current Jewish speculation about the role of that meal before the Exodus. In fact, Annie Jaubert saw in these verses traces of a ritual Passover covenant. The basis for such a theology can be seen in the so-called Book of Consolation of Jeremiah (Jer 30-31; 37-38LXX). It portrays God as saying that he is going to gather the people of Judah from the ends of the earth "on the feast of Passover" (Jer 38:8LXX in contrast to 31:8 in the Hebrew text). In similar fashion Wis pictures the '*fathers*' as knowing '*beforehand*' what God was going to do and how their faith in God's oaths was going to be vindicated. They expected '*the destruction of their enemies*' (vv. 6-7).

This digression contains a statement of the principle that governs the seven contrasts of Part IV, namely, that God glorifies his people '*by the same means*' he employs to punish his enemies (v. 8). This differs from the principle of divine talion that governed Part III, namely, that God punishes sinners in the same way they sin. The '*holy children of good men*' experienced the saving power of God's word in their Passover '*sacrifices.*' This term implies that the meal sealed a special covenant for the generation of Moses by agreeing to the '*divine law*' (v. 9). The Greek text actually uses the expression "the law of thy divinity." "Divinity" is a hellenistic abstract term for God recorded first in the Letter of Aristeas and common in late hellenistic philosophers. It gives a contemporary tone to the ancient Jewish rite.

In contrast to this display of confidence in God and perception of his control over sacred history, the contrast portrays the disarray of the Egyptians (v. 10). In meaning this verse belongs with verse 5. Yet the digression about the Jewish understanding of these events provides a wider horizon for evaluating the malice of the Egyptians. They exercised solidarity in evil: no social class was innocent. The Sage expects readers to remember his defense of God's freedom (see 12:12). How can the God who does not '*condemn him who does not deserve to be punished*' (12:15) now punish even '*slave*' and '*common man*' (v. 11)? The answer is that all Egyptians fall under God's '*utmost condemnation*' upon idolatry (12:26-27). No middle ground exists between worshiping idols and serving the living God.

What Egyptians experienced in the plagues is what all sinners can expect at the last judgment. When all families of the foolish lost '*their most valued children,*' that is, their firstborn, and experienced corpses '*too many to count,*' they formed a contrast to believers who enjoyed '*uncounted*' wealth from Lady Wisdom (v. 12, forming a flashback to 7:11 to stress the horror of their sin). The cause of this misery was the Egyptians' recourse to '*magic arts,*' the same sin that brought divine '*hate*' upon the Canaanites and punishment upon Egyptians (v. 17; see 12:4 and 17:7). The Sage continues to be preoccupied with the phenomenon of God's simultaneous love and hate for his creatures; it is a motif for motivating the Jews to keep faithful in confessing their God. Eventually sinners are forced to recognize his power that they previously rejected as saving (v. 13; the repetition of '*God's son*' produces a flashback to 2:18; 5:2-5; 16:16).

The point of this comparison is that the power of God's word is both destructive and saving. When it meets with ignorance and malice—much like the Spirit of wisdom that '*will not free a blasphemer*' (1:7)—its '*sharp sword*' inflicts death (v. 16). The second half of this contrast tells how the divine word worked judgment within Israel when Korah and his followers, who revolted against Moses, were swallowed up (Num 16:1-35). With the final plague as basis for his presentation, the Sage pictures God's '*all-powerful word*' leaping down from his '*royal throne*' (v. 15, recalling Lady Wisdom on her throne in 9:10).

The Punishing Word

This ferocious word is in some ways the obverse side of both the Lord's Spirit (1:7) and Lady Wisdom, who portrayed God's saving presence for his people. It '*leaped*' down in the middle of the night like the lightning God used to arm creation against his enemies (v. 15; see 5:21). The final statement of this image adds a fantastic detail: the divine word '*touched heaven while standing on earth.*' Commentators dispute the allusion. Some see it as referring to Homer's description of Strife (*Iliad* 4:443); others link it to Jacob's ladder (Gen 28:12). More probably it is simply a variation of the hellenistic commonplace of the gigantic figures in divine epiphanies, because its effect on the Egyptians is explained (vv. 17-19). It recalls the fears and apparitions that '*greatly troubled them*' in the darkness (see 17:3-15). To the theme of the large number of dead is added a further detail that God predicted to the firstborn the reason for their death. They shared this knowledge with others so that all the Egyptians came to know '*why they suffered*' (v. 19). The phrase '*not unknowing*' ironically reverses the theme of idolatry as not knowing God.

At this point the contrast shifts to the situation of the chosen people and devotes almost the same number of verses to describing what happened to them (vv. 20-25, a total of 20 stichs; if the eleven lines in the digression are included, the description of the '*righteous*' is a longer section). For the first time within this series of contrasts the Sage pictures God as inflicting punishment on his own people. In Part III he had indicated that God punished his people to instruct them (12:21-22). Here he does not state any specific sin but presents their fault as the occasion for the intercession of Aaron, described in the Book of Numbers (Num 17:1-15; 16:36-50LXX). The word translated '*plague*' comes from that biblical scene (v. 20; Num 16:48LXX). Divine '*wrath*' in this section is personified—like God's Word above—and would be better capitalized (vv. 20, 23, 25).

Aaron, assuming his '*ministry*' as '*shield,*' engages as his people's champion in an apocalyptic struggle that recalls God's own activity in taking '*holiness as an invincible shield*' (v. 21, recalling 5:19). The ability of '*prayer*' as well as the liturgical rite of '*incense*' practiced in the Temple of Jerusalem to propitiate God would speak to the situation of the Jews in Egypt. This scene provides a dimension not found in the other six contrasts, namely, that it is God who designates his priests as agents in bringing about '*propitiation.*' Liturgical '*ministry*' is not magic that forces God to submit to mortals. Rather, it is a '*shield*' provided by God himself to keep his people alert to the danger of being turned from his saving will. The speed of Aaron in being '*quick to act*' against evil points out the danger of '*wickedness*' to '*obscure what is good*' by repeating the term that described God's intervention in the case of Elijah, whom he took '*quickly*' from the earth (v. 21; see 4:10-14).

The way God exercises his care varies according to concrete situations, but he always remains faithful to the '*oaths and covenants given to our fathers*' (v. 22; see 16:11). Again the tension of dealing with God as both '*punisher*' and '*champion*' is evident in the double manifestation of '*word.*' When it came from God upon the Egyptians, it '*filled all things with death.*' Yet the prayerful, propitiatory '*word*' of Aaron '*subdued the punisher*' sent by God upon his own people. Because the argument is subtle, commentators disagree about how to interpret the text. In fact, to solve one aspect of the problem the RSV substitutes the term '*wrath*' for '*multitude*' (v. 22, assuming an interchange of two letters in Greek).

Because the principle involved about the place of intercession in general and of propitiation in particular is vital to the religious life of the chosen people, the Sage concludes this contrast by explaining how the '*shield*' of Aaron's liturgical '*ministry*' functioned (vv. 23-25). It stood between the living and the dead to '*cut off*' God's anger, vividly described in the biblical account (Num 17:5-16LXX, which puts the number of dead at 14,700). Rather than repeating biblical details, the Sage turns his attention to the '*robe*' and '*diadem*' of Aaron, to show their significance for encouraging his young readers to be faithful to God and to the covenant.

The '*robe*' had on it '*the whole world*' plus '*the glories of the fathers*' engraved in twelve stones (v. 24). On the '*diadem*' was the '*majesty*' of God. Hellenistic Jewish writers like Philo speculated on the cosmic symbolism of the priestly garments, and this text reflects that speculation. How these robes were decorated is still disputed. Some commentators hold that the '*glories*' were the names of the twelve patriarchs after whom the tribes of Israel were named; others see them as symbols of their deeds. That kind of speculation about obscure verses of the Bible was popular in hellenistic Judaism and would have been familiar to the original audience of Wis. Only in a learned environment could this ferocious apologetic command a hearing.

A literary inclusion formed by repeating the word '*test*' marks the close of this contrast (vv. 25 and 18, where the same word is translated '*experience*'). The vocabulary chosen makes this concluding scene of God's providence toward his people serve as a flashback to the picture in the prologue of his creative power that wards off destruction from the universe (1:13-14).

6. SEVENTH CONTRAST: GOD USES CREATION ITSELF TO SAVE AND DESTROY
Wis 19:1-21

19 But the ungodly were assailed to
the end by pitiless anger,
for God knew in advance even their future actions,
[2]that, though they themselves had permitted
thy people to depart
and hastily sent them forth,
they would change their minds and pursue them.
[3]For while they were still busy at mourning,
and were lamenting at the graves of their dead,
they reached another foolish decision,
and pursued as fugitives those whom they had begged
and compelled to depart.

[4]For the fate they deserved drew them on to this end,
and made them forget what had happened,
in order that they might fill up the punishment which their torments still lacked,
[5]and that thy people might experience
an incredible journey,
but they themselves might meet a strange death.

[6]For the whole creation in its nature was fashioned anew,
complying with thy commands,
that thy children[a] might be kept unharmed.
[7]The cloud was seen overshadowing the camp,
and dry land emerging where water had stood before,
an unhindered way out of the Red Sea,
and a grassy plain out of the raging waves,
[8]where those protected by thy hand
passed through as one nation,
after gazing on marvellous wonders.
[9]For they ranged like horses,
and leaped like lambs,
praising thee, O Lord, who didst deliver them.
[10]For they still recalled the events of their sojourn,
how instead of producing animals the earth
brought forth gnats,
and instead of fish the river spewed out vast
numbers of frogs.
[11]Afterward they saw also a new kind[b] of birds,
when desire led them to ask for luxurious food;
[12]for, to give them relief, quails came up from the sea.

[13]The punishments did not come upon the sinners
without prior signs in the violence of thunder,
for they justly suffered because of their wicked acts;
for they practised a more bitter hatred of strangers.
[14]Others had refused to receive strangers
when they came to them,
but these made slaves of guests
who were their benefactors.
[15]And not only so, but punishment of

some sort will come upon the former
for their hostile reception of the aliens;
[16]but the latter, after receiving them with
festal celebrations,
afflicted with terrible sufferings
those who had already shared the same rights.
[17]They were stricken also with loss of sight—
just as were those at the door of the righteous man—
when, surrounded by yawning darkness,
each tried to find the way through his own door.

[18]For the elements changed places with one another,
as on a harp the notes vary the nature of the rhythm,
while each note remains the same.[c]
This may be clearly inferred from the sight
of what took place.
[19]For land animals were transformed
into water creatures,
and creatures that swim moved over to the land.
[20]Fire even in water retained its normal power,
and water forgot its fire-quenching nature.
[21]Flames, on the contrary, failed to consume
the flesh of perishable creatures that walked among them,
nor did they melt the crystalline,
easily melted kind of heavenly food.

[a]Or *servants* [b]Or *production* [c]The meaning of this verse is uncertain

Suddenly the scene shifts back to the Egyptians, toward whom the divine '*anger*' manifests itself as '*pitiless*.' The Sage justifies God—or more exactly, God's '*anger*'—because he foreknows '*their future actions*.' The RSV supplies '*God*' but, since the Greek text does not have any noun, the subject is better taken as God's '*anger*,' spoken about in the third person. This interpretation would keep the apostrophe to God in the second person intact (v. 5). God now appears superior to Lady Wisdom, who only '*infers*' the future (see 8:8).

The final contrast is obscure because it becomes so

involved. The Sage does not specify what particular type of divine activity God performs to benefit his chosen ones and to destroy their enemies at the same time. The style becomes impressionistic and leaves more to the imagination of readers. By this time they are expected to be able to complete the picture from their familiarity with Jewish tradition. Only by sensitivity to the Sage's habitual pattern can readers follow his creative adaptation. This final contrast is most difficult to follow because he broadens his perspective even more than in the fourth one about the manna, through which God '*preserves those who trust in thee*' (16:26).

In the Exodus God '*fashioned anew...the whole creation*' to save his people (v. 6). But then he turned his creation into choas to destroy their enemies. As in all the other contrasts the principal actor is God, who directs specific creatures in two opposite directions: to save and to annihilate. First comes the Egyptian sin that provoked the destructive response of God. After resisting a whole series of divine punishments, they finally '*permitted*' the Israelites to depart and even '*hastily*' sent them forth. But God knew '*in advance*' that '*they would change their minds and pursue them*' (vv. 1-2). That '*foolish decision*' is what stirs up his final punishment (v. 4). In '*reaching*' this decision the Egyptians serve to illustrate the very first warning the Sage gave at the beginning of Wis, not to '*bring on*' destruction by an ungodly way of life (1:2, alluded to here in v. 3 by the same rare compound). Unfortunately, the RSV misses this literary link that helps tie the entire exhortation together.

The Egyptians begin their inevitable clash with God by a self-destructive '*lamenting*' (v. 3—a new compound, the first of many the Sage introduces into the Bible in this section). They rush into '*the fate they deserved*' because their deeply rooted sin enslaved them in much the same way as sin destroyed the ancient Canaanites (vv. 4-5, recalling 12:10). To convey the inescapable punishment of sin, the Sage again speaks in terms of '*fate*' (v. 4; see 17:17). Greek philosophers pictured '*fate*' as controlling even the gods. Although he introduces the Stoic personification of Fate, the Sage does so to proclaim the Lord's supreme control over the world and those he created. '*Forgetfulness of favors*' was one of the vices ascribed to idolaters (see 14:26), whereas God sent reminders to his own to convert them (16:11). What is going to happen—arranged by God who is in control of human destiny—is symbolized by the '*incredible journey*' of the Exodus, already referred to in the fifth contrast (v. 5; see 18:3).

This finale of the syncrisis section focuses on God's activity at the crucial moment of that '*journey*,' the crossing of the Red Sea. His intervention took the form of a series of cosmic '*commands*' by which '*the whole creation*' was refashioned for the salvation of his people (v. 6). The intervention employs images already found in the manna sign, in which '*creation*' also served God's plan (16:24). The Sage mirrors contemporary science to describe this divine recreative activity as a reshaping of the primary elements of the universe. Hellenistic science taught that differences in beings resulted from the way their elements were grouped. Hence, the Sage speaks to God as having '*fashioned anew*' created matter by '*thy commands*' rather than as violating the laws he gave to '*nature*' (v. 6).

This method of expression shows how the Sage dealt with the question of miracle in his sophisticated society. God does not violate the laws of '*nature*' but by his infinite power and wisdom makes them benefit his own '*children*' (v. 6). The alternate reading of the RSV, '*servants*' reflects the ambiguity of the same Greek word *pais*. Elsewhere the Sage employs it in both of its meanings. The translation '*children*' produces a flashback to the claim of the upright to be a '*child of God*' (2:13). On the other hand, the translation '*servants*' assumes an allusion to the servant of Isaiah 41:8.

In this context of cosmic renovation, the '*cloud*' over the Israelite camp is best seen as referring to the formless void at the beginning of creation. As in the first creation, God's word made '*dry land*' emerge from it (v. 7; see Gen 1:1, 9). Imaginative details then color the progress of God's cosmic intervention, which commentators compare to the description of Pliny's account of fruit trees growing in the Red Sea (*Natural History* 13.25). The basin of the Red Sea—already mentioned in the aretalogy about Lady Wisdom (10:18)—becomes '*an unhindered way*' in the form of '*a grassy plain*' (v. 8). All this was an act of God's '*hand*' that '*protected*' his own. These terms '*protected*' and '*hand*' link this crossing to the earlier scene of the final reward of the upright who reached heaven only because of the same kind of divine protection (v. 8; a flashback to 5:16).

Linking the Seven Contrasts

The text presents the Exodus as a great liturgical procession that recalls the joyful description of the Exodus in Isaiah 63:12-14. It repeats the image of '*leaping*' from the fifth contrast (see 17:19). This is part of the technique of tying all the comparisons together as a majestic portrayal of God's power—the basis of his people's trust. In turn, they voice that trust by '*praising thee, O Lord, who didst deliver them*' (v. 9). This implicit statement of their obedient response rests on belief that all creation is directed to God's praise and glory and that all humans perform a unique role in the plan of God.

In the opening contrasts of Wis, the ungodly had mockingly challenged God to '*deliver*' the righteous (v. 9; see 2:18). Later the Sage portrayed Lady Wisdom as delivering the just throughout the course of history (10:6, 9, 13, 15). Now he climaxes his exhortation with this vivid picture of God bringing his entire creative power to effect the liberation of his people—a theme that has guided the entire presentation since 9:18 (vv. 6-21).

Continuing to recapitulate as many themes as possible from the entire work, the Sage pictures the Israelites as singing about God's saving acts while they march through the Red Sea and the desert (vv. 9-12). In recalling the plagues, he introduces a Greek idea that remembering past trials increases satisfaction when they are over. This summary also introduces features of the plagues not mentioned earlier, like the mention of '*gnats*' and '*frogs*' (v. 10; see Ps 105/104LXX). They form a contrast with the '*quails.*' The Greek text does not describe them as a '*new kind*' of bird (the reading selected for the RSV text), but says they were made available by a new "production" (as in the RSV margin).

One feature of the recapitulation not possible to reproduce in a translation occurs when the Sage describes the '*quail*' as '*luxurious*' food. He does this by cleverly altering a single letter of the Greek word that described them in the second contrast (v. 11; see 16:2-3). In making this change he also introduces the Greek expression for "the good life," a common designation for the luxurious abundance of hellenistic kings.

The changes in nature are described in this way to recall that the punishments of the ancient Egyptians show them to have been even more blameworthy than the Canaanites. For Egyptians committed '*wicked acts*' against the Israelites who had lived among them for many years as '*guests who were their benefactors*' (v. 14). The Sage coins a new compound to give their sins a special name, '*hatred of strangers*' (v. 13). Such creativity updates the Exodus story for young Jewish students and warns them against being deceived by their sophisticated contemporaries.

Such polemics complicate this seventh contrast, which could have ended here. The remaining lines read like an attempt to bring Part IV to an appropriate close. They continue to allude to sacred history in three ways:

1) by picturing the Egyptians as worse even than the Canaanites who inhabited the city of Sodom (vv. 13-17; see Gen 19:1-11). But these allusions to Scripture are too subtle for any except trained biblical students to appreciate because of the Sage's stylistic device of omitting proper names. The sharing of '*rights*' refers not to political status but to religious freedom enjoyed by believers (v. 16).

2) by repeating vocabulary from the narrative that opened this final set of six contrasts. It forms an inclusion by repeating three words: the verb '*shared*' (v. 16, translated as

'*partake*' in 16:3) and the nouns '*desire*' (v. 17, recalling 16:2) and '*quails*' (v. 12, found in 16:2).
3) by linking the cosmic changes that occurred in conjunction with the Exodus and Israel's desert experience with the manna to the fire miracle found in the center of these contrasts (vv. 18-21 with 16:16-23). By affirming that these cosmic changes took place while nature somehow remained the same makes the final flashback in Wis. The situation in nature recalls the activity of Lady Wisdom who, while '*remaining in herself*' brought about change, just as nature did during the Exodus (vv. 18-19 with 7:27).

This expansion of the final contrast is not directed explicitly to God as is the entire syncrisis, but it recalls earlier sections of the Book of Wis. The '*punishments*' that came upon those '*sinners*' for their '*wicked acts*' is expressed in vocabulary that recalls the liberation of Enoch from '*sinners*' by God lest the '*fascination*' of '*wickedness*' pervert his innocence (v. 13 and 4:10-14). A similar danger faced the original readers of Wis in their Egyptian milieu.

Evidently these concluding reflections caused difficulty for scribes copying the book over the ages because a great variety of readings occurs in extant manuscripts. The RSV notes indicate that verses 18 and 21 are uncertain. No doubt part of the difficulty is that this section contains eight words never found elsewhere in the Bible. The Sage ends with a bold image when he calls the manna by the Greek term that designates the food of the gods. '*Heavenly food*' is a pale translation for the original expression, "ambrosial food," a new way to identify the biblical term (v. 21).

7. CONCLUDING PRAISE
Wis 19:22

> [22]For in everything, O Lord, thou hast exalted
> and glorified thy people;
> and thou has not neglected to help them at all times and in
> all places.

After that series of intricate and elaborate contrasts, the

Sage quickly draws his protreptic or rhetorical exhortation to a close with a brief prayer of thanksgiving. It is addressed to the '*Lord*' and acknowledges his constant care over his chosen people. Significantly, he closes his book with the same literary feature of litotes or understatement with which he opened it. Thus, the statement, '*Thou has not neglected to help,*' must not be interpreted as a flat anticlimax to the affirmation that God '*hast exalted and glorified thy people.*' Rather, it is a subtle expression of trust providing a delicate balance to the opening word of praise of the Lord who '*manifests himself to whose who do not distrust him*' (1:2).

A similar combination of understatement appears in speaking of Lady Wisdom's gift of '*glory*' in dealing with Joseph in Egypt (10:14, where the RSV translates the term as "honour"). Wisdom '*stood by*' Joseph just as God stands by the people always and everywhere (10:11, where the same verb is translated as "help"). This final couplet also contains an allusion to hellenistic religion. The goddess Hera enjoyed the title of "she who stands by" to portray her as defender of her clients. The Sage's original readers would not miss this way of exalting the God of Israel—one of the many allusions lost upon modern readers.

For Further Reading

1. General Works

Ernest G. Clark, *The Wisdom of Solomon*. The Cambridge Bible Commentary on the New English Bible. New York: Cambridge University Press, 1973. Brief but competent notes.

John F. Craghan, "The Book of Wisdom," *Old Testament Reading Guide* 29. Collegeville: Liturgical Press, 1979. The text of the New American Bible with excellent introduction and notes.

Eugene H. Maly, "The Wisdom of Solomon," *The Bible Today* 18 (May 1980) 154-159. A concise update on the background and purpose of the book.

James M. Reese, "In Praise of Wisdom," *The Bible Today* 18 (May 1980) 160-165. How Lady Wisdom is portrayed in the Book of Wisdom.

Joseph Reider, *The Book of Wisdom.* New York: Harper and Brothers, 1957. One of the best available commentaries.

Roger Schoenbechler, *The Book of Wisdom.* An Interpretative Version in Measured Rhythm. Collegeville: Liturgical Press, 1975. A free verse translation with introduction.

David Winston, *The Wisdom of Solomon: A New Translation with Introduction and Commentary.* Anchor Bible 43; Garden City, N.Y.: Doubleday and Company, 1975. A fresh translation with detailed introduction, bibliography and philological notes, but lacking a theological synthesis.

2. Specialized Works

Alexander A. DiLella, "Conservative and Progressive Theology: Sirach and Wisdom," *Catholic Biblical Quarterly* 28 (1966) 139-154. Insights into the openness of the Sage.

Thomas Finan, "Hellenistic Humanism in the Book of Wisdom," *Irish Theological Quarterly* 27 (1960) 30-48. Shows the influence of Hellenism on the book.

James M. Reese, *Hellenistic Influence on the Book of Wisdom and its Consequences.* Analecta Biblica 41; Rome: Biblical Institute Press, 1970. Original research on the background and theology of the Book of Wisdom.

Addison G. Wright, "Wisdom," in R.E. Brown, J.A. Fitzmyer, R.E. Murphy, *The Jerome Biblical Commentary*, 1:556-568. Englewood Cliffs, N.J.: Prentice-Hall, 1968. A critical commentary that stresses the Semitic influence on the book.

SONG OF SONGS

Introduction: The Song of Songs

1. Literary Genre, Unity and Purpose

The first question confronting readers of the Song of Songs is whether they are dealing with a single work or with a collection of short lyrics, an anthology along the lines of the Book of Psalms but shorter and containing different types of poetry. Modern critics are radically divided on this question. Many opt for an anthology. But even they vary greatly in their estimate of the number of lyrics collected. Some go as high as 52, although the common estimate hovers around 30. They see the collection as being held together by a common theme of love or by word links between individual poems. The collection is random and grew over a period of time, perhaps even centuries.

At the same time, many commentators argue that the Song is a single literary work. For example, Roland E. Murphy has called attention to many literary signs pointing to a unified composition, and he recently published a study of the text itself. In a careful analysis of the Song J. Cheryl Exum proposed that it is a careful arrangement of related poems that form an integrated celebration of the reality of love. She argues for a complex organization of the whole with individual sections constructed to balance others. Her continuing research refines her conclusions and she no longer insists on a single author. She suggests that a group of poets reworked love songs from oral tradition into an artistic whole, without eliminating all contradictions between earlier stages.

Some commentators see in the Song an elaborate allegory. For example, the French exegete A. Robert and his school interpret it as a sophisticated allegory about the relationship of Israel after the Exile with the Lord. Another esoteric form of allegorizing appears in the Jewish tradition. It attempts to decipher the Song according to a secret code of the Cabala.

This commentary accepts indications throughout the text as pointing to the conscious effort of the biblical writer to modify, arrange and coordinate pre-existing lyrics in order to produce a single literary work that celebrates love as the strongest force in God's creation. These indications include refrains, repetitions of words, themes and primary literary forms, learned allusions to persons, places and events linked to Israel's destiny, plus other stylistic devices of Israelite wisdom that will be noted in the commentary.

The introduction of such learned features makes the Song of Songs unique among the lyrics of love surviving from the ancient Near East. As a result, the unity of the Song in its final form exists on a variety of levels—as J.C. Exum notes—such as tone, theme, imagery, character, style, language and poetic structure. That articulation of the work's integrity permits readers to isolate smaller literary units. It also grounds the variety of approaches commentators are still developing to discover the "surplus of meaning" of the Song.

This view of unity requires that certain approaches to the Song be excluded. For example, there is not enough evidence in the text to affirm that it is a drama with a true plot. Nor does it tell the story of a concrete courtship involving Solomon or any other historical character. On the contrary, the biblical poet celebrates love itself by a skillful integration of several lyrical forms.

The majority of these primary units are love lyrics, similar to those that have survived from ancient Egypt. But other factors were at work also. Scattered among these lyrics are elements that link love to ritual and cult, possibly to celebrations of the dead conducted with feasting and dancing. In other words, the Song shows traces of a learned religious dimension. At least two pieces belong to the dream narrative form (3:1-5; 5:2-8).

Research on the vocabulary of the Song of Songs dispels any illusion that it is merely a collection of popular love ditties. Proportionately, it has more rare words than any other biblical book. These include almost 50 *hapax legomena,* that is, words not found elsewhere in the Bible. Such words make passages difficult to understand and create the type of ambiguity that fosters variety in interpretation. The meaning of many of its verses and images is still disputed.

All these indications point to the final editor of the Song as a member of the wisdom tradition in Israel. This editor indicates his own understanding of the significance of the Song as a whole by including four proverbial expressions that exalt love as creation's most powerful force (8:6-7).

In the original setting when the lyrics were first composed, the love they celebrated was that between a man and a woman as equally capable of fulfilling each other. The biblical sage accepted that insight but recognized that it does not exhaust the power of love as God's supreme gift to creation. The biblical Song of Songs invites readers to explore richer voyages into that love. Revelation of the power of love on every level of existence is what commentators have discovered in the Song down through the ages.

The lack of any direct reference to the Lord in the Song becomes understandable when it is viewed in the light of its prehistory. Only in one of the four appended proverbs is there an allusion to Israel's God. It speaks of the expression of love as "the flame of Yahweh" (8:6 in the Hebrew). The Revised Standard Version (RSV) translates this expression as a superlative, '*a most vehement flame.*' In this translation the reader cannot recognize the deliberate contrast between the names of the living God and the god of death. And so the polemic against the cult of the dead is also missed.

Cultic celebrations like the *hieros gamos* (sacred marriage) between gods and goddesses or between a divine being and a mortal were linked to fertility of land, flocks and humans in pagan religion. Research on rites of this nature, such as the ritual concerning Ishtar, reveals similarities to parts of the Song. These discoveries led some commentators to designate it as a ritual drama celebrating the power of love over death. M. Pope favors a more tempered approach that links the Song to those funeral feasts that included wine and song. He points out possible links between it and hymns in honor of the goddess in Tantric rituals of India, but also warns that these areas demand further investigation.

Funeral rites often featured women, who also have prominent places in the Song. Its frequent references to the fertility of the bride could reflect a polemic against pagan rites of surrounding cultures. Rather than seek for fertility in magic or in rites of nature, the biblical author sings of God's gift of love as the source of all fruitfulness (see 8:6).

But what is the specific focus of the Song on love? Here commentators are divided. Many concentrate on its natural—or better, anthropological—dimension as a celebration of the power of eros. Some evangelical Christians even present the Song as if it were a modern sexual manual to guide the faithful in face of a permissive society. Such an approach is anachronistic, for it ignores the mores of ancient Israelite culture that was not conscious of the individualism and psychologism of modern western society.

When the Song focuses on mutual intimacy it does so by way of indirection, using metaphors and other figurative language. Often it is difficult even to designate the character speaking. All its voices speak out of the horizon of Israel's belief in God as author of life who endows creatures with creative spontaneity. Human activity is complex and operates on many levels of meaning at the same time. The flowing interaction between the man and the woman throughout the Song proclaims that mutual fidelity originates in love. As Phyllis Trible concludes, the Song reads almost like a commentary on the creation and fall narrative of Genesis 2-3 and declares that humans cannot live solely in the garden of erotic love.

The multilevel dimension of the Song contributed to its being allegorized at later periods of history. But resort to allegory to explain its primary meaning is not a valid method because the Song does not set out primarily to tell the story of Israel's marriage to the Lord. On the contrary, it was the Song's insertion into the Bible that encouraged a variety of allegorical interpretations in both Jewish and Christian traditions. Details on some of these interpretations will be treated in the third part of this introduction.

2. Date and Author

Concerning the author of the Song, contemporary critical commentators agree on one point: it was not Solomon. His name was added to the title at some period in its manuscript history. Several reasons have been suggested for this attribution, but none of them is completely satisfactory. For example, the name of Solomon gives authority to the Song. Or, he was famous for his large harem, similar to the one mentioned in the Song. He was a traditional patron of Israel's wisdom literature, the collection in which the Song was preserved, first in oral form and later in writing.

Most commentators agree that the Song went through stages before it reached the form preserved in the Bible. But their opinions differ as to how it evolved. Shorter love lyrics circulated over a considerable length of time in wisdom circles. Some of these lyrics could have originated at the time of Solomon because they resemble lyrics composed in Egypt before 1000 B.C.

Nothing in the text itself is decisive for fixing the date of composition. The mention of the ancient capital of the northern kingdom of Israel, Tirzah (6:4), is simply one of the learned allusions that wisdom authors could have introduced at any time—before or after the fall of Samaria in 722 B.C.

Certain linguistic arguments favor a date after the end of

the Babylonian Exile in the fifth century B.C., at least for final editing. For example, it contains the Persian word for '*orchard*' (4:13; a better term would be "park"). The Song always uses the form of the relative that is rare in other biblical books. Some of its linguistic features are more similar to other Semitic languages than to biblical Hebrew. These features do not determine any date of composition but illustrate that the Song had its own literary history.

Its final author was a member of the corps of Israel's sages, who must have been familiar with it from his course of studies. The sages were at the service of Israel's political authorities, who also supervised its religious affairs and who helped in the education of priests and levites for their roles in society. One area of life that had to be studied was the place of love and marriage in God's plan for creation. Israelite religion could not accept the approach of their pagan neighbors toward love, linked as it was to pagan myths, fertility cults and sacred prostitution.

As frequently happened in biblical literature, the author of the Song incorporated many inherited features of the lyrics of contemporary love literature, but brought them within the horizon of Israelite beliefs. He attributed the power and qualities of love to the Lord as creator who bestows gifts lavishly upon both men and women. This editing was in conformity with the original purpose of the small primary units of the Song. Such an enlargement of meaning was a different process from the allegorizing interpretations of later Jewish and Christian commentators, who dealt with the Song as proclaiming a prophetic message of instruction and warning.

3. History of Methods of Interpretation

From the time of Solomon a body of praxis or wisdom literature began to grow within the archives of the Temple of Jerusalem. This wisdom literature ranged from scientific knowledge about building construction to moral directions on how to succeed at court and how to avoid the pitfalls of wine, women and song. It was in this wisdom tradition that the lyrics eventually assembled to form the Song of Songs were first collected.

The demands and expressions of love were of crucial importance to Israel's sages, but they never isolated elements of wisdom from their overarching view of reality. They dealt with human love in the context of their creation theology. Their celebration of human love in the final version of the Song could not fail to generate further reflection and creative insights. Not only the original text itself but also the variety of commentaries it evoked have exercised a profound influence on both Jewish and Christian spiritualities.

For centuries after its composition, only the primary meaning of the text was considered; in fact, some Jews used snatches of it in drinking songs. The great hellenistic Jewish commentators Josephus and Philo, who fostered allegorical interpretation of Scripture, did not comment upon it. Nor is the Song referred to directly in the New Testament. M. Pope dates the earliest allegorical commentaries of the Song as normative for its interpretation among the Jews from the period between the destruction of the Temple of Jerusalem and the revolt of Bar Kokhba, that is, between 70 and 132 A.D.

Hippolytus of Rome (170-235 A.D.) wrote the first full Christian allegorical commentary on the Song as portraying the marriage of the Church to the Incarnate Word, but only fragments of this work remain. The great Christian allegorical commentator Origen (184-253 A.D.) was influenced by the Jewish rabbis of that period. Origen's commentary was based on his belief that the Song was a formal allegory about perfect knowledge and the unity between the Incarnate Word and either the Church as a whole or the individual believer.

From Origen flowed the rich tradition of the spiritual interpretation of the Song, which produced over 1,200 commentaries. By contrast, during the era of the Fathers of the Church, Theodore of Mopsuestia (350-428 A.D.) stands almost alone in teaching the so-called naturalistic or anthropological meaning. He supported his approach by pointing out that the Song was not read in either Jewish or Christian liturgy. However, by the seventh century the Jewish Targum or Aramaic paraphrase of the Song interpreted it as an allegory of Israel's sacred history, and it was being read in the liturgy of the eighth day of Passover.

In the Latin Church Gregory the Great (540-604) used it to expound a form of morality. According to H. de Lubac, Rupert of Deutz (d. 1135) was the first to devote a whole commentary to the Song as celebrating the marriage of the Word to the Church in its origin, that is, in the incarnation. His commentary is sometimes mistakenly called the first mariological interpretation. The 86 sermons of Bernard of Clairvaux (1095-1153), which treat only the first two chapters of the Song, are the most famous medieval commentary.

De Lubac calls the commentary of Thomas of Vercelli (1224), who followed the tradition of Ps-Dionysius, the first purely mystical interpretation. The commentary of John of the Cross (1542-1591) is the most famous one in the mystical tradition. The critic Northrop Frye warns against dismissing it as some do as a "strained allegorical wrenching" of the text. On the contrary, he sees it as forming part of the history of the text. Teresa of Avila commented only on verses she knew from the divine office or from sermons. She does not quote the text but gives personal reflections on her mystical type of prayer.

In modern times Paul Claudel has continued the spiritual tradition of mystical interpretation of the Song. This tradition still exercises a guiding influence on the devotion of many Christian contemplatives. Roland Murphy has recently called attention to the value of the spiritual exegesis of the Song for both Jewish and Christian communities in a survey he published in *Catholic Biblical Quarterly* (October 1981; pp. 505-516).

Today most professional biblical commentators adopt an anthropological method of interpretation. Yet they ordinarily refuse to oppose the "naturalistic" to the "spiritual" method or to play off sexual love against human affection. Rather, they seek to discover the full mystery of love as it reveals itself in human passions, desires and movements as celebrated in the interpersonal relationships of the Song.

Commentary

1. TITLE; MUSINGS OF THE WOMAN
Cant 1:1-8

1 The Song of Songs, which is Solomon's.

[2]O that you would kiss me with the kisses of your mouth!
For your love is better than wine,
[3] your anointing oils are fragrant,
your name is oil poured out;
therefore the maidens love you.
[4]Draw me after you, let us make haste.
The king has brought me into his chambers.
We will exult and rejoice in you;
we will extol your love more than wine;
rightly do they love you.

[5]I am very dark, but comely,
O daughters of Jerusalem,
like the tents of Kedar,
like the curtains of Solomon.
[6]Do not gaze at me because I am swarthy,
because the sun has scorched me.
My mother's sons were angry with me,
they made me keeper of the vineyards;
but, my own vineyard I have not kept!
[7]Tell me, you whom my soul loves,

where you pasture your flock,
where you make it lie down at noon;
for why should I be like one who wanders
beside the flocks of your companions?
[8]If you do not know,
O fairest among women,
follow in the tracks of the flock,
and pasture your kids
beside the shepherds' tents.

The title '*Song of Songs*' is simply the ordinary form of the superlative in Hebrew. It introduces this poetic composition as "the most beautiful song." The title attributes it to '*Solomon*' because of his connection with wisdom and his reputation for having so many loves (see 1 Kgs 11:1-2). By placing the poem among the wisdom writings of Scripture, the compilers of the Bible suggest a method of interpreting it. In its evident meaning the Song reveals the divine meaning of the sexual dimension in human beings as related to their lived experience.

The Song opens with the woman's excited outburst for the '*kisses*' of her beloved. She speaks to him as if he were present although the flow of the events makes his absence evident (vv. 2-4). Her excitement is even more evident in the Hebrew text, which makes her alternate between two forms of direct address, namely the ordinary second person '*you,*' and the indirect form that uses the third person title '*king.*' For simplicity and clarity, the RSV translation puts all her statements into the familiar '*you*' form.

This opening scene introduces leaders to both the heroine and hero of the Song. When she speaks about his '*name,*' she is using a Hebrew expression to proclaim his exalted state—now available to her like '*wine*' and '*anointing oils*' (vv. 2-3). Appeals to the senses of taste, smell and touch will be prominent throughout the Song as one form of its indirect mode of expressing intimate longing. On the immediate level the woman wants first of all to experience his affection, his '*kisses.*' His acts of '*love*' are '*better than wine*' (v. 2). In the context '*better*' means sweeter. His '*kisses*' are like a sweet drink that nourishes her love (see 4:11; 7:9 and comments on 5:16).

In the spiritual interpretation of the Song, the term '*kiss*' became the code term for a wide range of explanations of all levels of love that unite the human soul with God and especially with the Incarnate Word. Such developments are part of the "surplus of meaning" that true classics create as they are read by a tradition. Although the Song deals primarily with human love, '*kisses*' express and represent love at every level. Historically kisses were one form of cult practice. The prominence of the term in the Song is one factor that points to the origin of at least parts of it in ancient cult.

The identity of neither the woman nor the '*king*' is revealed at any point of the Song. Given its final form as an expression of biblical wisdom, such a complete masking of the identity of its two leading protagonists makes them symbols of dimensions of practical human wisdom in the realm of loving rather than concrete individuals. When the Song applies the title of '*king*' to the man, it does so as an exercise of the literary technique of "royal fiction" that was a feature of Egyptian love poetry. Love gives a royal status to its recipients.

In no way then does the title '*king*' identify the man in the Song with Solomon. Expressions like '*curtains of Solomon*' (v. 5) and '*litter of Solomon*' (3:7; see also 8:11-12) are literary features of the wisdom tradition to link these lyrics with the patron of wisdom literature.

In her opening outburst the woman celebrates love's power to arouse and transform humans beyond any other activity. Love is the overwhelming gift of God to mortals to unite them to one another in his wise plan for his creatures. Even the mention of the man's '*name*' stirs up the '*maidens,*' that is, the peers of the woman narrator (v. 3). She imagines union with her '*king*' in his '*chambers*' (v. 4). Moving toward intimate union, which is the basic dynamism of love, is the most common characteristic of the lyrics of the Song of Songs.

The quick change of scene (v. 5) shows that the opening

outburst does not describe an actual meeting. Rather, the Song appears as a series of reveries—including dreams—about the ecstatic experience of love. Nothing within the text provides basis for viewing it as a drama with real characters interacting and moving toward crisis and resolution.

Frequent shifts in time, place and topic do not coalesce into a single narrative. For example, the woman is frequently pictured as defending herself to the '*daughters of Jersualem*' (v. 5; see 2:7; 3:5, 11; 5:8, 16; 8:4). Her '*swarthy*' appearance is the result of sunburn acquired while performing her charge of caring for '*the vineyards*' (v. 6). This task was imposed by her '*mother's sons,*'who were '*angry*' with her for some unnamed reason (v. 6; an apparent resolution in 8:8-10). Like a piece of fruit left too long in the sun, she is '*scorched.*' The figurative and literal use of the term '*vineyard*' in the same sentence alerts readers for unusual shifts in the text, which shifts into symbolic language without warning.

The three proper names in verse 5 are the first of many that appear throughout the Song: '*Jerusalem,*' the tribe of '*Kedar,*' who was a descendant of Israel (see Gen 25:13), and '*Solomon.*' The large number of unusual proper names plays a significant part in the decision of some commentators to interpret the Song as an allegory of Israel's marriage to the Lord (see 4:1, 8; 6:4; 7:4-6; 8:11).

In a second abrupt shift the woman again addresses her beloved, '*you whom my soul loves*' (v. 7). She alludes to their meeting places at watering holes in pasture areas. In her imagination she recalls one of these encounters at a proverbial trysting place. But she is interrupted, evidently by the daughters of Jerusalem, although the text gives no indication of the speaker (v. 8; see 2:7; 3:5; 5:8, 16). Their presence acts as little more than a foil to articulate the desires of the woman, whom they encourage to search for her shepherd lover by following the '*tracts of the flock*' (v. 8).

In many ways this opening scene epitomizes problems of

interpretation encountered throughout the Song: the identity of the speakers; sudden shifts in setting; subtlety of literary allusion; degree of literal and figurative meaning intended. In general, commentators resolve such problems in terms of their approach to the Song as a whole. Of course, that method of interpretation creates the danger of circular reasoning and of imposing a conceptual unity upon a composition that grew out of smaller lyrics. Yet, the activity of the wisdom writer who joined these pieces encourages readers to use an active imagination in dealing with the final product.

2. DIALOGUE BETWEEN THE LOVERS
Cant 1:9—2:7

[9]I compare you, my love,
to a mare of Pharaoh's chariots.
[10]Your cheeks are comely with ornaments,
your neck with strings of jewels.
[11]We will make you ornaments of gold,
studded with silver.

[12]While the king was on his couch,
my nard gave forth its fragrance.
[13]My beloved is to me a bag of myrrh,
that lies between my breasts.
[14]My beloved is to me a cluster of henna blossoms
in the vineyards of Engedi.
[15]Behold, you are beautiful, my love;
behold, you are beautiful;
your eyes are doves.

[16]Behold, you are beautiful, my beloved,
truly lovely.
Our couch is green;
[17] the beams of our house are cedar,
our rafters are pine.

2 I am a rose of Sharon,
a lily of the valleys.

[2]As a lily among brambles,
so is my love among maidens.

[3]As an apple tree among the trees of the wood,
so is my beloved among young men.
With great delight I sat in his shadow,
and his fruit was sweet to my taste.
[4]He brought me to the banqueting house,
and his banner over me was love.
[5]Sustain me with raisins,
refresh me with apples;
for I am sick with love.
[6]O that his left hand were under my head,
and that his right hand embraced me!
[7]I adjure you, O daughters of Jerusalem,
by the gazelles or the hinds of the field,
that you stir not up nor awaken love until it please.

Suddenly the man is present and breaks forth in a celebration of the beauty of the woman, but in imagery foreign to that of modern American lyrics (vv. 9-11). Few women in today's western culture would consider being compared to a '*mare*' a compliment, although that comparison was common in ancient classical culture (v. 9). He addresses her as '*my love,*' a term of endearment found eight times in the Song between 1:9 and 6:4. She is pictured as wearing simple clothing, which he promises to replace by '*ornaments of gold*' (v. 11).

His promise opens a dialogue of mutual praise between the couple. No context is given, and the exchanges flow in a chain-of-consciousness freedom. Still showing an attitude of deference, the woman addresses her beloved in the stylized third person as '*king*' and '*beloved,*' and elaborates on her joy at being with him (vv. 12-14). '*Beloved,*' the most common designation of the man—over 25 times—is never used of the woman.

Her comparisons are based on three delightful fragrances. First, his presence is like the aroma of '*nard*' (again in 4:13, 14). Then it is like '*myrrh*' (also in 3:6; 4:6, 14; 5:1, 5,

13). Myrrh was put into a sachet '*bag*' and tied around the neck in such a way as to rest '*between*' the woman's '*breasts*'. Body heat made this aromatic resin melt to provide a continuous perfume. Finally, '*henna blossoms*' describe the delight that his presence brings to her.

He responds by praising her beauty, singling out her eyes as '*doves*' (v. 15; see 4:1). The basis of this metaphor is lost but the term '*dove*' appears as a term of endearment several times in the Song (see 2:14; 5:2; 6:9). Although the RSV presentation does not make it evident, the rest of this section is a series of rapid exchanges between the two.

The woman echoes the compliment and invites the man to lie on the '*green*' earth (v. 16). He takes up her image and imagines the trees of the area forming ornate '*rafters*' that make a luxurious house (v. 17). Nature is their palace. She continues the fantasy by describing herself as spring flowers—their identity is disputed by critics—on the fertile hill of '*Sharon*' or in the '*valleys*' of Jezreel (2:1). His love prompts him to correct her description by protesting that, compared to her, all other women are '*brambles*' (v. 2). She repays the compliment by calling him an '*apple tree*' in respect to other '*young men,*' because other trees promise no edible '*fruit*' (v. 3).

She seeks him for his '*shadow,*' which is ordinarily an image of protection. However, in the love poetry of the ancient Near East, this image denotes sexual union, which produces sweet '*fruit*' (v. 3; see 4:13, 16; 8:11-12). All these images are still in the realm of fantasy because she recalls that her '*beloved*' took her '*to the banqueting house*' and took steps to express his '*love*' for her by placing his '*banner*' over her (v. 4). The meaning of his expression is not clear; even ancient translators found it puzzling. One possible solution is to understand '*banner*' in the figurative sense of gaze or intention.

Overwhelmed by her fantasies, the woman feels faint and begs for '*raisins*' and '*apples,*' two foods whose taste or aroma help prevent fainting (v. 5). They act as a medicine when she is '*sick with love*' (v. 5; see 5:8). The only cure for love sickness—a malady mentioned also in ancient Egyptian lyrics—is the presence of the lover. So the woman wants to be '*embraced*' (v. 6).

But her beloved turns rather to the '*daughters of Jerusalem*' and charges them to respect the ecstasy of his chosen one (v. 7; a request repeated in 3:5 and 8:4; see 1:8). He entreats them by '*the gazelles or the hinds,*' animals symbolic of love, whose names are used as terms of endearment (see 2:9, 17; 8:14).

Obviously this exchange can be read on many levels. The final decision of the primary significance of the text is determined by the flow of the entire Song in its present form, taking into consideration especially the wisdom sayings in 8:6-7, which invite reflection on the meaning of love within creation. The repetition of this caution not to '*awaken love*' immediately before these proverbs (8:4) gives it special force as an expression of personal responsibility.

The allegorical interpretation adopted by Jewish rabbis and some Christian spiritual writers, and revived on a scholarly level by A. Robert, sees allusions to events in the history of Israel, like the Exodus and the Exile. However, the development of such secondary applications belongs rather to the history of the Song than to its original meaning.

3. MEETING AND SEPARATION OF THE LOVERS
Cant 2:8—3:5

[8]The voice of my beloved!
  Behold, he comes,
leaping upon the mountains,
  bounding over the hills.
[9]My beloved is like a gazelle,
  or a young stag.
Behold, there he stands behind our wall,
gazing in at the windows,
  looking through the lattice.
[10]My beloved speaks and says to me:
  "Arise, my love, my fair one, and come away;

[11]for lo, the winter is past,
the rain is over and gone.
[12]The flowers appear on the earth,
the time of singing has come,
and the voice of the turtledove is heard in our land.
[13]The fig tree puts forth its figs,
and the vines are in blossom;
they give forth fragrance.
Arise, my love, my fair one,
and come away.
[14]O my dove, in the clefts of the rock,
in the covert of the cliff,
let me see your face,
let me hear your voice,
for your voice is sweet,
and your face is comely.
[15]Catch us the foxes, the little foxes,
that spoil the vineyards,
for our vineyards are in blossom."

[16]My beloved is mine and I am his,
he pastures his flock among the lilies.
[17]Until the day breathes and the shadows flee,
turn, my beloved, be like a gazelle,
or a young stag upon rugged mountains.

3 Upon my bed by night
I sought him whom my soul loves;
I sought him, but found him not;
I called him, but he gave no answer.
[2]"I will rise now and go about the city,
in the streets and in the squares;
I will seek him whom my soul loves."
I sought him, but found him not.
[3]The watchmen found me,
as they went about in the city.
"Have you seen him whom my soul loves?"
[4]Scarcely had I passed them,
when I found him whom my soul loves.

I held him, and would not let him go
  until I had brought him into my mother's house,
  and into the chamber of her that conceived me.
[5]I adjure you, O daughters of Jerusalem,
  by the gazelles or the hinds of the field,
that you stir not up nor awaken love until it please.

This section of the Song has sustained unity in the form of the woman's seeking for her lover. In the first part she muses about the delights of union with him and imagines him inviting her to come (vv. 8-17; see 1:7-8). No chronological link between these lyrics and what has preceded them can be established. The Song is not a narrative of a courtship between two individuals but celebrates the role and power of love for perfecting human experience.

The woman begins by describing her emotional reaction to '*the voice of my beloved*' (v. 8)! That is, she shrieks that he is coming as she imagines him '*leaping*' and '*bounding*' toward her. She pictures him with the swiftness of a '*gazelle*' or a '*young stag*' (v. 9; compare the animals he had just mentioned in his entreaty in v. 7). His '*gazing*' at her is another figurative expression of desire for intimacy.

This desire transports her into a reverie of fantasizing about their coming meeting. The first part of the reverie is simply a repetition of his invitation (vv. 10-11). But then she continues, providing one of the rare descriptions of nature in the Bible. Her beloved's desire is like the rich Palestinian spring, '*the time of singing,*' a riot of sound and color and scent. It comes to replace the '*winter,*' which she specifies as the season of '*rain*' in keeping with the parallelism of Hebrew poetry that describes each item twice (vv. 11-12).

She uses figurative language to describe their lovemaking (vv. 13-15). This indirection of language is the Song's way of inviting reflection on the role of love in human existence. The ambiguity of expression creates many-leveled meaning, a characteristic of lyric poetry. All the acts of self-revelation by the lover to '*my dove*' portray awareness of the varieties of personal communication demanded for the growth of human love: by voice, expression, body language (v. 14).

She voices her fear that their union may be damaged and rendered fruitless as she imagines her beloved appealing to her to help in protecting '*our vineyards*' (v. 15). Together they try to '*catch . . . the little foxes*' that destroy the fruit of their union. Her long reverie reaches an exultant close in an exclamation of confidence that their union is secure (vv. 16-17; see 6:3; 7:10 for comparable sentiments).

The imagery in this climax is mixed. She pictures her beloved as both a shepherd who '*pastures his flock*' and as '*a gazelle or a young stag,*' repeated here to form a literary inclusion that brings her reverie to a close (vv. 9 and 17). As '*shepherd*' he has been guarding his flock all night '*among the lilies,*' employed here in the literal sense (v. 16; see 6:3), although her beloved's lips will later be called '*lilies*' (5:13). At the coming of '*day*' he bounds like an animal to reach her.

Once more a sudden shift from anticipated union gives way to another picture of physical separation of the lovers (3:1). This is one more indication that the Song is not telling a concrete story. The woman has just spoken about her lover as being with the flocks all night. Now she wants to find him but goes searching '*about the city*' (v. 2). Commentators disagree on the significance of this change in imagery. It remains part of the enigma of the Song. It is best read as a dream sequence.

Her fruitless search adds a note of realism in contrast to the dreamlike lyrics by which the woman had been describing her beloved's desire for her. The path of love is marked with difficulties, loneliness and blind alleys. In her desperation she seeks help from '*the watchmen of the city*' but gets no satisfaction (v. 3). Then, just as abruptly, she again finds him '*whom my soul loves*' (repeated in vv. 1, 2, 3, 4). This time she '*held him*' lest he escape and '*brought him into my mother's house*' (v. 4). This mysterious action has never been adequately explained, but it will be repeated later (see 8:2).

Once again the scene changes and the woman is asleep. Her beloved is present and repeats the entreaty formula that closed the previous section of the Song (v. 5; see 2:7; 8:4). This closing refrain not to disturb '*love*' embodies the underlying thrust of the Song as a wisdom composition. Without going into specific concepts about love, it invites reflection on God's self-revelation through the ecstasy of self-communicating love, as the maxims in 8:6-7 will indicate. How can love become a healing power in God's creation?

4. THE LITTER OF SOLOMON ARRIVES
Cant 3:6-11

[6]What is that coming up from the wilderness,
like a column of smoke,
perfumed with myrrh and frankincense,
with all the fragrant powders of the merchant?
[7]Behold, it is the litter of Solomon!
About it are sixty mighty men
of the mighty men of Israel,
[8]all girt with swords and expert in war,
each with his sword at his thigh,
against alarms by night.
[9]King Solomon made himself a palanquin
from the wood of Lebanon.
[10]He made its posts of silver,
its back of gold, its seat of purple;
it was lovingly wrought within
by the daughters of Jerusalem.
[11]Go forth, O daughters of Zion,
and behold King Solomon,
with the crown with which his mother crowned him
on the day of his wedding,
on the day of the gladness of his heart.

As elsewhere in the Song this new scene begins with a state of separation between the couple, and moves toward union (see 2:8; 8:5). C. Gordis sees this lyric as the oldest unit of the Song, a hymn composed for a wedding of the historical Solomon, but most commentators understand '*King Solomon*' in the figurative sense explained below. At first the obscure object stirring up dust in the desert seems to be a caravan. But then the poet imagines it raising a '*column of smoke*' like incense coming from the burning of '*fragrant powders,*' including the '*myrrh*' already mentioned as one of the woman's perfumes (v. 6; see on 1:13).

John White found that myrrh trees were planted in Egyptian temple groves, and he points out parts of the Song that are similar to Egyptian religious lyrics. Those who view the Song as a cultic piece interpret this scene as describing a religious procession. In contrast to previous parts, the narrator is the voice of the poet speaking as a spectator at this procession. As the object approaches, he recognizes it as '*the litter of Solomon,*' that is, the special ceremonial carriage accompanied by a select group of specially chosen body guards (vv. 7-8).

The term translated '*palanquin,*' found only here in the Bible, was not understood even by ancient translators. It seems to have come from the Sanskrit and to have designated some kind of colorful portable throne of elaborate construction, described in detail (vv. 9-10). In this context the designation '*King Solomon*' does not imply that it belonged to the historical king but identifies an ornate style of construction. Instead of '*lovingly wrought within,*' the Hebrew may mean "made of leather," a phrase that fits the context better (v. 10). A similar Arabic word means leather, and the author may have deliberately picked an uncommon term to play on the litter as an expression of love, because such portable thrones were adorned with love scenes.

Other commentators see the whole scene as a metaphorical description of the woman herself, luxuriously adorned for her marriage (see 1:11; 8:5). The text has been compared to the procession bringing the rich Canaanite bride (1 Macc 9:37-39), but the basis of that interpretation is weak, because this is not a historical narrative but a lyric.

The shadowy chorus is invited to witness this pomp. Here alone are the members called '*daughters of Zion,*' the mountain upon which Jerusalem was built (v. 11). In keeping with forms of the love poetry of the ancient Near East, the expression '*King Solomon*' functions as a literary "royal fiction" to designate the bridegroom. Again, the Song breaks off with no definitive union between the couple.

5. IN PRAISE OF THE BRIDE
Cant 4:1—5:1

4 Behold, you are beautiful, my love,
behold, you are beautiful!
Your eyes are doves behind your veil.
Your hair is like a flock of goats,
moving down the slopes of Gilead.
[2]Your teeth are like a flock of shorn ewes
that have come up from the washing,
all of which bear twins,
and not one among them is bereaved.
[3]Your lips are like a scarlet thread,
and your mouth is lovely.
Your cheeks are like halves of a pomegranate
behind your veil.
[4]Your neck is like the tower of David,
built for an arsenal,[a]
whereon hang a thousand bucklers,
all of them shields of warriors.
[5]Your two breasts are like two fawns,
twins of a gazelle,
that feed among the lilies.
[6]Until the day breathes and the shadows flee,
I will hie me to the mountain of myrrh
and the hill of frankincense.
[7]You are all fair, my love;
there is no flaw in you.
[8]Come with me from Lebanon, my bride;
come with me from Lebanon.
Depart from the peak of Amana,
from the peak of Senir and Hermon,
from the dens of lions,
from the mountains of leopards.

[9]You have ravished my heart, my sister, my bride,
you have ravished my heart with a
glance of your eyes,

with one jewel of your necklace.
[10]How sweet is your love, my sister, my bride!
how much better is your love than wine,
and the fragrance of your oils than any spice!
[11]Your lips distil nectar, my bride;
honey and milk are under your tongue;
the scent of your garments is like the scent of Lebanon.
[12]A garden locked is my sister, my bride,
a garden locked, a fountain sealed.
[13]Your shoots are an orchard of pomegranates
with all choicest fruits,
henna with nard,
[14]nard and saffron, calamus and cinnamon,
with all trees of frankincense,
myrrh and aloes,
with all chief spices—
[15]a garden fountain, a well of living water,
and flowing streams from Lebanon.

[16]Awake, O north wind,
and come, O south wind!
Blow upon my garden,
let its fragrance be wafted abroad.
Let my beloved come to his garden,
and eat its choicest fruits.

5 I come to my garden, my sister, my bride,
I gather my myrrh with my spice,
I eat my honeycomb with my honey,
I drink my wine with my milk.

Eat, O friends, and drink:
drink deeply, O lovers!

[a]The meaning of the Hebrew word is uncertain

Beginning with phrases found in 1:15, the man breaks into a lyrical and yet systematic description of his bride's beauty, descending from her dove-like '*eyes*' and black '*hair*' (v. 1). With exaggerated imagery he paints the movement of her hair as it tumbles down '*like a flock of goats*' on '*the slopes of Gilead,*' a mountian mentioned again in 6:5. Modern commentators usually designate this lyric as a *wasf,* a lyric devoted to praising either a bride or a bridegroom in contemporary Syrian wedding celebrations (4:1-5; see 5:10-16). But recent studies of ancient Egyptian love poetry have uncovered similar techniques and imagery. At times the comparisons are based more on plays on words than on clear images.

As the RSV note indicates, no satisfactory explanation of the comparison in verse 4 has been discovered because the '*tower of David*' has not been identified. Possibly the woman's intricate neck piece suggests shields hung upon a military fortification during times of peace to adorn its walls (see Ezek 27:11). But K. Crim suggests a different metaphor. The woman is beautiful enough to make a thousand warriors lay down their weapons in surrender.

The comparison of the woman's breasts to '*two fawns*' appears again (v. 5; see 7:3; contrast 8:8). In this context the mention of a '*gazelle*'—used of the male in 2:8, 17—refers to shape rather than to speed. The comment about the '*fawns*' grazing '*among the lilies*' appears to be an automatic addition of a stereotyped phrase to bring the description to a close (see 2:16).

The text then moves directly into the Song's favorite theme of seeking and finding. This time it is developed by means of the language of courtship, but expressed indirectly. The man anticipates ecstatic union with his '*love*' as a '*mountain of myrrh*' and a '*hill of frankincense*' (v. 6, repeating phrases from 1:13 and 3:6); he describes the time of intimacy in the same poetic phrases found in 2:17.

Verse 6 reads much like a short snatch of a preexisting song, but the editor of the Song has been able to integrate it into the continuity and movement of the whole. Such repetition of phrases invites readers to consider the whole Song as a joyful celebration of the love of a man and a woman in the unfolding of God's creative activity. Even if this verse incorporates once independent lyrics, it fits in well with the movement of the Song at this point. The insertion contributes to the continuity of the overall theme of mutual love.

Another new celebration of praise begins abruptly with a variation on the opening phrase of this section of the Song, as the man once more proclaims that his '*love*' is '*all fair*' (v. 7; this same term is translated '*beautiful*' in 1:15 and 4:1). When he adds that she has no '*flaw*' he deliberately chooses a word that resonates meaning on a variety of levels: physical, moral, personal—all of which form part of the experience of love.

For the first time he calls the woman '*my bride,*' a term found six times between 4:8 and 5:1 but nowhere else in the Song. Such fluctuation in vocabulary supports the opinion that the Song was put together from previously existing lyrics. Technically, '*bride*' designates a woman who is pledged to a man rather than one who is actually married. But in Egyptian love poetry this term is used in the figurative sense of a lover—the sense that '*bride*' has in these verses.

The figurative terminology carries over in the use of proper names for the four mountains, joined in lyric exuberance with the '*dens of lions*' and the '*mountains of leopards*' (v. 8). The terms continue the man's efforts to find adequate praise for his '*love.*' Such terminology does not conform to that of popular love songs. In the expression '*lions*' M. Pope sees a mythical allusion to the Semitic goddess of the hunt, who was also the goddess of love. The same joining of figurative language to terms of endearment like '*my sister*' and '*my bride*' is a feature of ancient Egyptian love poetry (v. 9).

The Hebrew word translated as '*sweet*' (v. 10) appears elsewhere in the Song, but is usually translated as '*beautiful*' (1:15; 4:1; 6:4). It is part of the Song's using imagery from the realms of touch, taste and smell to describe lovemaking, as when it is compared to '*wine*' (v. 10; see 1:2, 4). The comparison is extended by adding '*honey and milk,*' terms that recall the richness of the promised land when it flowed in spring with '*milk and honey*' (v. 11; see Exod 3:17; Lev 20:24). Comparisons to the delights of smell are perhaps what evokes the picture of the woman as a '*garden*' (v. 12; see 4:15, 16; 5:1; 6:2, 11).

The specification that the garden is '*locked*' and its '*fountain sealed*' fits in with the picture of the woman as '*bride*,' destined to be faithful to one lover (v. 12; see Prov 5:15).

Verses 13-15 elaborate on the '*garden*' image, first by enumerating a variety of aromatic plants that signify the bride's extraordinary fruitfulness. Her designation as an '*orchard*' in the RSV translation could be rendered more poetically by "park" or even by "paradise," because the word is of Persian origin (v. 13). The text attributes equal force to the love of both man and woman by comparing her to '*henna*,' to which he was compared in 1:14. '*Saffron*' appears nowhere else in the Bible. The other scents are exotic rather than those to be expected in popular love lyrics—another indication of the learned character of the Song. This hint as to the origin of at least this part is strengthened by the fact—as Winandy notes—that such a combination of plants would not be found in a real garden.

To complete the description of the bride as '*garden*,' the poet returns to the metaphor of a '*fountain*' which now grows into '*living water*' and even into '*streams from Lebanon*' (v. 15). The tenor of the image is that she will never cease to be fruitful. It is a tribute to the inexhaustible creativity of love.

At this point the lyrics shift into an emotional apostrophe to express emotional response to this long description of the '*bride*' (v. 16ab). It could be spoken either by the bride who invites the '*winds*' to carry these intoxicating aromas to her beloved so that he may be drawn to experience her delights. Or the man may be addressing the '*winds*' to invite them to carry these scents to him—another indirect image of mutual union. In either case, the final two lines of verse 16 are the bride's invitation to her beloved to enjoy her person, in much the same way as she used the image of the vineyard of herself (see 1:16).

The garden image was a commonplace for lovemaking in ancient Near Eastern poetry, and the beloved recognizes that this third-person invitation is addressed to him. He accepts the joyful call to union in the same figurative language that embraces touch, taste and smell (5:1; see 4:10-11). His strong response is marked by the emphatic use of the personal pronoun '*my*' that occurs eight times in four lines. In connection with '*spice,*' the '*myrrh*' here refers to seasoning the food to be eaten (compare the '*spiced wine*' of 8:2).

After this detailed description of mutual desire, the long section ends with a couplet pronounced by the poet: he invites the lovers to take full advantagc of their coming union (v. 1 ef). No doubt the wisdom writer intends it as a general invitation to readers to taste the sweetness of love. The couplet also serves as a literary marker to separate two different types of poems. By this arrangement the editor anticipates his final reflections on the unique power of love in human relationships (see 8:6-7). Instead of '*0 lovers,*' it is possible to understand the Hebrew term as "love," and to translate, "drink deeply of love."

6. DREAM REPORT: UNION WITH AND LOSS OF THE BELOVED
Cant 5:2-8

2I slept, but my heart was awake.
Hark! my beloved is knocking.
"Open to me, my sister, my love,
my dove, my perfect one;
for my head is wet with dew,
my locks with the drops of the night."
3I had put off my garment,
how could I put it on?
I had bathed my feet,
how could I soil them?
4My beloved put his hand to the latch,
and my heart was thrilled within me.
5I arose to open to my beloved,
and my hands dripped with myrrh,

my fingers with liquid myrrh,
upon the handles of the bolt.
[6]I opened to my beloved,
but my beloved had turned and gone.
My soul failed me when he spoke.
I sought him, but found him not;
I called him, but he gave no answer.
[7]The watchmen found me,
as they went about in the city;
they beat me, they wounded me,
they took away my mantle,
those watchmen of the walls.
[8]I adjure you, O daughters of Jerusalem,
if you find my beloved,
that you tell him I am sick with love.

In this new scene the woman is once more separated from her beloved. The term '*bride*' no longer occurs nor is any time frame indicated. Some translations understand the text as speaking of present time, but the RSV renders it as a description of a past happening. It seems best to interpret the woman as recalling a dream that embodied an experience of union with her lover and then her loss of him, a movement similar to 2:8—3:5.

The dream takes place in her '*heart*' which serves as both the point of contact and the symbol of the encounter. It portrays his longing to be admitted to intimacy, a desire expressed in the usual indirect figurative manner characteristic of the Song. The terms of endearment are common in ancient Egyptian love poetry as well as in other parts of the Cant: '*my love*' (eight times from 1:9), '*dove*' (1:15; 2:14; 6:9), '*my sister*' (4:9, 10, 12), '*my perfect one*' (6:9).

For a shepherd accustomed to living in the fields at night, the motives the man alleges for being received appear trivial. They are voiced simply to set the tone for the dream dialogue. Keeping up the playful mood, the woman refuses to admit him because she does not wish to disturb her comfort or '*to wash her feet,*' another phrase that is an indirect statement of intimacy (v. 3; see 2 Sam 11:8). She intends to be playful and is anticipating the sexual intimacy that is dramatized under the figure of penetrating the door latch, an action that '*thrilled*' her (v. 4). The interaction between the two persons is conveyed by repeating the personal pronouns '*I*' and '*my*' in their interchange. The woman moves toward fulfilment of union and prepares to '*open to my beloved*' (v. 5). The '*liquid myrrh*' that she drops was evidently received from him, since myrrh appears on the man's lips below (v. 13). Although that is a separate scene, similar vocabulary and characters invite readers to interpret one part in terms of the other. All contribute to the overall portrait of love.

Throughout this and other scenes the poet is careful to avoid explicit sexual expressions common in the love poetry of neighboring civilizations. He treats the sexual experience under the mantle of Israel's creation wisdom. The possibilities of personal love are among God's greatest gifts to those he created in his own image.

Suddenly the mood of the situation darkens; the lover is no longer seeking entrance but has disappeared (v. 6). This change introduces the "seek and find" motif found in 1:7-8 and 3:1-4, probably another dream sequence. The woman expresses her consternation by repeating '*my beloved*' (v. 6). The added statement that her '*soul failed when he spoke*' does not fit the situation because he had already disappeared. Hence, the Hebrew word translated '*spoke*' should probably be understood as a similar rare form that means "fled."

The shock the woman experienced is described by the term '*failed me*'; her '*soul*' abandons her like her beloved. Unable to believe that he has really fled, she seeks him, calling out to him not to play such a joke on her.

The dream takes an ominous tone as the woman is apprehended by the night '*watchmen,*' who make their rounds in the '*city.*' This verse repeats a similar situation in 3:2-3. However, this time the watchmen '*beat*' and '*wounded*' her—to be understood in the wide sense of mistreated her for roaming around the city at night (v. 7). They even took away her '*mantle,*' the outer garment that served as protection against the elements.

Why the poet repeats with variation such a sequence has not been satisfactorily explained, but it does indicate that the Song is not simply an anthology of popular lyrics. On the other hand, such repetitions scarcely justify elaborate theories of sophisticated structure. The woman's willingness to endure these hardships for her beloved illustrates the proverbs at the end that extol the unique power of love (see 8:6-7).

In desperation she cries out to the '*daughters of Jerusalem,*' once more conveniently present as a sounding board, for help in finding her lover, because she is '*sick with love*' (v. 8; see on 2:5). The phrase repeats words she spoke to them before, but this time they express the sadness of lost love. Her plea to them to say this on her behalf to her '*beloved*' shows that she hopes for reunion with him. Whether she is awake now is not clear. In any case the scene ends and the Song moves into another form of lyric in which the woman praises her beloved.

7. DESCRIPTION OF THE BRIDEGROOM
Cant 5:9—6:3

[9]What is your beloved more than another beloved,
O fairest among women?
What is your beloved more than another beloved,
that you thus adjure us?

[10]My beloved is all radiant and ruddy,
distinguished among ten thousand.
[11]His head is the finest gold;
his locks are wavy,
black as a raven.
[12]His eyes are like doves
beside springs of water,
bathed in milk, fitly set.[a]
[13]His cheeks are like beds of spices, yielding fragrance.
His lips are lilies, distilling liquid myrrh.

[14]His arms are rounded gold, set with jewels.
His body is ivory work,
encrusted with sapphires.
[15]His legs are alabaster columns,
set upon bases of gold.
His appearance is like Lebanon,
choice as the cedars.
[16]His speech is most sweet,
and he is altogether desirable.
This is my beloved and this is my friend,
O daughters of Jerusalem.

6 Whither has your beloved gone,
O fairest among women?
Whither has your beloved turned,
that we may seek him with you?

[2]My beloved has gone down to his garden,
to the beds of spices,
to pasture his flock in the gardens,
and to gather lilies.
[3]I am my beloved's and my beloved is mine;
he pastures his flock among the lilies.

[a] The meaning of the Hebrew is uncertain

The reply of the '*daughters of Jerusalem*' to the bride's plea to find her beloved takes the form of a double question, which is introduced as a stylistic device to advance the minimal story line of the Song (v. 9). It permits the woman in turn to sing a *waṣf* or stereotyped description of her spouse's physical beauty (vv. 10-16; compare 4:1-5). The mutual admiration of the couple, which is shared equally by both, places both loves on an equal footing. Their unbounded affection and mutual attraction celebrate love as the strongest human bond.

To acknowledge her unique dignity, the '*daughters*' address the bride as '*fairest among women*' (v. 9; see 1:8; 6:1). Her long ode about her bridegroom begins with a brief overview to praise him in general terms (v. 10). Then she enters into details about his head, proceeds down to the feet and concludes with another general expression of praise (vv. 10-16).

His skin gleams with a '*ruddy*' glow. She does not say why. It could be because of his exposure to the sun; it could be the result of some artificial makeup; or it could be a divine favor. In any case, he outshines '*ten thousand*', that is, an entire city. Her ode goes on in hyperbolic fashion to glorify his every physical quality in a way that makes it hard for modern readers to visualize his appearance. With little consistency she speaks of his head as '*finest gold*' and of his hair as '*black as a raven*' (v. 11; see the head of the statue in Dan 2:32). A standard comparison is utilized for his eyes: '*like doves*' (see 1:15; 4:1, both of the woman).

As the RSV translation notes, the final part of verse 12 is "uncertain." As translated, it applies to his eyes, but it could also be a description of his teeth—white like '*milk*' and '*firmly set*'—which are not mentioned in the poem. The whole picture of the beloved has a certain statue-like quality, with his eyes like jewels '*set firmly*' in his face as inlays of stone, as will be explained below.

Both sight and smell feature in the description of the '*cheeks,*' which support a perfumed beard (v. 13; see 1:10 for the woman's cheeks). A use of stereotyped expressions is evident in the description of his lips as '*lilies,*' the spring flower to which the entire woman was compared (see 2:1). His lips drip the same '*liquid myrrh*' found on her fingers (see 5:9). Included in this ode is the hint that whatever words drop from these '*lips*' have profound power to move.

The picture of his arms celebrates both their strength and their beauty as gleaming '*gold*' (v. 14). The Hebrew word for '*jewels*' is the same as the name of the city Tarshish, a legendary seaport at the western end of the Mediterranean Sea. So some translations take the term as a proper name. Such an allusion, especially if deliberately ambiguous, indicates how the poet reached out to contemporary learning. Similar points of style occur as far back as Sumerian cult texts referring to love and sacred marriage. At times both

Jewish and Christian commentators allegorized proper names in the Song, but that method marks a later stage in interpretation and is not the original meaning.

As mentioned above, some critics suggest that the beloved is portrayed here as a divine statue. The lower part of his '*body*' namely, his stomach, is '*ivory work encrusted with sapphires,*' that is, with lapis lazuli, a kind of limestone with blue grains (v. 14). His '*legs*' appear as '*columns*' of white marble, translated as '*alabaster*,' which are '*set upon bases of gold*' (v. 15). It is more plausible to trace the influence of such vocabulary to ancient Near Eastern poetry than to search for allusions to the structure of the Temple of Jerusalem, as A. Robert does.

The remainder of this ode is a general description of what moderns would call personality traits of the bridegroom. His overall '*appearance*' (v. 15; a term applied to the woman in 2:14) is so strong that it reminds her of the might of Lebanon '*cedars*' (v. 15, recalling that their trysting place was adorned with such trees in 2:17). The word translated '*speech*' actually means "palate," and is probably a figurative expression for "kiss" rather than '*speech.*' In fact, the RSV translates it as '*kiss*' in 7:9. If this understanding is correct, the woman is saying that his kisses are '*sweet*' and '*altogether desirable*' (v. 16).

The forceful manner in which the bride ends this *waṣf* communicates how pleased she is with her description of her '*beloved*' and '*friend*' (v. 16). Impressed by her performance, the '*daughters of Jerusalem*' pursue their dialogue with this '*fairest among women,*' a title linked to the Sumerian goddess Inanna in one of the sacred marriage poems. They ask her a second set of questions, which are similar in form and rhythm to their first set but differ in content (6:1; compare 5:9). They seem to convey a certain irony also, for if her beloved is solid as a statue, where could he have '*gone*' or '*turned*'? But they may also allude to the descent into the nether world theme (see 6:11).

The woman answers them in an entirely different style—. another indication that the biblical poet has drawn upon a variety of previously existing sources to compose the Song. Yet he has carefully completed, arranged and edited this material to convey the qualities of love that make it the crowning gift of God's wisdom. The bride's brief reply is an expanded variant of her words in 2:16, and correspond to the irony of the question (6:2-3). Her beloved has never really left her, despite the dream scene.

Her reply reveals the depth of her union with her beloved. He entered '*his garden,*' an image of her as bride (see 4:12; 5:1) to enjoy the '*beds of spices*' (6:2, repeating a phrase from 5:13). Thus this complex section of the Song ends on a note of intimate union. The activity of the beloved is repeated from 2:6, but in reverse order. All of this indirect imagery expresses the mutual fidelity of the couple, as the concluding exclamation of union attests (6:3; compare 7:10). However, this formula of mutual union is not close enough to the prophetic formula of Israel as God's people and of Yahweh as Israel's God to argue—as A. Robert does—that the original sense of the Song develops the image of Israel's marriage to the Lord (see Jer 7:23).

8. DOUBLE DESCRIPTION OF THE BRIDE
Cant 6:4—7:9

[4]You are beautiful as Tirzah, my love,
  comely as Jerusalem,
  terrible as an army with banners.
[5]Turn away your eyes from me,
  for they disturb me—
Your hair is like a flock of goats,
  moving down the slopes of Gilead.
[6]Your teeth are like a flock of ewes,
  that have come up from the washing,
all of them bear twins,
  not one among them is bereaved.
[7]Your cheeks are like halves of a pomegranate
  behind your veil.
[8]There are sixty queens and eighty concubines,

and maidens without number.
[9]My dove, my perfect one, is only one,
the darling of her mother,
flawless to her that bore her.
The maidens saw her and called her happy;
the queens and concubines also, and they praised her.
[10]"Who is this that looks forth like the dawn,
fair as the moon, bright as the sun,
terrible as an army with banners?"

[11]I went down to the nut orchard,
to look at the blossoms of the valley,
to see whether the vines had budded,
whether the pomegranates were in bloom.
[12]Before I was aware, my fancy set me
in a chariot beside my prince.

[13]Return, return, O Shulammite,
return, return, that we may look upon you.

Why should you look upon the Shulammite,
as upon a dance before two armies?[a]

7 How graceful are your feet in sandals,
O queenly maiden!
Your rounded thighs are like jewels,
the work of a master hand.
[2]Your navel is a rounded bowl
that never lacks mixed wine.
Your belly is a heap of wheat,
encircled with lilies.
[3]Your two breasts are like two fawns,
twins of a gazelle.
[4]Your neck is like an ivory tower.
Your eyes are pools in Heshbon,
by the gate of Bath-rabbim.
Your nose is like a tower of Lebanon,
overlooking Damascus.
[5]Your head crowns you like Carmel,
and your flowing locks are like purple;
a king is held captive in the tresses.

[6]How fair and pleasant you are,
O loved one, delectable maiden!
[7]You are stately as a palm tree,
and your breasts are like its clusters.
[8]I say I will climb the palm tree
and lay hold of its branches.
Oh, may your breasts be like clusters of the vine,
and the scent of your breath like apples,
[9]and your kisses like the best wine that goes down
smoothly, gliding over lips and teeth.[b]

[a]or *dance of Mahanaim* [b]Gr Syr Vg: Heb *lips of sleepers*

This section of the Song begins abruptly without any editorial link to the description of the bridegroom, who suddenly becomes the speaker. He offers two long *waṣf*-like descriptions of the beauty of his bride, one after another. The first presents a static view (6:4-9; compare 4:1-7), and the second pictures her in a dance (7:1-8). Both end with a short expression of his desire for intimate union with her (6:11-12 and 7:9).

The arrangement provides an argument for those commentators who hold that the Song is an anthology of love lyrics. Yet, features of the work in its present form—like order, repetition, cross references and learned allusions—indicate that the poet had a plan in his manner of presenting his material. As John White states, the Song conveys a lesson of mutual love and celebrates the beauty of fidelity absent from Egyptian love poetry. It flows from sages who believed that the fear of the Lord is the beginning of wisdom.

The first *waṣf* begins with the emphatic word '*beautiful,*' an adjective applied to the woman several times (v. 4; see 1:8, 15; 2:10, 13; 4:1, 7; 5:9; 6:1). The word is found for the last time at the end of this description, thus forming a literary inclusion (v. 10). This is also the last time that the woman is addressed as '*my love*' (v. 4; see on 1:9).

The mention of the two capitals of the northern and southern kingdoms of Samaria and Judea—'*Tirzah*' and '*Jerusalem*'—gives a historical dimension to this lyric in keeping with the poet's linking his Song to the wisdom ideal of Israel. M. Pope, however, sees the word '*Tirzah*' as a verb meaning "you are very pleasing," and deletes '*Jerusalem*' as an editorial insertion when '*Tirzah*' was taken as a proper name. If original, the choice of the ancient capital of Israel, '*Tirzah*' rather than Samaria, points to a time of animosity between the Jews of Judea and the Samaritans—thus suggesting a rather late date for the Song. Such polemics are a far cry from the style of popular love lyrics.

The military aspect of her appearance—'*terrible as an army*'—can be explained by appealing to cultic influence (v. 4). In several ancient Near Eastern civilizations the goddess of war and love was the same. As noted above, some military image also lies behind the image of the woman's neck as the '*tower of David*' (see 4:4). Several phrases of the earlier description of the bride are repeated in the first lyric of this section: '*hair*' like the '*flock of goats*' on '*Gilead*' (v. 5; see 4:1); '*teeth*' like fruitful '*ewes*' (v. 6); '*cheeks*' like '*halves of a pomegranate*' (v. 7; see 4:3).

The second half goes its separate way as it makes allusion to a harem, perhaps to recall that of Solomon (see 1 Kgs 11:3). That king had more wives than numbered here and his harem did not include '*maidens*' (v. 8; a different term is used in v. 9 in the Hebrew text). J.C. Exum sees a link between the '*sixty queens*' and the '*sixty mighty men*' who accompanied '*the litter of Solomon*' (v. 9 and 3:7). In context, these numbers serve to heighten the praise of the '*dove,*' unique recipient of the man's faithful love, the '*only one,*' who evokes praise even from '*the queens and concubines.*' A. Robert concludes that the vocabulary places the '*darling*' in a class with the wise widow praised in Proverbs 31:28 (v. 9).

Another isolated snatch of a lyric follows this first ode (v. 10). The quotation marks in the RSV translation indicate that it stands in isolation from the two *waṣfs*, but nothing in the text provides any hint as to the speaker. In its present position this apostrophe marks a fitting reaction to and states a new dimension of the man's praise. It compares the bride to the three periods of time that make up a day: the glory of the '*dawn,*' the brightness of the '*sun*' in daylight, and the softness of night in the beauty of the '*moon.*' Coming at this point, the final line of verse 10, a repetition of verse 4c—'*terrible as an army with banners*'—must refer to stars, considered as hosts of the heavens by the ancients.

The celebration of such beauty draws from the beloved a desire for union, which he again expresses in indirect language, using the metaphor of exploring '*the nut orchard,*' since nuts were linked to fertility (v. 11, although the produce mentioned are not nuts). A cultic overtone is present in the verb '*went down*' according to M. Pope, who sees an allusion to the underworld (see on 6:1).

Commentators agree that verse 12 is the most difficult in the Song. The beloved is overcome with love '*before I was aware,*' but his reaction is not clear. In fact, this verse was unclear even to the ancient Greek translators. All attempts to make sense out of the Hebrew are only educated guesses. The '*chariot*' may point to a hidden cultic allusion, such as a procession (see 3:6-11).

The second description of the bride is introduced by a four-fold appeal to '*return*' (v. 13, which is 7:1 in the Hebrew numbering). This appeal is directed more to arouse reader attention than to call the woman. She is addressed as a '*Shulammite,*' a term found only here in the Bible. Of the many explanations given, three merit attention. First, it may designate her obscure place of origin, possibly a linguistic transmutation of the village from which the beautiful Abishag was recruited to nurse the aging David (1 Kgs 1:3). Second, some Greek translators understood the term as a form of the Hebrew word for peace, *shalom,* although the context does not point to any allegorical significance. Thirdly, '*Shulammite*' may be a variation of the name of a Semitic goddess, linking the Song to ancient cult. Yet, no one can say with certainty why she bears this title here.

Whatever the signficance of '*Shulammite,*' she is urged by an unidentified audience to perform a ritual dance, possibly a sword dance associated with the celebration of marriage. As the RSV note mentions, the name of the dance is sometimes translated as proper name, '*dance of Mahanaim,*' a Levitical city and religious shrine. The name means "two camps" (see Josh 21:38).

As she begins this dance, the chorus sings another *waṣf* in praise of her beauty (7:1-7). Because the bride is pictured as dancing, the lyrics begin to describe the motion of her '*graceful feet,*' that is, her dance steps. The title '*queenly maiden*' is part of the "royal fiction" and refers to her role in the dance rather than to her social position.

The movements of her '*thighs*' assume shapes that only a '*master hand*' could shape (v. 1). The term actually means a master craftsman, a term found again in the Bible only in Prov 8:30 to designate God's personified wisdom. This linguistic link to the biblical sages is a clue to their role in composing the Song.

The words of the dance praise the bride's beauty directly, but indirectly they celebrate her fruitfulness. '*Rounded bowls*' were part of the cultic vessels of ancient shrines (v. 2). '*Lilies*' were mentioned above (2:1), and the first part of verse 3 repeats 4:5, also in praise of the woman. Her neck is again compared to a '*tower*' this time of '*ivory*' (v. 4; in 5:4 '*ivory*' was used of the man's body). At this point the usual complementary phrase found in the other verses of the lyric is missing; it was probably lost in copying.

The bride's eyes this time are not '*doves*' but '*pools of Heshbon,*' perhaps because they reflect like clear water or because Heshbon had two reservoirs (v. 4). Such comparisons are not clear or appealing to modern readers, but are in keeping with the style of other ancient Near Eastern lyrics. Two further comparisons link the Song with names from Israel's history (vv. 4-5).

In ancient writing '*purple*' embraced a wide range of shades, including crimson. The '*purple*' of the woman's '*flowing locks*' designates not so much the color as their gleam that is worthy of a '*king*'—to keep the "royal fiction" for the bridegroom (v. 5; see 1:4). Elsewhere the woman's hair is presumably black (see 1:5; 4:1; 6:5). Such inconsistency of imagery could point to different sources of the

Song, whose details were not harmonized. The biblical poet was not offering realistic portraits of a specific couple but was celebrating the role of love in God's creation.

As in the previous ode, the final verses offer summary praise of the woman (vv. 6-7). They begin with an exclamation similar to that in 4:10, naming two qualities found in her: she is '*fair and pleasant*' (v. 6; words translated '*beautiful*' and '*lovely*' in 1:15-16). The final image of the bride as a '*palm tree*' adorned with '*clusters*,' that is, of dates, pays tribute to her stately figure (v. 7).

Having praised her so graphically, the beloved breaks forth in passionate desire to taste her fruit. His decisive, '*I say*,' is equivalent to the modern English, "I say to myself," or "I decided" (v. 8). The intensity of his desire manifests itself as he enumerates all the delights union with her promises by using the images of grapes, '*apples*' and '*wine*' (v. 9). As above, the sense of smell is added to these metaphors for personal intimacy (see 1:3, 12; 2:13; 4:10-11). For '*kisses*' see on 5:16.

In an attempt to clarify an obscure passage, the RSV makes two modifications in verse 9. It eliminates "for my love" and reads with the Greek '*lips and teeth*' instead of the Hebrew "lips of sleepers." Poetic vocabulary and lack of context account for variations in the preservation of the text and these affect modern translations.

9. DESIRE FOR MUTUAL UNION
Cant 7:10—8:4

[10]I am my beloved's
  and his desire is for me.
[11]Come, my beloved, let us go forth into the fields,
  and lodge in the villages;
[12]let us go out early to the vineyards,
  and see whether the vines have budded,
whether the grape blossoms have opened
  and the pomegranates are in bloom.
There I will give you my love.

[13]The mandrakes give forth fragrance,
and over our doors are all choice fruits,
new as well as old, which I have laid up for you,
O my beloved.
8 O that you were like a brother to me,
that nursed at my mother's breast!
If I met you outside, I would kiss you,
and none would despise me.
[2]I would lead you and bring you into
the house of my mother,
and into the chamber of her that conceived me.[a]
I would give you spiced wine to drink,
the juice of my pomegranates.
[3]O that his left hand were under my head,
and that his right hand embraced me!
[4]I adjure you, O daughters of Jerusalem,
that you stir not up nor awaken love
until it please.

[a]Gk Syr: Heb *mother; she* (or *you) will teach me*

The scene changes abruptly once more and the lovers are alone. The text gives no indication of the relation of this scene to previous events, but verse 12 could indicate that they are married. The woman speaks throughout. She begins by repeating the first half of a phrase that occurred in two earlier places in the Song about belonging to her '*beloved*' (v. 10; see 2:16; 6:3). Instead of completing the statement about mutual belonging, however, she speaks of his '*desire*' for her, a term found again in the Bible only in Genesis 3:16 and 4:7 about the '*desire*' of Eve for Adam and of sin for Cain. In attributing this great urge to the man toward the woman, the Song recognizes equality in the attraction between the sexes.

Her following suggestions portray how intensely she reacts to the '*desire*' that her beloved has for her (compare 2:12-14). In the beginning of the Song it was the man who brought the woman into his chambers (see 1:4). By now placing the initiative toward union in the woman, the Song affirms that her role in fostering the love relationship is equal to his. She proposes a triple program of activity: first, to visit '*the fields*'; then, to spend the night '*in the villages*' (v. 11; the same term is translated '*henna*' in 1:14 and 4:13); and finally to '*go out early to the vineyards*' and examine them (v. 12; see 1:6 for the image). All these terms are used metaphorically, as the woman's explicit statement, '*I will give you my love,*' affirms.

In describing this three-fold program she incorporates expressions that her beloved used in 6:11—another indication that both parties are equally committed to fostering love. To encourage their intimate union, she calls attention to the '*fragrance*' of the '*mandrakes,*' a popular aphrodisiac in the ancient Near East (v. 13; the term for '*mandrakes*' in Hebrew is similar to love. They are mentioned in the Bible again only in Genesis 30:14-16 as the price Leah paid for a night with her husband Jacob). The woman also prepared '*choice fruits*' for their enjoyment, a term already found as a metaphor for her charms (v. 13; see 4:13, 16).

The final stanza of this lyric introduces a new image, as the woman wishes that her bridegroom were her '*brother*' (8:1). Two explanations are offered for this unusual wish that sounds so strange to contemporary readers. Either it alludes to social conditions of the time, which allowed only blood brothers and sisters—not even spouses—to display affection in public. This is a reason why ancient Egyptian love poetry often uses the terms brother and sister to express affection. Or her wish may be a remnant of the cultic origins of this lyric, recalling that the lovers were originally a god and goddess.

This cultic explanation would provide a motive for the visit that the bride suggests to '*the house of my mother*,' probably for the cultic celebration and feasting that mark the completion of their marriage (vv. 2-4). M. Pope suggests funeral celebrations as the origin of banquets that were marked by drinking and revelry. Earlier the Song spoke about bringing the beloved '*into my mother's house*' (see 3:4). In both cases the action is linked to the command not to '*stir*' or to '*awaken love until it please*' (v. 4). Here the Hebrew text has an added note that the mother '*will teach me*' (RSV note to v. 2). Such instruction is hard to work into the text and was evidently not understood even by ancient scribes. The RSV has replaced it with a phrase from the Greek translation about leading the husband '*into the chamber*' of her mother. This phrase is found in 3:4 and provides a better balance with the mother's '*house*.'

The traditional division of the next line is also disturbed, and the translation of the two final lines of verse 2 in the RSV is a conjecture or scholarly guess to keep a spirit of celebration in the passage (see 4:10 and 5:1 for possible parallels). The '*daughters of Jerusalem*' are mentioned for the last time, although they had not been hinted at in this section, where the bride enjoys her beloved's presence.

The final verse of this section introduces two earlier expressions from the Song. The first is the word of mutual embrace. At this point it is better understood as expressing the reality of perfect union rather than simply a longing for it (v. 3; see 2:6). The second is the plea that no one wake '*love*' (v. 4; see 2:7; 3:5). In the other two cases this command was spoken by the man; here the bride speaks. On this note of her desire for mutual union the lyric selections of the Song end abruptly. These final couplets summarize the fidelity that the poem celebrates throughout. The remaining verses will comment on the place of love in the creative plan of God.

10. REFLECTIONS INSPIRED BY THE WISDOM OF THE SONG
Can 8:5-14

> [5]Who is that coming up from the wilderness,
>   leaning upon her beloved?
> Under the apple tree I awakened you.
> There your mother was in travail with you,
> there she who bore you was in travail.
>
> [6]Set me as a seal upon your heart,

as a seal upon your arm;
for love is strong as death,
jealousy is cruel as the grave.
Its flashes are flashes of fire,
a most vehement flame.
[7]Many waters cannot quench love,
neither can floods drown it.
If a man offered for love
all the wealth of his house,
it would be utterly scorned.

[8]We have a little sister,
and she has no breasts.
What shall we do for our sister,
on the day when she is spoken for?
[9]If she is a wall,
we will build upon her a battlement of silver;
but if she is a door,
we will enclose her with boards of cedar.
[10]I was a wall,
and my breasts were like towers;
then I was in his eyes
as one who brings peace.

[11]Solomon had a vineyard at Baal-hamon;
he let out the vineyard to keepers;
each one was to bring for its fruit
a thousand pieces of silver.
[12]My vineyard, my very own, is for myself;
you, O Solomon, may have the thousand,
and the keepers of the fruit two hundred.

[13]O you who dwell in the gardens,
my companions are listening for your voice;
let me hear it.
[14]Make haste, my beloved, and be like a gazelle
or a young stag upon the mountains of spices.

Another abrupt change of scene opens up a series of five concluding incidents or reflections that center upon the identity of the woman and upon the mystery of love.

1. The first scene begins by repeating a question that had been asked twice before: at the coming of the '*litter of Solomon*' and at the coming of the woman (see 3:6 and 6:10). Assuming that the author wished to recall various scenes from the Song, we can look upon this scene as a dramatic reprise. The bride and the bridegroom are now embracing in the '*litter*' that is '*coming up from the wilderness,*' where they had been together (v. 5). She takes her husband not to '*the house of my mother*' (see 8:2), but rather to the '*apple tree*' where she had '*awakened*' him and where he had been born (v. 5; compare 3:4).

The English translation does not make clear who is speaking, but in the Hebrew the man is being spoken about. Many modern commentators change the text to make the man speak about the woman, but there is no justification for this change from the Hebrew. A. Bea saw this part of the Song as referring to various ceremonies connected with celebrating their marriage.

The '*apple tree*' may be a figurative term for the mother's house where the man was born because it is linked to love (see 2:3, 5; 7:8). When the bride wants to be set as a '*seal*' upon the '*heart*' and '*arm*' of her husband, she is asking to be the very symbol of his personal identity. Seals of various shapes were used in the ancient Near East to identify the possessions and actions of their owners. A similar request is found in one of the ancient Egyptian love poems.

2. From the woman's request the text moves immediately into a series of four proverbs in Hebrew verse form, that is, in the form of parallel phrases that make related statements about love. These point to a wisdom writer as the one who put the Song into its final form as a way of teaching about the mysterious power that God has given to love.

The word for '*love*' here is not the narrow term found in the opening words of the woman when she spoke of '*love*' in the sense of embraces as '*better than wine*' (1:2). Rather, the term for '*love*' is the one used to identify the one '*whom my soul loves*' (1:7). That is, she spoke of '*love*' in the broadest sense as the quality that moves toward union on every level of interpersonal relations. These four sayings celebrate the qualities which the sage has distilled from the displays of mutual love gathered in the Song itself. By expanding the notion of love he celebrates its centrality in creation.

a) '*Love is strong as death,*' that is, irresistible. Love is not just any superlative performance; it is superior to the strongest force of dissolution imaginable. '*Death*' is best understood as the personified king of the underworld, the god Mot, especially since the term is used in parallel with "sheol," translated in the RSV as '*the grave,*' the prison that refuses to give up its inhabitants (v. 6; see Hosea 13:14). Death shows its strength by its '*jealousy,*' which is not confined to sexual competition, but is better seen as the consuming zeal that will stop at nothing, and that ruthlessly eliminates any rivals seeking to challenge its domination over human existence.

b) '*flashes of fire.*' The '*flashes*' of love include all its vehemence that penetrates like lightning and is as destructive as a storm (v. 6). This proverb about love may also be based on a personification of the gods of nature, to whom its unpredictable and often violent manifestations are compared. The phrase '*most vehement flame*' is a superlative made by combining the divine name Yahweh, its only occurrence in the Song. The ambiguity is deliberate—to bring out the victory of Yahweh over all gods of nature.

c) It withstands '*many waters.*' The phrase '*many waters*' is a common biblical idiom to refer either to the sea or to a violent demonstration of water, like a storm or '*floods.*' In a metaphorical sense '*many waters*' can mean any overwhelming trouble. In this cosmological context love receives a cosmic dimension that is capable of triumphing over the forces of chaos. No kind of difficulty, even those capable of destroying the entire creation, can overthrow love.

d) the final proverb about '*love*' is expressed in an unfilled condition, namely, in terms of the situation of someone who wished to buy '*love*' by offering all his wealth to obtain it. But the conclusion of this situation is ambiguous. It can be interpreted in at least three different ways. First, as the RSV understands it, that the intended lover will reject his approach of buying love and the one making the offer will end up '*utterly scorned*' (v. 7). Second, that the person deciding to obtain love will not consider the loss of wealth worthy of the least concern in comparison. Third, the conclusion can be understood as a question. Then it is the approving comment of observers who ask whether anyone would despise the person who risks all for love. The question expects them to reply "no." Love with its mysterious powers is worth all the pain it demands. Perhaps the enigma of Proverbs 30:19—'*the way of a man with a maiden*'—influenced the author in bringing this material together to form the Song of Songs.

3. The third scene can be interpreted as the activity of those who wish to finalize the union of the man and woman (vv. 8-10). For a second time the woman's brothers speak. Now they are presented as scheming to get the best bridal price for her. At first they are disappointed because she is so small, but then they figure a way to make the best out of the situation. They will protect her virginity if she is still a '*wall*' that is, not ready for marriage. But if she is a '*door,*' that is, able to receive lovers, they will make sure that she is not violated before the marriage contract.

The woman responds coolly to their scheming by affirming her maturity and integrity: she is a '*wall,*' yes, but with '*breasts like towers*' (v. 10). Hence she is able to appeal to her beloved as the one who offers '*peace,*' in the Semitic sense of abundant concrete favors. This '*peace*' obviously includes a generous bridal price, as the next section explains.

4. Verses 11-12 deal with an enigmatic detail that is difficult to fit into any kind of narrative. The location '*Baal-hamon*' appears nowhere else in the Bible. Baal is the Semitic word of "lord," and this name may designate a divinity. The price demanded for each of the '*keepers*' is enormous—equivalent to the produce of a thousand vines (see Isa 7:23). Possibly this verse was inserted to illustrate the value of love (see v. 7).

In response to this tax, the unidentified speaker, probably the man of the Song, protests that he has '*my vineyard, my very own*' to care for. This statement recalls the lament of the woman that she did not keep '*my own vineyard*' (1:6). Readers will assume that the one who gave '*Solomon*' the '*thousand pieces of silver,*' and even added '*two hundred*' for the '*keepers of the fruit*' is her beloved, who has already expressed his ardent desire to possess her as his '*very own,*' his unique wife. This short insert seems to be one of the early wisdom interpretations of the Song. It proclaims once again the incomparable gift of love that was expressed in the four maxims above. In the history of the text it became the basis for a variety of allegorical interpretations (see Introduction, Section 3).

5. Verses 13-14. The final enigma incorporates phrases from 2:9 (see also 2:14 and 6:3), but does not identify the speaker. The author is using the technique of literary allusion to make a comment on the Song as a whole. A. Robert holds that verse 13 is a prayer addressed to the Lord under the title of '*you who dwell in the gardens,*' that is, it is a plea to God as infinite Wisdom to instruct his people—perhaps that they may understand this Song itself.

If so, the final verse reinforces this plea by giving a short paraphrase of the Song. Now the '*beloved*' is Yahweh himself as the Spouse of Israel who offers the gift of prayer as intimate union with himself. In other words, the biblical author takes the initiative to give this literary composition he has forged from preexisting lyrics and editorial additions a deeper meaning. This verse must have encouraged the spiritual and allegorical interpretations that were so popular in both Jewish and Christian spiritualities. It indicates that the final author already recognized the "surplus of meaning" of these lyrics and encouraged readers to seek and find it—just as the characters sought and found love.

FOR FURTHER READING

Albert Cook, *The Root of the Thing*. Bloomington: University of Indiana, 1968. An evaluation of the two basic approaches to the Song—devotional and anthropological.

John F. Craghan, "The Song of Songs," *Old Testament Reading Guide 29*. Collegeville: Liturgical Press, 1979. A concise commentary by a scholar to provide an explanation of the New American Bible translation in popular language.

Robert Gordis, *The Song of Songs and Lamentations*. Revised and Augmented Edition. NY: Ktav, 1974. Interprets the Song as an anthology of 29 poems in ten different literary genres as celebrating love and nature.

Roland E. Murphy, "Interpreting the Song of Songs," *Biblical Theology Bulletin* 9 (July 1979) 99-105. Offers observations on the structure, movement and meaning of the Song along with contemporary applications.

Marvin H. Pope, *Song of Songs*. Anchor Bible 7c. Garden City, N.Y.: Doubleday and Company, 1977. This is an encyclopedia of the Song consisting of three parts: a new translation; a comprehensive introduction that includes commentaries published before 1800; detailed notes that comment on the entire spectrum of approaches to the Song.

MORE TECHNICAL WORKS

Two scholarly articles dealing with the structure of the Song, but reaching different conclusions, appeared in the same periodical, *Zeitschrift für die Alttestamentliche Wissenschaft:* J. Chryl Exum, "A Literary and Structural Analysis of the Song of Songs," 85 (1973) 47-79, and William H. Shea, "The Chiastic Structure of the Song of Songs," 92 (1980) 378-396.

Nicholas J. Cerella, *The Kiss, Sacred and Profane. An Interpretative History of Kiss Symbolism and Related Religio-Erotic Themes.* Berkeley: University of California Press, 1969. Contains valuable references to the history of the interpretation of the Song

Roland E. Murphy, *Wisdom Literature.* Grand Rapids: Eerdmans, 1981. Includes a technical form-critical study of the Song.

W.E. Phipps, "The Plight of the Song of Songs," *Journal of the American Academy of Religion* 42 (1974) 82-100. Reviews the various types of interpretation of the Song.

Phyllis Trible, "Love's Lyrics Redeemed," in *God and the Rhetoric of Sexuality.* Philadelphia: Fortress Press, 1978. Her reflections on pp. 144-165 seek to make the Song speak to modern readers.

John B. White, *A Study of the Language of Love in the Song of Songs and Ancient Egyptian Poetry.* Missoula, MT: Scholars Press, 1978. A doctoral dissertation that gives important background on the language of the Song.